LEVINAS AND THEOLOGY

Emmanuel Levinas was a significant contributor to the field of philosophy, phenomenology, and religion. A key interpreter of Husserl, he stressed the importance of attitudes to other people in any philosophical system. For Levinas, to be a subject is to take responsibility for others as well as yourself and therefore responsibility for the one leads to justice for the many. He regarded ethics as the foundation for all other philosophy, but later admitted it could also be the foundation for theology. Michael Purcell outlines the basic themes of Levinas' thought and the ways in which they might be deployed in fundamental and practical theology, and the study of the phenomenon of religion. This book will be useful for undergraduate and graduate students in philosophy, theology and religious studies, as well as those with a theological background who are approaching Levinas for the first time.

MICHAEL PURCELL is senior lecturer in Systematic Theology in the School of Divinity, University of Edinburgh. He is author of *Mystery and Method: The Other in Rahner and Levinas* (1998).

LEVINAS AND THEOLOGY

MICHAEL PURCELL

University of Edinburgh

CAMBRIDGE
UNIVERSITY PRESS

CAMBRIDGE UNIVERSITY PRESS
Cambridge, New York, Melbourne, Madrid, Cape Town, Singapore, São Paulo

Cambridge University Press
The Edinburgh Building, Cambridge CB2 2RU, UK

Published in the United States of America by Cambridge University Press, New York

www.cambridge.org
Information on this title: www.cambridge.org/9780521012805

© Michael Purcell 2006

First published 2006

Printed in the United Kingdom at the University Press, Cambridge

A catalogue record for this book is available from the British Library

ISBN-13   978-0-521-81325-9 hardback
ISBN-10   0-521-81325-5 hardback
ISBN-13   978-0-521-01280-5 paperback
ISBN-10   0-521-01280-5 paperback

'The just will flourish like the palm-tree
and grow like a Lebanon cedar.
Planted in the house of the Lord
they will flourish in the courts of our God.'
—Psalm 92

'Tout est grâce.'
—Georges Bernanos

Contents

List of abbreviations of Levinas' works   *page* ix

   Introduction   1

1. Levinas, phenomenology, and theology   7

2. Ethics, theology, and the question of God   45

3. Incarnate existence   73

4. Existence as transcendence, or the call of the infinite:
   towards a theology of grace   95

5. The economy and language of grace: grace, desire,
   and the awakening of the subject   110

6. The liturgical orientation of the self   135

7. Eucharistic responsibility and working for justice   155

Notes   168
Select bibliography   191
Index   197

Abbreviations of Levinas' works

AQS	*Autrement que savoir*
BPW	*Basic Philosophical Writings*
CPP	*Collected Philosophical Papers*
DEHH	*En découvrant l'existence avec Husserl et Heidegger*
DF	*Difficult Freedom*
DQVI	*De dieu qui vient à l'idée*
EE	*Existence and Existents*
EI	*Ethics and Infinity*
EN	*Entre nous*
GDT	*God, Death, and Time*
HAH	*Humanisme de l'autre homme*
HO	*Humanism of the Other*
IOF	*Is Ontology Fundamental?*, in *Basic Philosophical Writings*. The article was first published in 1951.
IRB	*Is it Righteous to be? Interviews with Emmanuel Levinas*
MS	'Meaning and Sense' in *Basic Philosophical Writings*
NineTR	*Nine Talmudic Readings*
NTR	*New Talmudic Readings*
OB	*Otherwise than Being*
OE	*On Escape*
OGCM	*Of God who Comes to Mind*, 2nd edn
PN	*Proper Names*
SMB	*Sur Maurice Blanchot*
TI	*Totality and Infinity*
TIHP	*Theory of Intuition in Husserl's Phenomenology*
TO	*Time and the Other*
US	'Useless Suffering'

Introduction

Emmanuel Levinas died on 25 December, 1995, a curiously strange Christian day which celebrates incarnation and the acknowledgement of the divine in the human, and the human in the divine. A god walks and wanders the way of humanity and occupies the wilderness and strangeness of the human.

A funeral oration was delivered by Jacques Derrida that same day. In that Derrida quotes from Levinas' own writings on 'uprightness' (*droiture*), taking from Levinas' commentary on the Tractate Shabbath Levinas' description of consciousness as

the urgency of a destination leading to the Other and not an eternal return to self . . . an innocence without naivety, an uprightness which is also absolute self-criticism, read in the eyes of the one who is the goal of my uprightness and whose look calls me into question. It is a movement towards the Other that does not come back to its point of origin the way a diversion comes back, incapable as it is of transcendence – a movement beyond anxiety and stronger than death. This uprightness is called *Temimut*, the essence of Jacob.

Derrida continues:

This same meditation also sets to work . . . all the great themes which the work of Emmanuel Levinas has awakened in us, that of responsibility first of all, but of an 'unlimited' responsibility that exceeds and precedes my freedom, that of an 'unconditional yes'.[1]

Derrida recalls a conversation on the rue Michel Ange in Paris, where in response to Derrida, Levinas remarks,

You know, one often speaks of ethics to describe what I do, but what really interests me in the end is not ethics, not ethics alone, but the holy, the holiness of the holy.[2]

Derrida rightly points to 'all the great themes' which Levinas' thought has awakened, for philosophy (and theology) is an awakening. This book attempts to outline some of them, particularly as they might relate to theology. Levinas was both a philosopher in the phenomenological tradition, but also a religious thinker in a Jewish tradition. He also mistrusted Christian theology, first, because it compromised the transcendence of the divine, but secondly, and more importantly, because, by taking God as its proper object of study, it avoided the detour of the human. So also, his mistrust of any mysticism which would seek access to God without the encounter with the human. For Levinas, God could only be encountered in terms of the human. Hence his constant saying that 'God arises as the counterpart of the justice rendered to the other person.'

Why is Levinas significant for theological reflection? In the *Preface* to the second edition of *Of God who Comes to Mind*, Levinas notes,

We have been reproached for ignoring theology; and we do not contest the necessity of a recovery, at least, the necessity of choosing an opportunity for a recovery of these themes. We think, however, that theological recuperation comes after the glimpse of holiness, which is primary.[3]

For Levinas, 'ethics is first theology'. Or, put otherwise, theology must first of all be ethics. It is both ethical in intent and ethical in origin. One might say that ethics is 'fundamental theology'. Ethics, as Levinas understands the term, is fundamental to theology and opens on to what is often called 'fundamental' or 'foundational' theology, that is, a theology which takes its point of departure in the one who is able to receive some form of revelation. The question of God cannot be asked without raising the prior question of the one who is able to ask the question of God. Theology begins as theological anthropology, and to reflect on the human person is already to be involved in an ethical enterprise.

But further, in paying attention to the significance of the human, Levinas enables theology to be liberated from a tendency towards the purely theoretical and directs its concerns to practical engagement in human concerns. Theology, like ethics, involves *praxis*. It is 'the wisdom of love in the service of love'.

There is a further reason why Levinas is significant for theological reflection: significant work is being done in Continental Europe – particularly in France and Belgium – on the theological development of Levinas' phenomenological and ethical reflections. One thinks of figures such as Jean-Luc Marion, Michel Henry, and Jean-Louis Chrétien in France, and Roger Burggraeve in Belgium, to say nothing of the new generation of theologians and philosophers of religion who advance theology in a phenomenological voice, some of whom figure in this present work.

For these reasons, Levinas is worth careful attention by theologians and aspiring theologians. He offers to theology a new voice, a new grammar of response and responsibility, a new lexicon for articulating the human in its tendency towards the divine which, for Levinas, cannot avoid an ethical commitment to the other person here and now.

EMMANUEL LEVINAS

Who, then, is Emmanuel Levinas? These are simply the bare bones of biographical detail. Others have written substantial biographical volumes.

Emmanuel Levinas was born on 12 January 1906 (30 December in the Julian Calendar) in Kaunas (Kovno), Lithuania, into an orthodox Jewish family. During the First World War, the family emigrated to Karkov in the Ukraine, before returning to Lithuania in 1920.

In 1923, he went to Strasbourg, France, where he began his philosophical studies, and where he met Maurice Blanchot. In 1928–29, he was at Freiburg to follow courses offered by Husserl and Heidegger, and, in 1930, completed his thesis on 'The Theory of Intuition in the Phenomenology of Husserl'. Also in 1930, he became a French citizen.

He was imprisoned during the war in a German prisoner-of-war camp, Stalag 1492.

In 1947, he was named director of L'École Normale Israélite Orientale. In 1961, he became a professor at the University of Poitiers, and in 1967, professor at the University of Paris, Nanterre. In 1973, he was named a professor at the Sorbonne.

What of the influences which formed his own thinking? Levinas notes three main ones: first, his reading of great Russian authors. Thus, one finds frequent references to Dostoievsky's *Brothers Karamazov* and the words of Markel, younger brother of the elder Zossima:

Darling mother . . . there have to be masters and servants, but let me be the servant of my servants. Let me be the same as they are to me. And let me tell you this, too, Mother: every one of us is responsible for everyone else in every way, and I most of all.

Secondly, the Hebrew Bible, especially Talmudic texts and Rabbinical commentary: Levinas' Talmudic writings involve painstaking and detailed reflections on the Talmud, and like its authors, return time and again to these texts which grapple with the human existential. In Levinas, the existential acquires a phenomenological articulation. Levinas' method of constant iteration ('like a wave breaking constantly against a shore', as Derrida would have it) no doubt reflects this Talmudic training.

Thirdly, the historical experience of emigration across Russia, and then to France, the rise of Hitler and National Socialism, and the experience of the Holocaust. The effect of the never-to-be-forgotten antisemitism – the type of 'every hatred of the other person' – cannot, nor should it, be underestimated in Levinas' writings. In the inscription and dedication in *Otherwise than Being, or Beyond Essence*, Levinas writes

To the memory of those who were closest among the six million assassinated by the National Socialists, and of the millions of all confessions and all nations, victims of the same hatred of the other man, the same antisemitism. (*OB*, vii)

Then, in Hebrew, the more personal dedication which lists Levinas' father, Yekhiel ben Rabbi Avraham Halevi, his mother, Dvora bat Rabbi Moshe Halevi, his brothers, Dov ben Rabbi Yehiel and Aminadav ben Rabbi Yekhiel Halevi, his father-in-law, Shmuel ben Rabbi Guershon Halevi, and his mother-in-law, Malki bat Rabbi Haim, all of whom, with the exception of his father-in-law, were victims of the Holocaust.

Of specifically philosophical influence is the thinking of Husserl, Heidegger, and Bergson.

A considerable volume of secondary literature continues to be produced on aspects of Levinas' thought. This is a small contribution.

One cannot begin to consider Levinas as a philosopher without acknowledging the phenomenological context within which his thought unfolds, and also the way in which he pushes beyond Husserl. This going beyond Husserl has provoked sharp criticism; hence the need to consider carefully the critique of Dominique Janicaud, and the 'theological turn in French phenomenology'. Chapter 1 considers the relationship between Levinas, Phenomenology, and Theology. A key point will be that ethics is not only 'first philosophy' but also 'first theology'.

This opens on to the relation between ethics, theology, and the question of God, which is considered in Chapter 2. These first two chapters set the context for any theological furthering or transposition of Levinas' thought.

Levinas is committed to the world. Existence is incarnate, and is lived out as responsibility for the other person. The nature of this incarnate existence is considered, both phenomenologically and theologically, in Chapter 3. Yet, to be is not only to be 'in-the-world'; it is to be in the world in a way which is *otherwise* than being. How this incarnate existence can be articulated ethically is considered in Chapter 4 which addresses the notions of transcendence and the appeal of the infinite, and the beginnings of a theology of grace. The theology of grace is a fundamental Christian doctrine. One could argue it is *the* fundamental and guiding doctrine. The ethical awakening of the subject, and the language and economy of grace is considered in Chapter 5 in terms of desire and phenomenological and theological awakening.

Transcendence, however, is not an escape from the world, nor an evasion of responsibility. 'The true life may be elsewhere' – or otherwise – 'but we are in the world'. Levinas expresses this in terms of the liturgical nature of subjectivity, where liturgy is understood as a work or service undertaken for and on behalf of the other person. This is considered in Chapter 6 on 'the liturgical orientation of the self'. The practical outcome of responsibility is the commitment to justice and working for an ethical community. The orientation of the self towards the other person – the one and the many – can also be articulated in terms of a eucharistic ethics. This, along with the nature of time and eschatology, is considered in Chapter 7.

Both for phenomenology and theology Levinas presents a challenge, an opportunity, and a language. The Carnegie Trust for Universities in Scotland is thanked for assistance in funding a research trip to Leuven, Belgium.

CHAPTER I

Levinas, phenomenology, and theology

Emmanuel Levinas first became prominent in the French philosophical environment as a translator and commentator of Edmund Husserl (1859–1938), and was largely responsible for introducing phenomenology to France.

Following studies in Strasbourg where he obtained his *licence* in 1927, he embarked on doctoral studies on Husserl, and in the academic session of 1928–29 went to Freiburg-im-Breisgau where he attended classes given by Husserl and Heidegger. His doctoral thesis, subsequently published in 1930, took as its theme 'The Theory of Intuition in Husserl's Phenomenology'. Husserl, meanwhile, had delivered a series of lectures in Paris in 1929. These, first published in French in 1931 as *Méditations Cartésiennes* in extended form, were translated and co-edited by Levinas, and became influential in the development of French phenomenological thought. Significantly, it was the translation of the fifth of the *Cartesian Meditations* which fell to Levinas that accounts for Levinas' ongoing interest in pursuing the intersubjective reduction in phenomenology, implicated but not pursued by Husserl.[1]

Simone de Beauvoir, in *La Force de l'âge*, gives a somewhat amusing account of this influence of Levinas on phenomenology in France, when she recounts Sartre's first encounter with phenomenology. Out with Raymond Aron, a student of Husserl, in Paris in 1932, apricot cocktails were ordered. According to de Beauvoir, Aron said to Sartre, 'You see, my little comrade, if you are a phenomenologist, you can talk about this cocktail, and that is philosophy.' This seemingly mundane incident, terribly ordinary, gives an indication of the value which Sartre recognised in phenomenology: the seemingly ordinary affairs of human existence have a significance which may be more than, or other than, ordinary. Levinas indicates something similar when he draws attention to the sincerity which characterises our life in the world. 'Life is a sincerity.' 'We breathe for the sake of breathing, eat and drink for the sake of eating and drinking, we take shelter for the sake of taking shelter, we study to satisfy our curiosity, we take a walk for the walk. All that is not for the sake of living; it is living.'[2] De Beauvoir continues:

Sartre grew pale with excitement, or nearly so. This was precisely what he had wished for years: to talk of the things as he touched them and that was philosophy. Aron convinced him that this was exactly what fitted his preoccupations: to transcend the opposition of idealism and realism, to affirm at the same time the sovereignty of consciousness and the presence of the world as given to us. He bought at the Boulevard St. Michel the work on Husserl by Levinas, and he was in such a hurry to inform himself that, while walking, he leafed through the book, whose pages he had not even cut.[3]

The book in question was the published version of Levinas' doctoral thesis, *The Theory of Intuition in Husserl's Phenomenology* (*TIHP*).

LEVINAS, HUSSERL, AND PHENOMENOLOGY

In his essay on 'The Phenomenology of Givenness and First Philosophy', Jean-Luc Marion indicates the three key formulas of classical Husserlian phenomenology,[4] which provide a helpful map or platform for considering Levinas and his use of phenomenological method. First, 'as much appearing, as much being'; in other words, objects are known insofar as they appear within consciousness, and according to the manner of their appearing. Secondly, 'Return to the things themselves'; in other words, phenomenology, through a reduction, attempts access to an object divested of ontological assumptions. The object, quite simply, is as it appears, and it is the reality of this object as it appears within consciousness which is to be clarified. Thirdly, 'intuition is a proper source of knowledge'; in other words, intentionality, or the attitude which is taken towards an object – the object as it appears within consciousness – is constitutive of knowledge. Marion will add, as a fourth 'principle', 'givenness' – objects are as they give themselves to us, which can be formulated 'as much reduction, as much givenness'. In other words, phenomenological method must first recognise the givenness of an object – the object as it first strikes us or imposes itself upon us, and thereafter reduce its appearing as such. Levinas, in his own use of phenomenological method and his defence of interiority on the basis of exteriority, will open the way for such as Marion. What then is the significance of Husserl for Levinas? Writing in *Signature*, Levinas comments,

Husserl brought a method to philosophy. It consists in respecting the intentions which animate the psyche and the modalities of *appearing* which conform to these intentions, modalities which characterise the diverse beings apprehended by experience. It consists in discovering the unsuspected *horizons* within which the real is apprehended by representative thought but also apprehended by concrete pre-predicative life, beginning with the body (innocently), beginning with culture (perhaps less innocently). (*DF*, 291–2)

Three things of significance are worth noting here, which correspond to the formulas which Marion identifies in Husserl. First, there is the link between appearing and reality: 'as much appearing, as much being'. Secondly, there is the concern with 'concrete life' which is to be subjected to phenomenological scrutiny: 'return to the things themselves'. Co-implicated here are also various horizons and frameworks which need to be reduced. If objects appear in consciousness as meaningful, these particular meanings point to other horizons and structures of meaning. There is also the difficulty of identifying or delimiting an object in the first place. Thirdly, there is the notion of intentionality: objects appear in a particular mode in conformity with a particular intention. In other words, thought is always 'a thought of something', hope is a 'hoping for something', desire is 'a desire for something'. Correspondingly, objects are always appreciated in terms of the particular manner in which a subject relates to them: objects make their appearance under a particular aspect, or they appear *as* thought of, hoped for, or desired. Husserl himself uses the example of the tree in his garden: A tree is never *just a tree*, but a tree apperceived and appreciated in a particular way and from a particular perspective. To say, however, that 'a tree is never *just a tree*' is to bring into play two contesting attitudes: the 'natural' or 'naive' attitude, and the 'phenomenological attitude' which seeks critically to overcome the 'natural attitude'.

Contesting the 'natural attitude' (or, naive realism)

Husserl had recognised that the 'naturalistic theory of being' is pervasive. He had started his philosophical career with studies in the philosophy of arithmetic and logic, but became convinced that although
the sciences seemed to display rigour in the pursuit of certainty, they
remained in themselves uncritical and unfounded. They claimed to
be evidentially based but the evidence which they offered was circumscribed by the confines and presumptions of their own particular discipline. Levinas comments that the sciences such as physics,
biology, psychology 'make use of a certain number of fundamental
notions' such as memory, perception, space, time etc., yet they do
not themselves clarify the meaning of these notions. Yet, these very
notions provide the framework within which the sciences operate and
'determine the necessary structure of different domains of being and
constitute their essence' (*TIHP*, 3). What Husserl recognised was the
need for a fundamental science – a 'first philosophy' – which would
provide critical grounding for all other sciences, 'a phenomenological
theory of cognition as a fundamental science, that is, a science which
systematically explores the ultimate basis of justification not only for
objectively oriented logic but for every science pure and simple.'[5] Levinas comments that 'for Husserl, the study of being is not exhausted
by the natural sciences and the regional ontologies' (*TIHP*, 4) such as
'the world of mathematics' or 'the world of biology'. These regional
ontologies are themselves founded on something more basic, and it
is phenomenology's task to investigate and expose the fundamental
notions which the various regional ontologies employ. Phenomenology, then, is an 'absolute science' whose task is to 'disclose the "sources"
from which the basic concepts and ideal laws of pure logic spring,
and back to which they must again be pursued in order to provide
them with the "clarity and distinctness" requisite for an epistemological understanding and critique of pure logic.'[6] Such a task means placing in question and contesting the 'natural attitude' which is often
evident in the sciences.

Naturalism – as 'a general philosophy, a theory of being' – assumes
that reality is always and everywhere the same. The constitution of
objects, the relations between them, and the categories of thought
are identical. Such a supposition of universality, Husserl recognised,

remained unquestioned by the natural sciences and regional ontologies. But the 'reality' is that 'the structure of being' – that is, 'the way things are' – 'which is the object of ontology is not everywhere the same: different *regions* of being [*Seinsregionen*] have a different constitution and cannot be thought of by means of the same categories' (*TIHP*, 3). '*To exist does not mean the same thing in every region*'; it is this insight into the relation between meaning and reality which is, says Levinas, 'one of the most interesting [theses] in phenomenology' (*TIHP*, 4).

Now, naturalism may be described as naive realism; it assumes that the object of which we are conscious really exists. For example, everyone will readily agree that the object which we are looking at is a blossoming apple tree. Husserl would not dispute the transcendence of the apple tree with respect to the subject. It is present not only in the interiority of consciousness but also possesses its own exteriority with respect to consciousness. However, the apple tree which appears in consciousness has no fixed or single meaning. What appears in consciousness is not 'the *tree simpliciter*, the physical thing belonging to Nature', which 'can burn up, be resolved into its chemical elements etc.'.[7] The perceived tree is only ever given *as perceived*, and the meanings which it is capable of bearing are variable. Such meanings are given by a consciousness which is subjective, and also intersubjective. 'Nature reveals itself in successive apparitions, in multiple, changing, subjective phenomena (*subjektive Erscheinungen*)', or 'from a certain angle in which are already inscribed systematic possibilities of ever new perspectives' (*TIHP*, 5). Levinas refers to Husserl:

A spatial being can 'appear' only in a certain 'orientation', which necessarily predelineates a system of possible new orientations each of which, in turn, corresponds to a certain 'mode of appearance' which we can express, say, as givenness from such and such a 'side', and so forth.[8]

The natural attitude, however, still presumes an object 'out there' which is perceived by a subject, an exteriority to which an interiority relates, 'an objectivity that would be indifferent to the very existence of a subjectivity' (*TIHP*, 6). Immediately, such a naive understanding of 'the way things are' raises the epistemological problem of bridging the gulf between subject and objects, the problem of 'connecting them with subjectivity' (*TIHP*, 6).

To illustrate the difficulty, Levinas refers to Husserl's example of the perception of a table,[9] and comments that a 'natural attitude' will argue that '[e]ven though this side of the table which is offered to sight is only a subject view of an objective table, immutable in space and time, it is in no way a content of consciousness but rather its object.' For the natural or naive attitude 'this is a table', an object whose existence is independent of consciousness. Despite the fact that only a certain aspect of the table is presented to us, 'the whole object is implicated' (*TIHP*, 6). From a particular aspect, the move is quickly made to the affirmation of an object in its entirety, for our senses do not deceive us. What appears is contiguous with the reality. '*Everyone will readily agree*' that this is a table. The appearance of the thing accords with its reality. 'In some sense each appearance contains the *whole* thing' (*TIHP*, 7). What is at stake here is the 'ideal of objectivity that is already intimated in concrete perception' (*TIHP*, 8), an ideal to which naturalism is prey. 'By asserting the objectivity of the physical world, naturalism identifies the existence and the conditions of existence of the physical world with the conditions of existence in general' but, Levinas comments, 'while the world of the physicist claims to go beyond naive experience, his world really exists only in relation to naive experience' (*TIHP*, 9).

Now, Husserl criticises naturalism because it 'misinterprets the meaning of the existence of nature itself' (*TIHP*, 10), conceiving objectivity 'on the model of material things' (*TIHP*, 12). But this impacts on the way in which consciousness is understood, for the 'naturalised object' finds its corollary in a naturalised consciousness. 'If to be is to be in nature, then consciousness, through which nature is known, must also be part of nature inasmuch as it claims to exist' (*TIHP*, 13). Both nature and consciousness become ideal realities, and the ensuing epistemological problem stemming from such a naturalised ontology is, as indicated, the problem of the link between the world 'out' there and the interiorised subject, a problem endemic to naive realism. Naturalism – naive realism – presumes an object, which the conscious subject intends; consciousness, however, is subjective, relative, unscientific, and consequently is prone to error. What the naturalistic method, in its attempt to secure an objective world, fails to do is subject its own method to scrutiny. At 'the very heart of naturalism', writes Levinas, 'is its conception of existence' (*TIHP*, 16). Phenomenology thus becomes a critique of method, and contests naive conceptions of reality. Positively, it seeks to clarify the meaning of existence. In other words, phenomenology has both an epistemological and an ontological import. Levinas articulates the problem in these words:

> If *to be* means to exist the way nature does, then everything which is given as refractory to the categories and to the mode of existence of nature will, as such, have no objectivity and will be, a priori and unavoidably, reduced to something natural. (*TIHP*, 17)

The problem with the natural attitude, or 'naive' realism, is that the 'natural' becomes the model for understanding what it is 'to be', and meaning becomes something super-added, variable, indeterminate, and susceptible to error. For, if meaning is something super-added to the real, consciousness must adequate itself to a reality which already *is* in the objective world. Yet, what is given in consciousness is only ever given *as* . . . Being and meaning are co-implicated.

Intentionality

In his *Ideas Pertaining to a Pure Phenomenology and to a Phenomenological Philosophy*, Husserl cites the example of the blossoming apple tree in his garden to explain the notion of intentionality, that is, that consciousness is 'consciousness of something'. Yet, 'consciousness', which is 'something obviously understandable of itself', is also highly 'enigmatic'.[10] Things are not as simple or as simply given to thought as we might think. For example, 'Let us suppose that in a garden we regard with pleasure a blossoming apple tree, the freshly green grass of the lawn, etc.'[11] Already two aspects are indicated: we not only regard the blossoming apple tree, but we regard it *with pleasure*. The perception of the apple tree has an objective pole (the tree) and a subjective pole (the pleasure). This is an entirely natural attitude to take: there is the tree which is perceived, and there is the subject who perceives the tree with pleasure.

In the natural attitude, the apple tree is for us something existing in the transcendent realm of spatial actuality, and the perception, as well as the liking, is for us a psychical state belonging to real people. Between the one and the other real things, between the real person or the real perception, and the real apple tree, there exist real relations.[12]

Unfortunately, however, this natural attitude tends to reduce the relationship between an object and a subject to the problem of knowledge, and the ensuing epistemological and ontological difficulty is accounting for the way that the gap between the knowing subject and the object which is known is bridged. The 'between' which Husserl adverts to in his example is the problem of connecting the blossoming apple tree which really exists with the person who, walking in the garden, takes delight and pleasure in its sight and smell. The difficulty is that the natural attitude, which has a certain naivety about it, presumes a relationship between a subject and an object and neglects the fact that the attitude which is taken *towards* the object actually conditions our appreciation of what the object actually *is*. It may well be that the blossoming apple tree gives us pleasure – it *is* the tree under which my children played; but it might equally well be the case that it provokes anger in us, so much so that we wish to take an axe to its roots – it *is* the tree from which my young son fatally fell.

Husserl, then, suggests another, phenomenological, understanding of consciousness. Consciousness is always '*consciousness of*' and the object perceived is always the '*object perceived as*'. In other words, before ever there is a differentiation into a subject and an object, there is, on the 'subjective side', a consciousness which is never other than a *consciousness of*, and, on the 'objective side', an object which is only ever *perceived as*. This is described in terms of *intentionality*. Thus, with respect to the blossoming apple tree which Husserl notices, there is the act by which the tree is perceived (*noesis*) and the perception of the tree (*noema*), both of which can be described as a primary correlation between *noesis* and *noema*; and there is the actual tree, transcendent with respect to consciousness, but only ever accessible in terms of consciousness. Phenomenology, it must be stressed, as a 'science of meaning' which focuses on the intentional nature of consciousness does not deny the existence of the actual tree in the 'transcendent world' beyond consciousness. Rather, in the phenomenological attitude, the actuality of the transcendent world is placed in parenthesis, or 'bracketed'. 'The transcendent world receives its "parenthesis", we exercise the *epoché* in relation to positing its actual being'.[13]

Now, Levinas, considering the derivative nature of 'subject' and 'object', describes Husserlian intentionality like this: 'The precise function of intentionality is to characterise consciousness as a primary and original phenomenon, from which the subject and the object of traditional philosophy are only abstractions' (*TIHP*, 48). Again, 'each act of consciousness is consciousness of something: each perception the perception of a perceived object, each desire the desire of a desired object, each judgement the judgement of a "state of affairs" [*Sachverhalt*] about which one makes a pronouncement' (*TIHP*, 40). However, although in Husserl, *representation* tends to be the privileged understanding of consciousness such that *cogito* in its relation to the world is pre-eminently *theoretical*, Levinas draws attention to the fact that such states as 'I perceive, I remember, I imagine, I judge, I desire, I want'[14] are analogous states of Cartesian *cogito* which has to be understood 'in a pregnant sense'. The Cartesian *cogito* was not restricted to the theoretical but embraced the volitional and the affective.[15] Intentionality in Husserl, then, must be to be taken 'in a wide sense'. In his own work, Levinas will widen and extend the phenomenological scope or arc to the extent that life itself, in its many dimensions, is to be understood as intentional. Intentionality is the structure of *all our relations* with the world; it '*affects* . . . all the forms of our life'. Desire is always a desire for the desired; doing is always a doing of something; love is always a love of something loved; satisfaction derives from a satisfying relation with the satisfying. In other words, intentionality is not always and everywhere the same. There are differing ways of intending an object, differing ways of transcendence. Thus, Levinas can write that 'concrete life must be taken in all its forms and not merely in the theoretical form . . .; the real world is a world of objects of practical use and values' (*TIHP*, 44), a use and value which is not purely a 'subjective reaction'. Using and valuing are certainly ways of relating to the world, as Heidegger will clearly demonstrate in *Being and Time*, but '[i]t is precisely the very wide extension of the Husserlian notion of intentionality that makes it interesting'. Intentionality 'has a sense' which is not 'pure representation' (*TIHP*, 44).

Concrete life is not pure *theory*, although for Husserl the latter has a special status. It is a life of action and feeling, will and aesthetic judgement, interest and indifference, etc. It follows that the world which is correlative to this life is a sensed or wanted world, a world of action, beauty, ugliness, meanness, as well as an object of theoretical contemplation. (*TIHP*, 45)

For example,

> [t]he act of love has a sense, but this does not mean that it includes a
> representation of the object loved together with a purely *subjective* feeling
> which has no sense and which accompanies the representation. The character
> of the loved object is precisely to be given in a love intention, an intention
> which is irreducible to a purely theoretical representation. (*TIHP*, 44–5)

One might put this otherwise by saying that human life, as intentional, is characterised by transcendence.

Intentionality as transcendence

Because consciousness is always '*consciousness of* ' – that is, intentional – it bears an implicit reference to a reality which is transcendent to consciousness, although the affirmation of this transcendence
is placed in parenthesis in the phenomenological *epoché.* '*Intentionality is, for Husserl, a genuine act of transcendence and the very prototype
of any transcendence*' (*TIHP*, 40). In other words, *noesis* always and
already has a *noematic* correlate. Thought is never without an object.
Consciousness, in its widest sense, always 'intends something other
than itself; it transcends itself' (*TIHP*, 39). It is not simple subjectivity,
but finds itself always and already to be beyond itself. Here again the
notion of naturalism or naive realism which assumes that first there
is consciousness and thereafter something of which it is conscious is
being opposed. But, Levinas further explains, nor can intentionality
be viewed as a '*property* of consciousness' (*TIHP*, 40), as if there were
first a consciousness and then a movement or operation of consciousness which intended an object. The very nature of consciousness is
that it *is* intentional, or *eventful* or *eventmental*, as Marion will argue.
Thus, intentionality is not 'a bridge between the world and consciousness' as if the problem were one of bridging a gap between subject
and object. The problem is not one of explaining 'the connection
between some psychological event named "experience" and another
real being named "object"', or of answering the question 'How does
a subject reach a transcendent object?' for 'a subject is not something that first exists and then relates to objects' (*TIHP*, 41). Rather,
the subject is already beyond itself as transcendence towards what is
other than itself; it is always and already relational. As Levinas puts

it, '*Intentionality is what makes up the very subjectivity of subjects*'; and, 'the relation *between* subjects and objects constitutes the genuinely primary phenomenon' (*TIHP*, 43).[16] For Husserl, 'contact with the world' is 'at the very heart of the being of consciousness' (*TIHP*, 43).

In search of phenomenological adequacy

Husserl puts in question the notion of knowledge as a simple, naive *adequatio intellectus et rei*, in which a knowing subject relates to an external object. The notions of subject and object are already derivative. Yet, thought tends towards an adequacy of understanding. If 'the world of transcendent *res* necessarily depends on [*ist angewiesen an*] consciousness' in terms of the *noematico-noetic* correlation, and if adequacy remains a goal in terms of a better appreciation of and understanding of the world we inhabit, then the adequacy or otherwise of the apperception of any object in consciousness needs to be scrutinised. Husserl draws attention to the fact that *perception is inadequate*. An object given in consciousness is never perceived adequately. The tree that I perceive is not given in consciousness *as such*, wholly and entirely, but always from a particular side and angle. As Levinas puts it,

The aspects which we see at any given moment always indicate further aspects, and so on. Things are never known in their totality; an essential character of our perception of them is that of being inadequate. (*TIHP*, 21–2)

What this means is that each perception invites and leads on to further and related perceptions. 'Each moment of consciousness is surrounded . . . by *horizons* . . . "Each perception is an *ex-ception* [*jedes Erfassen ist ein Herausfassen*]".' In other words, whatever is perceived is always perceived as standing out against a horizon. 'Cogitation makes the *cogitatum* its own by extracting from it a background which constantly accompanies it and which may become itself the object of an *Herausfassung*' (*TIHP*, 19). Perception, then, is always partial. However, the 'partiality of perception' can be considered in two ways: first, from the more noematic point of view, objects only present a certain aspect to view; perception is always perception *of* an object from a particular perspective which can open on to other perspectives which contribute to the building up of a more complete, more adequate picture of the whole. Robert Sokolowski's example of 'The perception of a Cube as a paradigm of conscious experience' illustrates the complexity of perception. Faced straight on, a cube is apperceived as a square; it is only by bodily shifting position and changing perspective that the appreciation of the object as a 'cube' is built up.[17] Secondly, however, from the more noetic point of view, perception also demonstrates its partiality in another sense: the particular manner in which one intends an object determines what Husserl calls *'the very mode of the existence of external things'* (*TIHP*, 23), but, for Husserl, the determinative way of intending an object tends to be overly theoretical. Levinas will criticise Husserl for this overly theoretical approach to intentionality to the detriment of other manners of intending objects, whether practical, aesthetic, or ethical. The object is not simply a perceived object, but can be an object of use, beauty, value, and ethics.

There is, however, a further aspect of the inadequacy of perception to which Marion, in his treatment of 'givenness', draws attention. Building on Levinas' stress on the often disruptive effect which exteriority *as such*, or *kath'auto*,[18] can have on subjectivity, Marion stresses that objects give themselves *as such*, and it is this original and excessive givenness which is the point of departure for their appearing within consciousness. '[N]o appearing is excepted from the fold of givenness, *even if it does not always accomplish the phenomenal unfolding in its entirety.*'[19] For Marion, the connection between reduction and givenness will be the defining principle of phenomenology.

What appears gives itself, that is to say, it appears without restraint or remainder; it thus comes about [*ad-vient*], happens, and imposes itself as such, not as the semblance or the representative of an absent or dissimulated in-itself, but as itself, in person and in the flesh; what appears is emptied totally, so to speak . . . to the point of passing from the rank of image, from simple seeming or bereft appearance, to the one unique thing at stake. And if the phenomenon did not give itself as such, it would remain simply the other of being [*être*].[20]

In view of the excessive givenness of the object to thought, thought, which is always after the event of the advent of the object, is a constant attempt to be adequate.

Lived experience, and subject and object as derivative

Subject and object are derived notions. The naive attitude presumes the existence of a subject and an object, and the epistemological task becomes the 'pseudo-problem' of bridging the gap between the two. Husserl, however,

> tried to locate the existence of external things, not in their opposition to what they are for consciousness, but in the aspect under which they are present in concrete conscious life. What exists for us, what we consider as existing is not a reality hidden behind phenomena that appear as images or signs of this reality. The world of phenomena itself makes up the being of our concrete life. (*TIHP*, 24)

It is the sceptic who raises the possibility of knowledge as a problem. But the sceptical position presupposes 'the existence of an object and of a subject that must come into contact with each other' and thereby makes knowledge contact between the two. But,

> this problem is exposed as fictitious once we understand that the origin of the very idea of 'an object' is to be found in the concrete life of a subject; that a subject is not a substance in need of a bridge, namely knowledge, in order to reach an object, but that the secret of its subjectivity is its being present in front of objects. The modes of appearing of things are not, therefore, characters which are superimposed on existing things by the processes of consciousness; they make up the very existence of things. (*TIHP*, 25)

By stressing consciousness as a sphere of absolute existence, Husserl overcomes the problem of scepticism which doubts the correspondence of knowing and known. To say that consciousness, which is always consciousness as *a consciousness of*, has an absolute existence not only 'expresses the indubitable character of the *cogito*' but 'founds the possibility of an indubitable *cogito*' (*TIHP*, 30–1). This marks a key and important difference between Husserl and Descartes.

Descartes' consideration of the *cogito* is an epistemological endeavour. It is an analysis of knowledge. Within this analysis, sensibility is the site of error, and claims to knowledge based on an analysis of sensibility are 'relative and fallible'; it is the soul, not the senses, which opens onto knowledge, for 'the soul is easier to know than the body' (*TIHP*, 31). Descartes presumes the self-evidence of consciousness, but fails to interrogate its sources. Thus, in the Cartesian schema there is the move from the absolute existence of consciousness to the existence of God, whose veracity guarantees the evidence of the senses, and thereafter to the existence of the world which offers itself to consciousness through the senses. The *cogito* is the foundation from which all else follows. For Husserl, however, consciousness is always and already *consciousness of* and always and already implicates the existence of a world. Thus, unlike Descartes, existence does not follow from a *cogito*, but rather existence *allows* a *cogito*.

For Husserl, the necessary existence of consciousness does not follow from the *cogito*; rather, this necessary existence is none other than an existence that allows a *cogito*. The *cogito* is not merely a means to attain a first certainty so as to deduce the existence of the world outside the *cogito*. (*TIHP*, 31)[21]

In other words, prior to the *cogito* as a thinking substance, there is the absolute existence of *consciousness* which is always a *consciousness of*.

Now, Descartes' analysis proceeded epistemologically in view of an ontology. 'For such a philosophy, the question is not to know what it is to be, but to know whether such and such an object exists' (*TIHP*, 31). Husserl's analysis, on the other hand, proceeds phenomenologically in view of an ontology. In the Cartesian analysis, the question of the meaning of being is not raised, and naive realism and its sceptical opponents find fertile ground for debate and disagreement. But, 'to exist' is not always and everywhere the same, as Descartes had assumed. Descartes was attempting to build an impossible bridge between epistemology and ontology, along the model of traversing the gap between a knowing interiority and a knowable exteriority, separating 'the knowledge of an object' as it appears in lived experience from its being. Husserl, on the other hand, has a phenomenological understanding of being; being is as it appears in consciousness: the intentional object is the real object. Within consciousness, being makes its appearance in a variety of modes. Husserl's great insight was recognising 'the essential and fundamental difference between *being qua consciousness* and *being qua thing*' (*TIHP*, 26). Thus, in Husserl, Levinas comments 'there is for the first time a possibility of passing from and through the theory of knowledge to the theory of being' (*TIHP*, 32). The way this is achieved is through an understanding of *intentionality* as the fundamental character of absolute consciousness.

'But this is no longer Husserl . . .'

As he comes towards the end of *The Theory of Intuition in Husserl's Phenomenology*, Levinas draws together some of the main themes he has previously considered before raising some criticisms of Husserl which will influence his own subsequent philosophical reflections. Already noted is the distinction between the 'natural' attitude and the 'phenomenological' attitude. The 'natural' or 'dogmatic' attitude takes the existence of the world for granted, but such an attitude is '*essentially* naive' (*TIHP*, 121), and 'consists in accepting objects as given and existing, without questioning the meaning of this existence and of the "fact of its being given" [*Gegebenheit*]' (*TIHP*, 122). (In fact, it is the fact of the 'givenness' of what is given to consciousness and its reduction which will characterise the phenomenological endeavour in Levinas and beyond.) The 'natural attitude' overlooks and ignores the correlation of thought and its intentional object, and fails to recognise that existence and meaning are co-implicated. As such, the 'natural attitude' is uncritical. In focusing directly on the presumed objectivity of the object – that is, by taking a look and only taking a look – 'the genuine intention of life remains hidden' (*TIHP*, 123) and the significance of lived experience, or even the question of lived experience as significant, is passed over. The *naïveté* of the natural attitude demands a theory of knowledge for its remedy, but such a theory of knowledge already has ontological presuppositions.

In contrast to the 'natural' attitude, the 'phenomenological' attitude argues that life itself, and its meaning as it is experienced, must become the object of enquiry. What is the meaning and structure of our intentions, and how are they related? But this has ontological consequences. The epistemological problem of the naive attitude – 'How are we to understand the fact that the intrinsic being of objectivity becomes "presented", "apprehended", in knowledge, and so ends up by becoming subjective?' (*TIHP*, 124) – is, according to Husserl, entirely fictitious and absurd, '[f]or if consciousness is essentially intentional and "presence in front of being," rather than a reflection on being, how can we speak of a correspondence between the course of thought and the course of things?' (*TIHP* 124–5). 'The question – "How does thought transcend itself?" – expresses only a pseudo-problem' (*TIHP*, 125). The question is, then, how does one go beyond such a theory of knowledge.

Husserl certainly sought a theory of knowledge which clarified methods and put the sciences on a certain footing. In so doing, he also implicated imagination, willing, and desiring in the structure of intentional life and lived experience. But he also drew attention to the ontological dimension of his phenomenological project. The phenomenal object *is* the real object. The object *is* as it appears in consciousness, and consciousness is always consciousness *of* some object, although the question of its absolute existence apart from consciousness was placed in parenthesis in a phenomenological *epoche*. 'Since being is identical with the various objects of our cognitive as well as our volitional and affective life, the study of the objectivity of objects is reduced to the clarification of the very existence of being' (*TIHP*, 131). Phenomenological description of the mode of appearing of objects in consciousness – that is, careful attention to the '[n]oetico-noematic descriptions of the constitution of objects' – is already ontology.

Now, although Husserl emphasised the theoretical and the cognitive dimensions of intentionality, Levinas recognises that implicit in Husserl is the notion that 'the theory of knowledge, understood as an analysis of cognitive life, does not exhaust all of life'. Non-theoretical acts are also constitutive of objects and these contribute to 'a new and irreducible ontological structure'. Further exploration of these acts can 'show how they fecundate phenomenology and carry it beyond the theory of knowledge', into completely new 'dimensions of meaning' and value (*TIHP*, 132). There are elements in Husserl's system 'which seem to lead to a richer notion of existence than mere presence of an object to contemplative consciousness' (*TIHP*, 134).

In his criticism of Husserl, Levinas identifies two critical lacunae which will, in turn, provoke his own thinking beyond, but not necessarily otherwise than, Husserl.

First, in Husserl, there is the tendency towards *abstraction*. Husserl's phenomenological reduction 'does not attempt to perform a mere abstraction' but seeks, on the contrary, to engage with the lived experience of concrete human life. Nonetheless, Husserl 'does not think that the idea of pure immanence is contradictory and hence that consciousness could exist without a world' (*TIHP*, 150). Levinas, on the other hand, takes the intentionality of consciousness as a touchstone, and intentionality is '*necessarily transcendent*'. Following 'the general spirit of [Husserl's] philosophy', 'the world seems to be indispensable to a consciousness which is always a consciousness of something' (*TIHP*, 150–1).

Secondly, Husserl's phenomenological reduction remains on the level of an *egology*. But, concrete life is not a solipsistic life. Consciousness is not 'closed upon itself', and '[c]oncrete being is not what exists for only one consciousness. In the very idea of concrete being is contained the idea of an intersubjective world' (*TIHP*, 150–1). To describe objects in terms of an individual consciousness is to fail to attain 'objects as they are in concrete life' but only objects as an abstraction. The *egological reduction* 'can only be a first step toward phenomenology' (*TIHP*, 150). Concrete life implicates 'others'. The world we inhabit, the world in which we always and already find ourselves, is always and already a 'peopled' world, an intersubjective world. If the reduction is to be properly phenomenological, and if the 'philosophical intuition of subjectivity' is to be complete, then the field of transcendental *intersubjectivity* needs to be opened up by an intersubjective reduction (only briefly referred to by Husserl)[22] which goes further than the egological reduction. As he concludes,

While asserting the primacy of theory for Husserl, we have also emphasised that his essential thesis consists in locating being in concrete life. This is why practical and aesthetic life also have an intentional character and the objects constituted by them also belong to the sphere of being. The aesthetic and ethical categories are also constitutive of being and their mode of existence and of meeting consciousness have a specific structure. Of course, they are always founded on purely theoretical experience; the specificity of the being of these 'objects of value' etc., is not completely *sui generis* as long as there remains in them something of the brute thing. But isn't the possibility of overcoming this difficulty or fluctuation in Husserl's thought provided with the affirmation of the intentional character of practical and axiological life? (*TIHP*, 158)

BEYOND NAIVE REALISM TOWARDS A
'THEOLOGICAL ATTITUDE'

Husserl, as we saw, sought to go beyond the 'natural attitude' in view of developing a 'phenomenological attitude'. Phenomenology would seek to clarify the fundamental notions which the other sciences employed, and would thus merit the title of 'first' or 'fundamental' philosophy. Such an approach is not without theological import for, in the face of the naive and literal interpretations which revealed theology can so often delight in, there is a need also to adopt what might be termed a 'theological attitude' which, like its phenomenological cousin, attempts to clarify the notions which the various 'theologies' employ. Such a theology also claims to be 'fundamental' or 'foundational'. By way of illustration, the work of three theologians who adopt a phenomenological attitude can be suggested.[23]

Lonergan and theological method

The naturalistic attitude, which Husserl identifies, is akin to what Bernard Lonergan calls 'naive realism'. 'The naive realist knows the world mediated by meaning but thinks he knows it by looking'.[24] Lonergan's interest is fundamental theology. As fundamental, it needs to employ a method and a procedure which is properly scientific and so extricate itself from 'a list not of sciences but of academic disciplines'.[25] One cannot but read Lonergan phenomenologically. He describes his intent in *Method in Theology* thus:

First, we shall appeal to the successful sciences to form a preliminary notion of method. Secondly, we shall go behind the procedures of the natural sciences to something both more general and more fundamental, namely, the procedures of the human mind. Thirdly, in the procedures of the human mind we shall discern a transcendental method, that is, a basic pattern of operations employed in every cognition enterprise. Fourthly, we shall indicate the relevance of transcendental method in the formulation of other, more special methods appropriate to particular fields.[26]

In fact, Lonergan pays tribute to Husserl when he writes that 'Edmund Husserl (1859–1938) by his painstaking analysis of intentionality made it evident that human thinking and judging are not just psychological events but always and intrinsically intend, refer to, mean objects distinct from themselves'.[27] What is important for Lonergan is the working of the human mind, or the way in which objects appear in consciousness, and their meaning. Such objects are *concrete*, not abstract. '[W]e intend the concrete, i.e., all that is to be known about a thing'.[28] Said otherwise, it is the given object in its very givenness which is the object of phenomenological (and theological) reduction. One might say, knowing is summoned to be adequate to its inter- rogated object. Such a transcendental method 'is coincident with a notable part of what has been considered philosophy'. Yet,

Very precisely, it is a heightening of consciousness that brings to light our conscious and intentional operations and thereby leads to the answers to three basic questions. What am I doing when I am knowing? Why is doing that knowing? What do I know when I do it?[29]

The first question finds its response in cognitional theory; the second opens on to epistemology; the third is a question of metaphysics, but a metaphysics which is transcendental and heuristic rather than categorial speculation.

Lonergan relates meaning and reality. A significant part of his project is the clarification of meaning. Meaning 'can be clarified by a reduction to its elements'; it has 'various functions' and gives access to 'different realms'; it employs various 'techniques'. To illustrate the relation between meaning and reality, Lonergan considers the 'phe- nomenology of a smile'. A smile has a meaning which cannot be reduced to a particular configuration of lips and eyes. A smile is not a frown or a scowl or a stare or a glare or a snicker or a laugh. It is a smile, and, because its meaning differs from those associated with other facial contortions, 'it is named a smile'. But what makes a smile different from a snarl is its meaning. 'Because we all know that meaning exists, we do not go about the streets smiling at everyone we meet. We know we should be misunderstood'. Indeed, '[t]here is something irreducible to the smile. It cannot be explained by causes outside meaning'.[30]

A further element of meaning to which Lonergan draws attention is its intersubjective and incarnate nature, an element which will be par- ticularly exploited phenomenologically by such writers as Merleau- Ponty, Ricoeur, Irigaray, and even Derrida. A science of meaning – that is, a phenomenology – needs to recognise the functionality of meaning in society. Lonergan identifies meaning as cognitive, effi- cient, constitutive, and communicative. We inhabit a world which is already charged with meaning, which we appropriate, interpret, rework, and re-assign. Recognising this is to move from naive realism to critical realism, or to a phenomenological understanding of reality.

The world is given, but it does not ever give itself simply. Lonergan notes,

Different exigences give rise to different modes of conscious and intentional operation, and different modes of such operation give rise to different realms of meaning. There is a systematic exigence that separates the realm of common sense from the realm of theory. Both of these realms, by and large, regard the same real objects. But the objects are viewed from such different standpoints that they can be related only by shifting from one standpoint to the other. *The realm of common sense is the realm of persons and things in their relation to us.*[31]

It is this realm of 'common sense' – an embodied and incarnate realm – which Levinas, among others, will seek to address phenomenologically.

Karl Rahner's metaphysics of knowledge

Husserl sought to overcome the epistemological difficulties raised by the ontological presupposition of 'subject' and 'object'. The existence of a transcendent realm was not denied, but the question of its ontological status was placed in parenthesis in a phenomenological *epoché*. The point of departure was the object as it appears in consciousness. Subject and object are therefore derivative. Such an epistemological concern is not without its theological counterpart in Rahner. Rahner's doctoral work, eventually published as *Spirit in the World*,[32] is a work which is thoroughly phenomenological, and Husserl is an unacknowledged interlocutor. Rahner takes as his starting point Aquinas' consideration of the need for the intellect to 'turn to the *phantasmata*', that is, the contents of consciousness. In the *Summa Theologiae* (q. 84, a. 7), Aquinas had asked, 'can the intellect, using only the species it has and not turning to sense images, actually understand?' The answer shows a nascent turn to the phenomenological:

It is impossible for our intellect, in its present state of being joined to a body capable of receiving impressions, actually to understand anything without turning to sense images.

This *conversio* is a turning towards the contents of consciousness. Although Rahner employs a language which is overtly Heideggerian, the significant point is that in his consideration of Aquinas' theory of knowledge, he proceeds phenomenologically and relies on the phenomenological method which Husserl developed. The object as it appears in consciousness is the point of departure. A consequence of this is the recognition that the problem of knowledge as giving an account of how a 'subject' can relate to an 'object' is a pseudo-problem. Despite its overtly Heideggerian terminology, Rahner is perhaps more indebted to the work of Joseph Maréchal who, in *Le Point de départ de la métaphysique*, recognised that the emergence of a transcendental subjectivity in Kant had, as a consequence, the epistemological problem of how a transcendental subjectivity might possibly connect with a transcendent object, other than by attempting to 'throw a bridge' (*jeter un pont*) towards the exterior and the absolute.[33] Rahner outlines the problem thus:

> For the Thomistic metaphysics of knowledge the problem does not lie in bridging the gap between knowing and object by a 'bridge' of some gap: such a 'gap' is merely a pseudo-problem. Rather, the problem is how the known, which is identical with the knower, can stand over against the knower as other, and how there can be a knowledge which receives another as such. It is not a question of 'bridging' a gap, but of understanding how the gap is possible at all.[34]

In other words, given that the object as it appears in consciousness is the point of departure, notions of 'subject' and 'object', which are heavily laden with ontological presuppositions and presumptions, are derivative, and the epistemological problem of traversing the 'gap' is exposed, phenomenologically, as a problem which needs to be considered otherwise.

Jean-Luc Marion: traversing the 'gap' between phenomenology and theology

Jean-Luc Marion acknowledges his indebtedness to Levinas, and attempts in his own writing to straddle the divide between phenomenology and theology. What remains at issue is whether the attempt to traverse the 'gap' (if there be such a gap) between phenomenology and theology is also a transgression of the difference between phenomenology and theology, and whether or not theology trespasses into a phenomenological domain. Marion himself acknowledges that '[t]he relation between theology and phenomenology is an object of debate, even a polemic'.[35] Rightly, Marion notes that phenomenology's turn towards theology is impossible without a phenomenological predisposition. Phenomenology and theology are close, if recalcitrant, cousins, for they share the same origin in the phenomenality of the event of lived experience which they both attempt to articulate.

Marion poses two related questions, from phenomenology to theology, and from theology to phenomenology. It is sufficient simply to raise these questions for the moment. What phenomenology asks of theologians is 'why do [theologians] not undertake, or undertake so little . . . to read phenomenologically the events of revelation recorded in the Scriptures . . . instead of always privileging ontic, historic, or semiotic hermeneutics?'[36] What theology asks of phenomenologists is 'if appearing is always ordered to givenness according to the principle "As much reduction, as much givenness," if nothing is shown that is not given and nothing is given that is not shown, what does *to be given* ultimately signify?' Theology is as much a challenge to phenomenology as phenomenology is to theology. Their common origin is the givenness of lived experience, which demands both phenomenological and theological reduction, for 'givenness, being more essential, might also remain the most enigmatic'.[37]

ARE PHENOMENOLOGY AND THEOLOGY ALWAYS TWO?

Before proceeding further, Dominique Janicaud's[38] criticism of the 'theological turn' in French phenomenology cannot be left unacknowledged since it brings to the fore the difficult, if misunderstood, relation between phenomenology and theology, and the challenge which each offers to the other. The meeting ground for both will be the ethical origin of each. For Levinas, ethics will be both 'first philosophy' and 'first theology' and the point of departure for each is lived human experience.

Janicaud's criticism of the way in which phenomenology swerves into theology is put well by Steven Smith when he writes that Levinas' 'uncompromising treatment of God and neighbour . . . seems to negate the minimum conditions of sense and reason'. In other words, the scientific rigour of Husserlian phenomenology is compromised, for

How can there be a phenomenological description of something that is not evident, or an ontological description of something that is beyond being? If Levinas' analysis is neither phenomenological nor ontological, what is it? Why call it philosophy?[39]

Levinas, for his part, will stress that 'in spite of everything, what I do is phenomenology, even if there is no reduction, here, according to the rules required by Husserl; even if all the Husserlian methodology is not respected' (*OGCM*, 87). The ethics which Levinas will develop 'owe everything to the phenomenological method' (*TI*, 28). Yet, the method which Levinas employs is frustrating to a discipline which seeks to be rigorous. His method is a constant returning to the givenness of lived experience to explore and explore again those elements of human experience which remain as a remainder to the phenomenological reduction, and are therefore yet to be further reduced. It asks and asks again, employing excessive hyperbole. It verges on a philosophical Midrash. To use Derrida's image, it is the wave – the *same* wave – which unremittingly beats against the shore. Derrida writes of *Totality and Infinity*,

The thematic development is neither purely descriptive nor purely deductive. It proceeds with the infinite insistence of waves on a beach: return and repetition, always, of the same wave against the same shore, in which, however, as each return recapitulates itself, it also infinitely renews and enriches itself. Because of all these challenges to the commentator and the critic, *Totality and Infinity* is a work of art and not a treatise.[40]

This persistent and insistent theme which recurs and which refuses to go away is the theme of the ethical response that the other person provokes and, in so provoking, evokes a subjectivity.[41] The first question – 'the question *par excellence*' – is not 'why is there being rather than nothing, but how being justifies itself'.[42] For Levinas, how being justifies itself can only be answered in terms of ethics.

Now, Dominique Janicaud, who pursues Husserl's phenomenological rigour as a science, is critical of the elision of phenomenology and theology, which he characterises as 'the theological turn in French phenomenology'.[43] Although critical of writers such as Jean-Luc Marion, Jean-Louis Chrétien, and Michel Henry, Janicaud's severest

criticism is reserved for Levinas. Certainly, many of the notions which
Levinas employs such as 'substitution', 'responsibility-for-the-other',
'infinity', 'transcendence', 'liturgy', and 'revelation' are common cur-
rency in both Jewish and Christian theologies, and one could be
tempted to appropriate these notions which Levinas uses philosophically to theological ends, and in an uncritical way. As Janicaud
remarks, 'ulterior theological thoughts make use of . . . Levinas's
frank breakthroughs'.[44] The 'aplomb of alterity' which we find in
Levinas 'supposes a nonphenomenological, metaphysical desire', 'a
metaphysico-theological montage, prior to philosophical writing'.
'[F]aith rises majestically in the background'. In short, for Levinas,
phenomenology is not 'first philosophy', and Levinas' analyses are
profoundly unphenomenological. 'All is acquired and imposed from
the outset, and this all is no little thing: nothing less than the God of
the biblical tradition'. Thus the traduction of the phenomenological
reduction for pedagogic and apologetic ends, and the restoration of
theology 'in the most intimate dwelling of consciousness'.[45]

Janicaud's principal concern is that what Levinas undertakes owes
more to the undisciplined nature of theological enquiry than the
rigorous discipline of Husserlian phenomenology. Certainly, Levinas
exemplifies phenomenological study with 'a singular originality'[46] but
can what Levinas is actually doing be termed phenomenology? Certainly, the particular style of French phenomenology with its existential thrust is an open invitation to theology and phenomenology
to share a common bed; unfortunately, for Janicaud, the offspring
of such a coupling may lack both phenomenological and theological
pedigree. Indeed, for Janicaud, phenomenology in France began to
stray from the scientific discipline and rigour of Husserl's original
project almost as soon as Levinas ensured that it gained a foothold
in French philosophical thinking, with the appearance of Sartre's
Transcendence of the Ego (which Spiegelberg suggests is perhaps the
first properly phenomenological work in France). Phenomenology,
for Sartre, was altogether too abstract, 'too detached from concrete
situations and sociopolitical struggles'. Thus, 'Sartre abandoned [the
workplace of French phenomenological investigations] to turn resolutely towards politics and an ethics of engagement'.[47] With particular
regard to Levinas, Janicaud is critical of the 'philosophical aplomb'
with which Levinas 'loftily and categorically affirms' 'the primacy of

the idea of infinity, immediately dispossessing the *sameness* [*mêmeté*] of the I, or of being [*être*].' In fact, Janicaud contends, by displacing the self in favour of the other than the self, and in wanting to overcome 'the purely intentional sense of the notion of horizon',[48] Levinas is already deviating from the phenomenological rigour evident in Husserl. Yet, one must acknowledge that, for Husserl, the absolute existence of the other than the I is not denied but bracketed in the phenomenological *epoché*. Levinas will continue to describe consciousness in terms of intentionality and transcendence but will also draw attention to the givenness of the objects which consciousness intends, a point which Marion forcefully develops. Levinas himself makes this clear in *Totality and Infinity*:

> Intentional analysis is the search for the concrete. Notions held under the direct gaze of the thought that defines them are nevertheless, unbeknown to this naïve thought, revealed to be implanted in horizons unsuspected by this thought; these horizons endow them with meaning – such is the essential teaching of Husserl. What does it matter if in the Husserlian phenomenology taken literally these unsuspected horizons are in their turn interpreted as thoughts aiming at objects. (*TI*, 28)[49]

In short, for Janicaud, though 'more faithful to the spirit of phenomenology than Husserl himself', Levinas nonetheless 'takes liberties' with Husserl with his emphasis on 'overflowing the intentional horizon'.[50]

A few criticisms of Janicaud's critique are not misplaced. First, Janicaud, it seems to me, misunderstands the nature of theology and its enterprise. Marion correctly points out that 'it is necessary to distinguish strongly between two theologies that always confuse the polemics [concerning the relation between phenomenology and theology]: metaphysical theology (in which we could include "first philosophy") and revealed theology'.[51] '[T]he question of God is played out as much in the dimension of immanence as that of transcendence.'[52] Although Marion argues that a theology which is fundamental or philosophical is not immune from phenomenological critique and reduction since such a theology is 'based on real transcendence, causality, substantiality, and actuality', he goes on to argue that a revealed or dogmatic theology is also undertaken in 'the natural field of phenomenality, and is therefore dependent on the competence of phenomenology' since 'no revelation would take place without a manner of phenomenality'.[53] The questions which revealed theology addresses are not only 'based on given facts' but also presuppose a theology of revelation which, in turn, beckons a phenomenological turn in theology as much as it does a theological turn in phenomenology. The question of the phenomenal character of the phenomena on which revealed theology bases itself properly belongs to revealed theology itself; nevertheless, these also 'belong . . . rightfully to phenomenology, since revelation itself claims to deploy a particular figure of phenomenality'.[54] In other words, insofar as theology is a word about humanity in its dealings with God, or, minimally, a word about the religious dimension of human existence which opens on to questions of God, it cannot operate other than in a mode which is phenomenological. Further, if phenomenology is to be faithful to its own Husserlian origins and display scientific rigour and discipline it must also subject itself to scrutiny in its attempt at being an adequate method, and be attentive to the human situation in all its dimensions, including the religious existential.

Secondly, despite what Janicaud claims, phenomenology and theology may not always be two, or at least the distinction between them is not always clear-cut. Nor can it be. Both find their provocation in the singular givenness of a human existential which calls for a reduction which is both phenomenological and theological. Jeffrey Bloechl rightly urges wariness in understanding such terms as 'revelation' univocally, and also caution in 'illuminating Levinas's philosophy with his Jewish writings'. However, one must also be vigilant and resist the temptation to create a clear division between Levinas as phenomenologist-philosopher and Levinas as Jewish-religious thinker.[55] As Jean-Louis Chrétien notes, 'It is not enough to set up customs at the supposedly sure border between philosophy and theology; it is first necessary, in philosophy, to ask oneself about the very plotting of this border'.[56] Levinas similarly acknowledges, for example, that the themes of 'creation, omnipotence, rewards and promises', which he considers philosophically, also merit 'theological recuperation' (*OGCM*, ix).

Considering further that the 'revealed theology' which Marion considers stands in need of a theology of revelation which cannot be approached other than by the detour of the human existential and its phenomenality – that is, phenomenologically – Rahner is a helpful phenomenological and theological interlocutor. Basically, the (theological) 'question of God' cannot be asked without first placing in question the one who is able to ask the 'question of God'. The common origin of both phenomenology and theology is the human existential. For Rahner, the possibility of revelation has transcendental conditions. It presupposes both an openness to, and a capacity for, a revelation which gives itself in terms of the phenomenal. Thus, the subject is to be considered as a *hearer of the word* who is open to the possibility of revelation,⁵⁷ but whose very subjectivity is effected in the hearing. The very possibility of revelation presupposes a subjectivity as 'the place where a possible revelation might occur',⁵⁸ a subjectivity which is 'attentive to a possible revelation'.⁵⁹ In short, 'the natural human constitution is a positive openness for a possible revelation from God (and therefore the possibility of theology)'.⁶⁰

Despite Janicaud's criticisms, then, Levinas does present a phenomenological and theological challenge. It is not so much a case of 'hermeneutical violence', the *explicit* 'Abandonment of the phenomenological *method*', and 'a farewell to the Husserlian notion of rigour'.⁶¹ Rather, it is a case of expanding the scope of phenomenology and reconsidering the very nature of phenomenality. Indeed, as Janicaud acknowledged, 'although sometimes going beyond the letter of Husserl's theory', Levinas does mark out 'elements in [Husserl's] system which seem to lead to a richer notion of existence than mere presence of an object to contemplative consciousness' (*TIHP*, 134). It is this 'richer notion of existence' which needs to be considered both phenomenologically and theologically.

THE ETHICAL ENCOUNTER WITH OTHER AS FIRST
PHILOSOPHY AND FIRST THEOLOGY

Two further aspects of Levinas' thinking need to be brought to the fore: first, the practical nature of philosophy and theology, both of which are provoked by a first revelation of the other person; and, secondly, the ethical intent of scriptures which should not be viewed as opposing a reflection which is both philosophically and theologically rigorous. To state boldly that ethics is both 'first philosophy' and 'first theology' is to situate the origins of philosophy and theology in praxis. It is to privilege praxis as a point of departure for both philosophy and theology. Praxis is the situation in which one finds oneself when one encounters any other person. For Levinas, as soon as one faces the other person, the situation is at once ethical, and demands response and decision. While the decision is free on the part of the subject, its provocation comes first. It is not the case of freedom then responsibility; it is rather the summons to responsibility and then the decision freely made.

Theology, praxis, and scripture

How does one begin thinking? For Levinas, the answer is clear. He responds in *Ethics and Infinity*: 'from the reading of books', for books 'give one to think' since they 'give a certain, at times shocking, access to human questions and problems and possibilities' (*EI*, 21). The Bible is 'the book par excellence' (*EI*, 22). It is 'the Book of books wherein the first things are said so that human life has meaning' (*EI*, 23). It opens up dimensions of profundity and meaning which can be glimpsed in hermeneutics and feeling, in religious life and liturgy. However, in privileging the scriptures as the place wherein 'the first things are said', Levinas is not diminishing the significance of philosophical texts and reflection. In fact, these are 'closer to the Bible than opposed to it, even if the concreteness of Biblical themes [are] not immediately reflected in their philosophical pages' (*EI*, 23). Philosophy is not 'essentially atheist', and even if philosophy can no longer substitute verse for proof, 'the God of verse can, despite all the text's anthropological metaphors, remain the measure of the Spirit for the philosopher' (*EI*, 24).

What provocation, though, does scripture bring to thought? As a place where 'the first things are said so that human life has meaning', it opens on to a subsequent philosophical reflection which, though it has the 'right to the last word . . . is not the place of the first meaning of beings, the place where meaning begins' (*EI*, 25). The place where meaning begins is in the ethical encounter with the other person and the 'primordial responsibility "for the other"' which is both experienced in human relations, and enjoined by scripture. In its responsibility for the other person, there is *The Awakening of the I*. The summons which issues from the other person is both 'an irreducible possibility of the human and of God' for, in this original ethical encounter with the other person, there is 'the original awakening of an I responsible for the other', an 'authentic humanity' which is essentially *open* to both the human and the divine. This 'original ethical event would also be first theology.'[62]

This priority of the ethical in the scriptures is recognised by the Leuven moral theologian Roger Burggraeve, friend and interpreter of Levinas, when he notes, 'It is not the case that what the Bible says is true because it is in the Bible, but rather that it is in the Bible because it is true'.[63] Or, as Carmy and Shatz ask, 'Is an action right because God commands it, or does God command it because it is right? Is an action wrong because God prohibits it, or does God prohibit it because it is wrong?'[64]

In correpondence not published until after Levinas' death in 1995, Roger Burggraeve recalls writing to Levinas in 1975 about this 'pronounced separation between your philosophical and Jewish-Talmudic writings' and how some argue that 'your Jewish-Talmudic writings cannot be used to clarify your philosophical thought' because of 'an essential difference' between them. Burggraeve adds,

> I do not believe that one can separate these two kinds of writing and that such a separation is in no way justified. As you say yourself in your Jewish-Talmudic writings, you are seeking the ontological conditions of Jewish existence and the experience which provide the basis for Talmudic propositions. Even if the point of departure is materially different, Jewish existence, Talmudic Commentary, and experience as such, come together on the same philosophical level.

Burggraeve notes that Levinas' Jewish-Talmudic writings imply a philosophical dimension, and that both can be used at the same time, although each clarifies the other. Levinas responds that

> The difference is in the manner. What is communicated in Jewish writings *par chaleur* must be communicated in philosophy *par lumière*. In philosophy, one must not refer to verses and texts as proofs but as images or formulas which illustrate a thinking justified by analysis.[65]

In short, what Burggraeve argues is that 'the Bible gives to thought' rather than subverting thought. Nor can phenomenology and theology be in ultimate conflict, since the point of departure for both is the human existential which, in its ethical dimension, is the very provocation of thinking.

From a Jewish perspective, Richard Cohen will speak of 'scriptural reasoning'. Cohen notes that '[r]eason can reason as far as the transcendental but not as far as the transcendent'.[66] Cohen, like Burggraeve, argues that, in arguing the primacy of the ethical, Levinas

links transcendence, sociality, morality, and social justice. One thus recognises in Levinas' thought, as well as in his references, examples, and phrases, the deepest themes of Jewish ethics and spirituality, the grand gestures and minute details of prophetic and rabbinic morality, defining a redemptive history not only for Jews but for all human kind. In his metaphysical ethics Levinas weaves the specifics of the moral and holy language of Judaism into a compelling and critical web with the most advanced issues and idioms of contemporary continental philosophy . . . He persuades not by citing proof-texts, which would have no force in philosophical discourse in any event, but by giving voice to the prior and discordant claims of morality, to the very priority of its claim, as exerted by the one who faces, the other person to whom the morally elected self is obligated, the 'orphan, widow, and stranger', for whom and to whom one is responsible unto death.[67]

What Levinas puts in play is not so much the relation between faith and reason – a relation which is reflected in Christian theological concerns – but rather the more Jewishly inspired question of the relation between ethics and reason. Cohen writes,

Ethics exceeds reason . . . without being deduced from the limitations of reason. Ethics is not a consolation for reason's failure. Rather, ethics comes first, to the point that reason's capacities derive from the ethical relation.[68]

Ethics is not deduced from reason; rather, ethics is undergone; and it is reason's task to attempt an account of this. In other words, the ethical relation with the other person is the context within which reason operates. Ethics is access.

What Levinas intends, according to Cohen in his 'Introduction' to *New Talmudic Readings*, is a new humanism but that, in view of his religious writings, this can be termed a *biblical* humanism (*NTR*, 2). The close and attentive readings and commentaries upon Talmudic texts, and the frequent references to the Hebrew bible, witness a particular reflection which is profoundly ethical. The Law

which the scriptures enjoin prescribes the area within which *human*
behaviour is enacted, and offers guidance by way of *ethical* regulation
so that *human* life may be encouraged and flourish. The religion of
the Hebrew Bible is an ethical religion, and Torah has *ethical intent*.
Cohen suggests that humanism is 'directly a religious good, perhaps
even the highest, the greatest of religious goods, the very vocation
of the individual as *homo religiosus*, of humanity consecrated to the
task of returning to God'. Then, responding to Levinas' query at the
beginning of *Totality and Infinity* about whether or not we are duped
by morality, he makes the point that 'Humanity is not duped, but
elevated, by morality' (*NTR*, 3).

Two important points are worth emphasising here: firstly, the Law
is *formative* of the person, and thus there is a sense in which one must
love the Torah more than God, not because the Torah is more important
than God, but because the ethical life which the Torah prescribes is
the only access to God. 'God arises as the counterpart of the justice we
render to the other person'. Secondly, *to hear the Law* one must first *do
the Law*. Cultivating the *habit* brings understanding. In other words,
the keeping of the commandments promotes a humanism which is
both biblical and ethical. Cohen draws attention to the interplay of
the divine and the human in actively attending to the Law when he
writes that 'Biblical humanism . . . requires the meeting of the divine
and human through moral command manifest in moral action, hence
in human courts, divine command through human response, human
response as divinely commanded, absence and presence, preoriginality
and originality'. This is the lesson of the two tablets of the Law which
command duties towards God and humanity, and duties towards God
as duties towards humanity:

divinity as absolute mastery reduces humanity to absolute slavery, to sub-
humanity, to antihumanism. Tablets divine all too divine would have too
much authority, would fall to the ground unheeded, would not command
humans, would belittle humanity. . . Tablets human all too human, on the
other hand, would lack authority, would not *command* humans, would be
commanded by humans, by instinct and will to power. (*NTR*, 11)

As Levinas puts it, 'Without the signification they draw from ethics
theological concepts remain empty and formal frameworks' (*TI*, 37).
And thus, ethics is, as Levinas says, 'first theology'.

'Doing and hearing'

The keeping of the precepts of the Law brings instruction and renders a person attentive to the Law; in other words, *habitus* opens on to understanding. This seeming reversal of hearing and doing, such that doing assumes a priority, is important in Levinas' thinking. It is the ethical encounter with the other person which is thought's provocation. In following the ethical commands of the Law, and its concern for the poor, the widow, the orphan, and the stranger, a way to the divine is opened up. What is in play here is the notion of thought as an absolute origin. What characterises adult religion is its commitment to the ethical, and its adherence to the Law which prescribes the ethical. Thus, Levinas can write,

Ethics is not the corollary of the vision of God, it is that very vision. Ethics is an optic, such that everything I know of God must find an ethical expression. In the Holy Ark from which the voice of God is heard by Moses, there are only the tablets of the Law. The knowledge of the God which we can have and which is expressed . . . in the form of negative attributes, receives a positive meaning from the moral . . . The attributes of God are not given in the indicative, but in the imperative . . . To know God is to know what must be done. (*DF*, 17)

Doing comes before knowing. The importance of ritual is implicated here. Ritual is not, at first, slavish adherence to action, word, and gesture. Ritual is, at first, an undertaking in order that, in doing, understanding and transformation may follow in its wake. We do this in order to become what we do. Elsewhere we will speak of the *liturgical orientation of the self*. What characterises liturgy is that it is *'a movement of the Same towards the Other that never returns to the Same'* (*HO*, 26). It is essentially *for-the-Other*. Now, although Levinas intends this 'liturgical movement' in a philosophical sense, it is not unrelated to liturgy as ritual. One 'does' the liturgy in order to become what the liturgy is – a responsible movement towards what is other than the self. In other words, we do not hear and understand and then do; rather, in the doing, we reach an understanding. Participation in liturgy and ritual becomes a pedagogy. The 'daily regularity' of attending to the Law inclines us towards the neighbour and, at the same time, to God. What the 'austere discipline' of Jewish ritual law intends is justice. Levinas writes, 'The way that leads to God therefore leads *ipso facto* – and not in addition – to man; and the way that leads to man draws us back to ritual discipline and self-education. Its greatness lies in its daily regularity' (*DF*, 18). It is this inclination or orientation to the other that is the radical sense of liturgy as work.

An example of this can be found in a Talmudic reflection in which the essential nature of the Law is considered:

Ben Zoma said: 'I have found a verse that contains the whole of the Torah: "Listen, O Israel, the Lord is our God, the Lord is One".' Ben Namus said: 'I have found a verse that contains the whole of the Torah: "You will love your neighbour as yourself".' Ben Pazi said: 'I have found a verse that contains the whole of the Torah: "You will sacrifice a lamb in the morning and another at dusk".' And Rabbi, their master, stood up and decided: 'The law is according to Ben Pazi.' (*DF*, 19)

All three opinions are, of course, correct. In a certain way of thinking, the first is expressed in the second, and the second opens on the practicality of the third. But Levinas reverses the order: for 'the second indicates the way in which the first is true, and the third the practical condition of the second' (*DF*, 19). In other words, the undertaking of a work, properly liturgical, is the opening on to ethics and God. Theologically, one might be tempted to proceed in a deductive manner in which the theoretical structure is a movement from God to the neighbour, and then the practical implications of that movement, a 'theology from above'. However, 'the entire spirit of the Jewish Bible' is otherwise and reverses this; the relationship with the neighbour is achieved in the practice of social justice which the Law commands, and it is the relationship with the neighbour which opens on to the divine.

The pedagogical importance of doing for hearing

'Doing before hearing' gives understanding. *Before* ever understanding the content of its commands the demands of the Law are undertaken. In undertaking the Law (before ever a word is said), one comes to hear and understand what the Law commands, for 'one accepts the Torah before one knows it' (*NineTR*, 42). Such a disciplined adherence to the Law should not be understood as a burden that restricts

the scope of human freedom, nor as a 'blind orientation . . . where
the person betrays his vocation as person by absorbing himself in the
law that situates and orients him' (*HO*, 26). For Levinas, the structure of human freedom is otherwise, and the text of freedom must
always be read in the context of responsibility. It is not first that one
is free, and then responsible; rather, one is already responsible, and it
is this responsibility that delimits the scope of freedom. Freedom is
always and already responsible; it 'starts in a non-freedom which, far
from being slavery of childhood, is beyond freedom' (*NineTR*, 40).
Said otherwise, freedom finds itself coming after a situation which
precedes itself, coming after something which is already older than
itself, something which is anterior, and to which it responds.

This is further illustrated in a reflection on *The Temptation to
Knowledge as the Temptation of Temptation*. The knowledge which
modernity intends can be considered as the 'temptation of temptation'. Understanding, as the fruit of reflection, is essentially reflexive,
an act of interiority. It involves a disengagement from the world, and
demonstrates the first childhood of philosophy as an allergy to alterity. Rodin, in his solitary thinker, sculpts not only the emergence of
thought from its elemental base, as Levinas comments upon in *Existence and Existents*, but also a thinker whose hands, giving support to
thought, are cut off from involvement with the world. Thus, theory
is the dominant theme to the detriment of practice, and understanding becomes the condition of practice. For Levinas, it is otherwise.
Certainly, a thought that was 'simply and purely engaged' would be a
thought that was naive (*NineTR*, 34). Thought does require a certain
disengagement. It is a recollection of the self into itself, a withdrawal,
an event of separation. But, the question for Levinas is what provokes
thinking, and what should thinking think about.

Now, from a phenomenological perspective, philosophy, as the
quest for knowledge, is the quest to know the meaning of things.
Similarly, Jewish thinking – even from the ashes of the Holocaust –
embraces the notion of a world which is meaningful and purposeful. Levinas, writing in 'The Temptation of Temptation', affirms that
reality is meaningful. Expressed in terms of Talmudic commentary,
to discover the meaning of creation 'is to realise the Torah', with
attention to the ethics which the Law enjoins on Israel. In terms
of philosophy, it is argued that ethics orders ontology. 'The act by

which the Israelites accept the Torah is the act which gives meaning to reality'. The question of the meaning of Being – Heidegger's
Seinsfrage – 'finds its answer in the description of the way in which
Israel receives the Torah', for Mount Sinai was the moment when the
'to be' or the 'not to be' of the universe was being decided. Indeed,
to have refused to accept the Torah, to have refused the ethical intent
of creation, 'would have been the signal for the annihilation of the
entire universe' (*Nine TR*, 41) for the Torah, in its ordering of creation, subordinates creation to the ethical order. The acceptance of
the Torah is the establishment of the ethical order, and its eventual
fulfilment is the establishment of social justice. From the beginning
the end is implicated. Creation and eschaton come together in the
ethical purposefulness of the divine act: 'fruits come before leaves.
Marvel of marvels: a history whose conclusion precedes its development. All is there from the beginning' (*Nine TR*, 45). Israel refused
the 'temptation of temptation' – the temptation of knowing before
doing – and did not refuse to accept the Torah.[69]

Now, the phenomenological significance of this is that there is a
'reversal of the normal chronology of accepting and knowing' which
points to a 'a going beyond knowledge – a going beyond the temptation of temptation – but a going beyond different from that which
would be a return to childish naiveté' (*Nine TR*, 42). There is no place
for naive realism here. 'To go beyond the temptation of temptation
could not be the deed of an underdeveloped human nature. It is a
perfectly adult effort' (*Nine TR*, 42). The temptation of temptation
is the temptation to knowledge, that is, the temptation of hearing
as a prerequisite for doing, the temptation of knowing rather than
doing, of freedom rather than responsibility, of autonomy rather than
heteronomy – a temptation which subjects ethics to ontology.

Levinas' reflection then takes an explicitly philosophical turn (as if
the philosophical had ever been far away), in which the anteriority of
ethics is affirmed:

But here is where the logical integrity of the subject leads: the direct relation
with the true, excluding the prior examination of its term, its idea – that
is, the reception of Revelation – can only be a relation with a person, with
another. The Torah is given in the Light of a face. The epiphany of the other
person is *ipso facto* my responsibility toward him: seeing the other is already
an obligation toward him. A direct optics – without the mediation of any

idea – can only be accomplished as ethics. Integral knowledge or Revelation (the receiving of the Torah) is ethical behaviour. (*NineTR*, 47)

Implicated here is the notion of hearing before ever a content is given, of hearing a speaking before one understands what is heard. Irrespective of what is said, '[t]o hear a voice speaking to you is *ipso facto* to accept obligation toward the one speaking.' Similarly, doing before hearing is not the exclusion of understanding, but indicates a prior openness to what may be said, which is already an inclination or a 'movement towards the other which does not come back to its point of origin the way diversion comes back, incapable as it is of transcendence' (*NineTR*, 48).

Levinas concludes his reflection with considerations which are explicitly philosophical: first, the commitment to doing before hearing is an unconditional *yes*. This is neither naivety nor a flight from careful and considered thought. It is this phenomenon of an original responding of which we only subsequently become aware and bring to conscious reflection that phenomenology needs to be attentive to with an attention which is disciplined. 'In question here is a *yes* older than that of naive spontaneity. We think . . . that consciousness and seeking, taken as their own preconditions, are, like *naïveté*, the temptation of temptation, the tortuous path leading to ruin' (*NineTR*, 49).

Secondly, the modern question of human freedom is implicated, and the relationship between freedom and responsibility. Just as the doing which comes before hearing sets the context for understanding, so too the responsibility evoked when faced with the other person precedes and sets the context for freedom. 'Will it be said that this prior alliance was not freely chosen?' In asking such a question, 'one reasons as if the ego had witnessed the creation of the world and as though the world had emerged out of its free will. This is the presumptuousness of the philosopher. Scripture makes Job a reproach of it' (*NineTR*, 49). Like responsibility, the Torah is undertaken without having been chosen, 'an order to which the ego adheres, without having had to enter it, an order beyond being and choice. This is not to reduce the subject to servility before the mastery of the other person, but rather to establish the subject *as* responsibility. One must

remember that 'the distinction between master and slave already presupposes an established ego' (*NineTR*, 49). The origin of the subject
lies in responsibility for the other who is always prior and prevenient.
'To say that the person begins in freedom, that freedom is the first
causality and that the first cause is nobody, is to close one's eyes to that
secret of the ego, to that relation with the past which amounts neither
to placing oneself at the beginning to accept this past consciously nor
to being a mere result of the past' (*NineTR*, 49). To be free is already
to be a hostage.

Thirdly, there is the question of the divine withdrawal as the possibility of human ethical endeavour. In the keeping of the Law, one
puts onself in a position to hear. In this sense, hearing is indeed obedience. But this original obedience, as an original openness, commands
action on behalf of the other person. Paradoxically, in turning towards
the other person to whom the Law directs us, the Law finds a new
inscription and legitimacy in the face of the other person. We face the
other person, as commanded by the Law, to find the law inscribed
in the face of the other person. There is a sense, then, that, the law
having been given and yet being discovered in being obeyed, God
withdraws in order that the responsibility which I bear for the other
may not be annulled or compromised by the divine presence. 'The
personal responsibility of man with regard to man is such that God
cannot annul it' (*DF*, 20). Thus, for example, God does not forgive
the sin which harms the other person. Such forgiveness lies within the
realm of human relations. God withholds forgiveness in order that
humanity might forgive. Thus,

He Who has created and Who supports the whole universe cannot support
or pardon the crime that man commits against man. 'Is it possible? Did
not the Eternal efface the sin of the golden calf?' This leads the master to
reply: the fault committed with regard to God falls within the province of
divine pardon, whereas the fault that offends man does not concern God.
The text thus announces the value and the full autonomy of the human who
is offended, as it affirms the responsibility incurred by whomsoever touches
man. Evil is not a mystical principle that can be effaced by a ritual, it is an
offence perpetrated on man by man. No one, not even God, can substitute
himself for the victim. The world in which pardon is all-powerful becomes
inhuman. (*DF*, 20)

But this does not lead to despair, as if there were no hope, for despite the tragedies inflicted upon human beings by fellow human beings, Judaism maintains a positive understanding of humanity as responsibility for the other. 'Judaism believes in the regeneration of man without the intervention of extrahuman factors other than the consciousness of the Good and the Law . . . Human effort has unlimited possibilities' (*DF*, 20).

CHAPTER 2

Ethics, theology, and the question of God

Ethics is 'first theology'? Levinas suggests an interesting idea – 'an original ethical event which would also be first theology' – in a 1992 interview entitled *The Awakening of the I* (*IRB*, 182). Theology will only ever be worthy of the name when it is attentive to the holiness of neighbour, that is, when it is ethically redeemed. He also notes,

We have been reproached for ignoring theology; and we do not contest the necessity of a recovery, at least, the necessity of choosing an opportunity for a recovery of these themes. We think, however, that theological recuperation comes after the glimpse of holiness, which is primary. (*OGCM*, ix)

That glimpse of holiness is revealed in the other person, through whom alone one can gain access to God. In other words, ethics is not only 'first philosophy' but also 'first theology', and ethics, being first, provides the common point of departure for both phenomenology and theology. Said otherwise, theology cannot be undertaken other than by way of the human detour. What contribution, then, can Levinas make to a theology, ethically understood?

PHILOSOPHY AND RELIGION

It has already been noted that one should be cautious about using Levinas' religious writings to illumine his philosophical writings, but also that one should resist the temptation to separate Levinas, the phenomenologist-philosopher, and Levinas, the Jewish-religious thinker. The border between philosophy and theology does need to be patrolled with a certain vigilance, but there remains a crossing point for the simple reason that, given their common origin in a consideration of the human existential, both phenomenology and theology remain close cousins, and need to speak with each other. How then does one begin to classify, if such were possible, Levinas' writings? Even though Levinas admits, 'I always make a clear distinction in what I write between philosophical and confessional texts' and that 'it is necessary to draw a line of demarcation between them as distinct methods of exegesis, as separate languages',[1] making a clear distinction between Levinas' 'philosophical writings' and Levinas' 'religious writings' is altogether too simple. Better to recognise that, at times, Levinas writes in a style that is more strictly philosophical and, at times, in a style which is more strictly religious.[2] Nonetheless, it is the one Levinas who is writing, and from a singular ethical provocation.

The division of his writings in 'philosophy' and 'religion' can be accounted for in a variety of ways. First, a certain correlation between Levinas' biography and bibliography should be mapped. For example, his early work in the 1930s, associated with his doctoral studies on *The Theory of Intuition in Husserl's Phenomenology* (1930) had overt phenomenological intent. Fresh from doctoral studies and engagement with Husserl and Heidegger, Levinas continues to write and comment on phenomenology. During this period, however, he also becomes associated with L'Alliance israélite universelle, an association that remained 'a constant in Levinas' life',[3] and various essays with more religious themes begin to appear. Following the intervention of the 1939–45 war, his own philosophical project, and many of the themes which will be subsequently developed, begins to be outlined in works such as *Existence and Existents* (1947) and *Time and the Other* (1947). In this same year (1947), Levinas is appointed director of L'École Normale Israélite Orientale, and many of his writings in the 1950s tend to reflect a concern with specifically Jewish themes. Specifically philosophical writings continued nonetheless. In 1961, his professional university career begins – in Poitiers (1961), Nanterre (1967), and the Sorbonne (1973). Works on Jewish themes and Talmudic commentaries continued in this period, but this is mainly the period of *Totality and Infinity* and *Otherwise than Being*, as well as of engagement with other philosophers.

A second explanation for the distinction often made between his philosophical and religious writings, apart from their being addressed to two distinct constituencies, is the lack of recognition or the outright dismissal of religion within the academy, and the need for Levinas to establish his academic credentials (to the extent of using different publishing houses for the 'more philosophical' works and the 'Jewish' writings). Jeffrey Kosky comments that Levinas 'was delivering Talmudic lectures to Jewish audiences at a time when it was an academic heresy to speak about religion'.[4] Certainly, many 'early and popular commentaries on Levinas did not consider the religious dimensions operative in his work',[5] and 'the complex relation and often blurred boundaries between the philosophical and religious aims of Levinas' thought' oversimplified.[6] Robert Gibbs comments similarly when he notes that 'Levinas has been read as a philosopher, while the Jewish dimension of his thought has been largely ignored, or honoured by a mention and then ignored.'[7] The difficulty is the status of his religious thinking and writing and its relation to philosophy. Within Levinas' work, the question is whether or not Jerusalem and Athens can enter into dialogue and what translation might be needed if, as Levinas states, philosophy must always have the last word, even if it is not the place where meaning begins. Theologically, it is the question of the distinction and relation of revelation and reason, or religion and rationality, or theology and philosophy. Again, the ethical provenance of both phenomenology and theology needs to be kept to the fore.

ETHICAL HUMANITY AS THE POINT OF DEPARTURE FOR THEOLOGY

Theology, pursued from a phenomenological perspective, can have no other point of departure than in the subject who is capable of asking the question about God, or the subject for whom God can become a possible question. This does not mean that the subject is the absolute origin of theology, as if the question of God thereby became a projection. Rather, it means that the starting point for theological reflection on God takes its point of departure in the *here* of human subjectivity. The process of reduction may thereafter lead on to a consideration of the question of God.

Philosophically, Levinas articulates this in terms of the *posteriority of the anterior* (and its corollary, *the anteriority of the posterior*). What he means by this is that consciousness, as consciousness of, is *here*. It is the positioning of the self as a point of departure. Yet, though a point of departure, thought is neither original nor originating. Rather, through a transcendental reflection, consciousness comes to find itself already founded. In other words, a phenomenological reduction, the prior conditions of thinking are only ever uncovered subsequent to thinking. '[E]ven its cause, older than itself, is still to come. The cause of being is thought or known by its effect as though it were posterior to its effect' (*TI*, 54). For Levinas, the interiority of consciousness, which Husserl understands to be constituting and the transcendence of whose object was placed in parenthesis, finds itself, in Levinas, already to be constituted, intersubjectively, culturally, and historically, and already to be struck by exteriority. The present of consciousness finds itself to have a past, which is older, or anterior, to itself. The sheer youthfulness of thought (as a beginning) which is the event of separation, or the effecting of a *here*, discovers subsequent to that event a prevenient past which both provokes and sustains it.

Now, this past is described as the idea of infinity in us, which Descartes spoke of in his Third Meditation. There is discovered after the event of 'thought' as 'representation' something which precedes that event, and which can only be welcomed, and never grasped or represented. The infinite – known only in its excessive infinition, or its constant disappearing beyond the horizon – overflows thought. Said otherwise, consciousness or thought, in the very conceiving of its object, finds itself already to have been conceived. The emergence or the 'awakening' of consciousness, which is the auto-positioning of the subject and the event of separation, is already a transcendence,[8] and even in its first stirrings, consciousness is found to be already a movement, beyond itself, an intentionality towards an object, the existence of which is already implicated in consciousness as consciousness of.

Thus, as we have seen previously, with the event of consciousness, which is the effecting of a 'here', there is not first consciousness and then the discovery of a world as in the Cartesian project. The distinction between subject and object is already derivative. Consciousness, though the starting point for phenomenological reflection, finds itself to have emerged from engagement with a world which is always and already there, and always and already peopled. To use the language of ethics, the event of the other person provokes or 'pricks' consciousness into conscience, and is discovered through reflection to predate conscience. It is not that I first have a moral consciousness, or conscience, and thereafter turn my attention to the other person. Rather, the event of the other person, who is the provocation of conscience and thus its proper origin, is already an inclination to the other person who, preveniently, is always and already there.

Now, the question becomes one of the possibility of undertaking a 'theological reduction' on the basis of the ethical, or intersubjective, reduction which Levinas pursues. Is the move from ontology (Husserl) to ethics (Levinas) to theology a legitimate one, or must the reduction necessarily halt at the human since the crossing over to the divine would be a transgression? For Levinas, the affirmation of the self as separate is both the possibility, and first movement, of a transcendence which has already happened. The relationship with the world and with the other person is already implicated in the event of separation which enables the fact of an already prior transcendence to be glimpsed. The event of the other person – which may be described as an ethical awakening – predates the subject, but is only discovered 'after the event' of subjectivity, as it were. For Levinas, however, such an ethics can also be 'first theology', properly understood. The relationship with God is implicated in the responsibility I bear for the other person, and in the justice I work with others to achieve for the many. The question is the extent to which the phenomenological reduction can move from the egological to the intersubjective, and, within this, to something which might be termed 'the theological'.

TOWARDS THE 'THEOLOGICAL REDUCTION' ON THE BASIS OF ETHICS

Now, taking the human as the proper theological point of departure for theology requires a reconsideration of subjectivity. For Levinas, an adequate consideration of subjectivity can only ever be an ethical consideration. But this ethical reflection on human life with others can also be considered as a proto-theology, which can provide the basis for further theological reflection. What Levinas' ethically inspired thinking offers is 'a new humanism'; a new humanism which is also a 'biblical humanism'; a new humanism which recognises the religiosity of ethical subjectivity. For example, Tamra Wright stresses that what Levinas attempts cannot and should not be considered as theology,[9] but rather as intending 'a new humanism'. Roger Burggraeve points out that such a humanism resonates with the ethical text of scripture.

Jeffrey Kosky argues that what Levinas does can be considered as a philosophy of religion. All draw attention to the ethical dimension of religiosity in Levinas.

A new humanism?

Levinas is not doing theology, but intends a new humanism. Levinas could be said to agree with this when, regarding the transcendence of ethics, he admits that 'it would be false to qualify it as theological' (*TI*, 42). Levinas, Wright argues, is both Greek and Jew, but the 'rapprochement (despite their differences) of Judaism and philosophy' is possible only insofar as 'each can be understood as a response to the "pre-philosophical experience" of the self's inescapable responsibility for others'.[10] Concrete human life is the 'pre-philosophical' starting point for any kind of reflection. Philosophy attempts to articulate the meaning of human life, and becomes, in phenomenology, the science of meaning. As Levinas acknowledges, although philosophy always has the right to the last word, it is perhaps not the place where meaning begins. But this is no less true of theology which shares with philosophy a concern to say something about the meaning of existence. The concrete life of the human person in the very givenness of its various cultural, social, historical *and* religious dimensions – what we might call 'incarnate existence' – is the hinge which brings both philosophical and religious reflection together.

Levinas, then, intends a new ethical humanism, a new understanding of subjectivity, which acknowledges but goes beyond the modern subjectivity and the new humanism which the project of the Enlightenment oversaw and brought to birth. The achievement of the Enlightenment was the privilege which it accorded to the human. Humanity became the focal point of reflection; it was the highest value 'in the economy of the Real', and the measure of all other values. Recognition of, and respect for, other people, as well as for oneself became paramount, and this in turn demanded that human freedom be both affirmed and safeguarded. Thus, the humanism of the Enlightenment saw

a blossoming of human nature, of intelligence in Science, creativity in Art, and pleasure in daily life; the satisfaction of desires without prejudice for the freedom and pleasures of other men, and consequently the institution of a just law – that is to say, a reasonable and liberal State. (*DF*, 277)

Such a humanism, in which humanity has come of age, might be considered an 'adult religion'. It is one in which the God of monotheism is not yet dead, but is no longer required for the development and progress of human life. God and humanity are in a process of separation, even if the divorce is not yet final.

Now, the emergence of such an enlightened and adult religion in which God is either removed, or placed at a distance, from the human equation has two main consequences.

First, the question of God is separated from ethical engagement with the human, and theology becomes both abstract and metaphysical. In short, theology becomes, for Levinas, *theism*, which is 'the most dangerous of abstractions since it is the highest'. The quest for the divine, then, retreats into the immanence and interiority of subjectivity where one mystically engages in 'a private meeting with a consoling God'. But, the God whom monotheism intends – the God of Abraham, of Isaac, and of Jacob – has no private meetings. Or, in abstracting God from engagement with the human, one reduces God to an abstraction, accessible to and through thought, an abstraction in which the very transcendence of the infinite is compromised by the finite. What monotheism attempts, in its ethical injunctions, is neither mystical encounter nor theological abstraction, but rather, the bringing of the divine presence 'to just and human efforts, as one brings the light of day to the human eye, the only organ capable of seeing it' (*DF*, 274–5).

Secondly, the 'new humanism' of the Enlightenment elevates human freedom, independence, and autonomy, and the vocabulary that enables their particular voice. Notions of responsibility, dependency, and heteronomy do not figure largely in the project of enlightened modernity, and the transcendental subject who is divorced from and immune to engagement with others. Relying on 'naked intellect' and its tendency towards abstraction, it failed to achieve 'an adequate understanding of the meaning of being human' since it neglected 'to take into account the experience of the conquered and the persecuted'.[11] In subscribing to the text of human freedom as one of the highest goods of the new humanity, it neglected to consider the prior context of responsibility for the other person within which freedom is both enabled and operates. The consequences of this unleashed freedom – the fruit of modernity – are illustrated, somewhat harshly, by Levinas:

The idea of freedom 'progresses' in the following way. From economic freedom to sex education through all the degrees of this freedom; freedom as
regards to the obligations to which heterosexuality is still naturally attached,
and even the solitary ecstasy of drugs in which we have no further need of
interhuman relationships, and all responsibilities become undone. Spiritu-
alisation brought to its highest point is not solitude but the solitary ecstasy
of drugs, the spirit in the cloud of opium! Opium as the religion of the people. But we can sink even lower. Everything is allowed, nothing is absolutely
forbidden. Nothing, perhaps, is forbidden any longer as regards our dealings
with the other man. (*DF*, 285)

What is worth noting here is the link which is made between the
progress and growth of freedom and the retreat into the self and
consequent wilting of responsibility for the other person. It is this
theme of 'responsibility for the other person' – an ethical humanism –
which will become the focal point of Levinas' entire philosophy.[12]

In contrast to the 'new humanism' of the Enlightenment and the
adult religion of autonomy and freedom which it proposes, Levinas
proposes instead an understanding of subjectivity which is profoundly
ethical and enfleshed. Subjectivity is intersubjectivity. Human life is
life with others, and responsibility for the other person is the highest
good. Within such an ethical framework, God is reduced to a regulative ideal which has the function of delimiting our freedom in view
of a common good; rather, God emerges in the practice of responsibility for the other person as the guarantor of justice for the many.
For Levinas, God is not a moral *a priori*, but is always encountered *a
posteriori* and always at the juncture of our dealings with other people.
'The vision of God is a moral act. This optics is ethics' (*DF*, 275). Said
otherwise, the question of God does not find its answer in the realm of
theory (*theism*) but in the realm of practice, which always and already
implicates response and responsibility. Ethics is always primary, even
if often discovered lately. The significance of the particular Jewish
religious perspective within which Levinas operates is that the truths
and the ideals which provide a regulative framework for our engagement with others 'are embodied in the concrete commandments of
the Law'.[13] The first question is not 'what must I believe?' but, rather,
'What must I do?' There is something, not without significance, in
'loving the Torah more than God'. But, 'loving the Torah more than
God' is not to embark upon the way of theological fundamentalism,

for '[i]t is not the case that what the Bible says is true because it is in the Bible, but rather that it is in the Bible because it is true'.[14]

A biblical humanism

Now, the 'new humanism' which Levinas proposes resonates with the humanism of the Hebrew scriptures, for 'the bible gives to thought.' Roger Burggraeve, reflecting on 'the possibility and proper nature of biblical thinking', suggests that a mature faith entails 'a thinking interaction with the Scriptures which orient and inspire it'.[15] Further, the bible itself is 'a particular form of thinking . . . which has as much claim to speak in philosophy' as do other texts, but what characterises biblical thinking is its 'resistance to rigorous critical-reflective engagement'.[16] Scripture is an expression of *human*, and not simply *religious*, culture; it orients and founds 'our existential, historical, and cultural perspectives'; it speaks of 'a modality of human existence' which 'can never be purely instrumental or functional';[17] as such, it has its own powerful rationality and truth which critical thought must 'tenaciously' revisit in order to penetrate further. The Bible, as 'the place where meaning begins', recalls critical rationality to its source and its inspiration which is the inherent rationality and meaning of concrete human life with others. For its part, the rationality of late modernity, if it is truly critical, needs to engage with biblical rationality in a way which is neither uncritical acceptance nor uncritical dismissal. On the other hand, if the message of the Scriptures is to engage with the rest of the world without 'being sidelined or ridiculed' then it 'will always need to exercise the ascesis of critical rationality'.[18]

How, then, does Scripture give to thinking? If, as Burggraeve suggests, it is axiomatic that *to live by the Word, we must learn from the Word*, then this implies an 'existential engagement' with Scripture, and a recognition that Scripture too is the product of a certain existentiality, which should not be too readily dismissed. The text, resistant and irreducible to critical reason, commands a certain respect and attention. Burggraeve notes, 'one has need of keen attention which thinks, thinks through, and thinks again' in order to catch a glimpse of 'the message inhabiting Scripture, giving rise to thinking'.[19] Thus the Talmudic practice of constantly poring over texts in order to discover anew the meanings which reside within it. In such a continual reflection, it is the text as the bearer of original meanings which is in command. Its message, although spoken of in terms of revelation, is nonetheless a revelation given in human terms, recounting as it does a people's relationships with one another, and its shared life before God.

Scripture is a reflective witness to the experience of particular communities who recognise in the texts certain truths – at times difficult truths – about themselves, and which has achieved a certain canonical status for those communities. In terms of the *humanum*, that experience, though culturally and historically conditioned, is not absolutely alien. It may appear strange or foreign to us, but this becomes an increased demand to read and to think; to think through; to think about our own thinking and perhaps un-think it; and to think again. In fact, it is a hermeneutics of hermeneutics, an interpretation of interpretation which is called for, but a hermeneutics which acknowledges and respects the resistance which the scriptural text offers to thinking.

[T]o read the Bible reflectively is first to listen honestly to the text itself. It is to avoid immediately rejecting its suggestions, and instead to accept them without prejudice, from a philosophical standpoint. One then asks whether their meaning and implications can be justified rationally by what we already find in ourselves.[20]

Crucially, Burggraeve recognises that a reflective-philosophical reading of texts does not utter the first word, but speaks in response to a text which is already there, a text which is other than the situation in which we now find ourselves. Texts are an interpretation of human experience and invite critical engagement and attentive response. Burggraeve concludes his reflection – rightly, I think – by saying:

What Levinas says about intellectual lay Judaism is, in my view, largely applicable to the related concern of better realising a Christian way of life. There can be no mature Christian faith without a thinking relation to Scripture, which is evident from the rich tradition of hermeneutics in Christian reflection. . . Thinking from and about the Bible follows and responds to a source of thinking which is at once an experience and a tradition: Scripture . . . 'From beneath', the reflective approach to Scripture is already open to a heteronomous source of meaning; 'from above', it is also already open to a transcendent aim.[21]

Similar points are made by Carmy and Shatz in 'The Bible as a source for philosophical reflection'.[22] On the face of it, the Bible would appear to offer itself as a source for philosophical reflection, since many of the themes it raises are themes which are often to be found in philosophical discourses: creation, the problem of evil and suffering, the nature of the human person, ethical behaviour, and so on. Yet, the manner and the style in which so many of these issues are expressed in the scriptures is far removed from the propositional and logical nature of philosophical reasoning, and 'often juxtaposes contradictory ideas, without explanation or apology', with this 'philosophical deficiency' thereby giving offence to critical philosophical reflection.[23] Carmy and Shatz affirm the Bible as 'the primary source for Jewish philosophical reflection', stressing that it 'indeed warrants philosophical attention'. Yet, a philosophical appreciation of the scriptures can only be achieved 'by meeting the Bible on its own ground, in terms of its actual contents – as a compendium of divine law, as a narrative of God's rendezvous with humankind and with a singular people, as the drama of humanity's yearning for the creator and God's revelation to humanity'. Only then 'can we acquire the power to interpret the text in the light of later generations' intellectual framework and existential concerns'.[24] In keeping the commandments, one must still speak 'of God who comes to mind' (*de Dieu qui vient à l'idée*). Such a speaking involves describing the *ethical*, in the sense in which Levinas *describes* the ethical.[25] Such a description requires close attention to phenomenological rigour. Indeed, Marion's plea that theologians should 'read phenomenologically the events of revelation recorded in the Scriptures' to which we have already adverted, needs to be taken seriously by theologians and phenomenologists alike.[26]

TOWARDS A PHILOSOPHY OF RELIGION?

In trying to negotiate a path between phenomenology and theology, Jeffrey Kosky presents Levinas' work in terms of a philosophy of religion. This is helpful for two reasons: first, philosophy of religion tends to be a discipline which makes extensive use of phenomenological method; secondly, it enables a consideration of the religious dimension of Levinas' project, unencumbered by theological baggage which is unnecessarily dogmatic, and thus responds to the criticisms which Levinas will raise against theology as he conceives it.

Levinas' philosophical project, Kosky argues, can be considered as a *philosophy of religion*, and also, it might be added, as a *fundamental theology*; however, the significance of these notions needs to be considered on the basis of an *ethical* metaphysics. Both Nietzsche and Heidegger had signalled the 'end of metaphysics', and the severing of the link between morality and religion. Might the 'new humanism' which Levinas espouses offer a way of bringing together again morality and religion on the basis of ethics? 'Would another interpretation of the ethical subject open a new significance of religious categories?'[27] Such an ethical understanding of the subject would be articulated 'in terms that are undeniably and unmistakenly religious', for 'religious traditions and theological forms are not as foreign to contemporary discourse as [many postmoderns] would like to believe'.[28] Besides, a phenomenology which attempts to be adequate to concrete life with others cannot pretend that religious traditions and theological forms play no part in social life. Levinas, Kosky suggests, 'offers a way to think and speak about religion within the contemporary horizon of thought'.[29] This is not a reduction of religion to ethics, nor is it a 'godless morality'. Rather, it is a new way of considering religion and God on the basis of the ethical subject which the phenomenological reduction of intersubjectivity has reached. What Levinas provokes is a rethinking of morality 'without denying the postmodern horizon of thought (the end of metaphysics and the death of God)'.[30] In a sense, this is an attempt at a theological minimalism which keeps theological commitments to a minimum *and* a phenomenological maximalism. Kosky's thesis, simply put, is this: '*the analysis of responsibility opens on to a philosophical articulation of religious notions and thus makes possible something like a philosophy of religion*'.[31]

Levinas's phenomenology opens the possibility of a religiosity that lives on in a postmodern or postmetaphysical age . . . [A] possible religiosity opens at the end of metaphysics insofar as the phenomenology of subjectivity describes its genesis in responsibility. There is no religion without responsibility . . . and Levinas' phenomenology, by uncovering the responsibility that undoes modern metaphysical thought, thereby saves religiosity for the postmetaphysical or postmodern age.[32]

What is significant in Kosky's reading of Levinas is his stress on the *phenomenological* import of Levinas' writing, and his refusal either to reduce religion to ethics or subsume ethics within the theological. Responsibility for the other person – a point reached by way of a phenomenological reduction – provides the new lexicon and grammar for religion and theology, even though the phenomenological and theological syntax may at times may be a struggle.

In other words, a rigorous phenomenological analysis which attempts to approximate to *adequacy* in its consideration of the phenomenon of the human subject as responsible for the other person must pay attention to the meanings of the religious phenomena which accompany and are proximate in the existential of the human. It is worth quoting Kosky at some length since, it seems to me, that what he correctly places in question is the relationship between phenomenology and theology.

A broader range of phenomena appear within [the] subject than its previous figure (consciousness). These phenomena include religious meanings that have traditionally been consigned to the unintelligibility of faith or else reduced to the intentions (conscious and unconscious) of the self. I argue that Levinas' ethical philosophy can be applied to a philosophy of religion which relieves theological thought of sacrificing the significance of religious notions at the threshold of intelligibility and understanding. This philosophy of religion gives significance to religious meanings by reducing them to the responsible subject where they appear. Achieved through a reduction to subjectivity, the significance of religion is accessible to those not committed to a particular religious tradition.[33]

Thus, the need to pay careful attention to the meanings which religion articulates and which theology attempts to express, and to extend phenomenological analyses beyond the purely theoretical and cognitive, which are nascent but not developed in Husserl, first into the domains of aesthetics and ethics as Levinas indicates at the end of his study on Husserl (*TIHP*, 158), but, beyond these, into the related domains of religious and theological meaning. Such a phenomenology 'describes neither a positive, determined religion nor actual, historic religious experience'; rather 'when the subject of phenomenology is taken to be responsibility, phenomenology reaches a subject that is open to the appearance of the unconditional, of what is not given in plain evidence of a present made by consciousness, and of what is impossible to account for by reflection on the self'.[34]

But nor can the significance of Levinas be restricted by considering him as a *Jewish* philosopher, as some have argued. Kosky, correctly I think, argues that Levinas, although Jewish, should not be considered as a 'Jewish philosopher'. First, Levinas himself disavows this label: 'I am not for all that an especially Jewish thinker. I am a thinker *tout court*' (*AQS*, 83); secondly, to situate his thinking within the framework of Judaism is to overlook the fact that the religiosity of the subject is discovered by way of a phenomenological reduction which Levinas pushes beyond its Husserlian limits. Just as Levinas stresses that his own work does not lie under the authority of the Bible but under the authority of phenomenology (*AQS*, 78–9), – for 'it is not true because it is in the Bible, but in the Bible because it is true' – so Kosky argues that

Levinas's analysis of responsibility can be seen as a discourse on religion that, at least in its intentions, holds forth without recourse to the authority of any faith or religious tradition. . . . [T]he religiosity met in Levinas's phenomenology of responsibility is not an actual religion but the possibility or nonnoematic meaning of religion.[35]

In other words, Levinas' analysis offers a prolegomena or point of entry to any proper understanding of religion on the basis of phenomenological analysis.

Kosky pushes further, however. Such a phenomenological analysis cannot be considered simply as a secular transformation of religion into ethics on the basis of the responsible subject. Intentionality is already a transcendence. Responsibility for the other person presupposes the advent of the other person who provokes what Levinas terms 'a turgescence of responsibility' within the subject, or perhaps, more accurately, effects a subject *as* 'a turgescence of responsibility'. *Transcendence*, and its meaning, remains a focus. The precise point of the reduction pursued by Levinas is that it does not end in self-enclosed interiority, but finds that interiority is already breached by a transcendent alterity, a *transcendence-in-immanence*, which is the constant provocation of the subject as ethical. Hence, the subtitle of *Totality and Infinity*: 'a defence of interiority on the basis of exteriority'. Although the starting point of the reduction, as in Husserl, is a consciousness which is always a consciousness of, Levinas argues that the reduction proceeds by showing that consciousness is always and already beyond itself in the transcendence of intentionality, and, further, that it is this very relationship with an exteriority which enables the affirmation and guarantee of subjectivity – a notion entirely derivative, as we have seen. Interiority is affirmed on the basis of exteriority. While Levinas may acknowledge that 'this is no longer Husserl', it should be remembered that Husserl's phenomenological epoché was not a denial of transcendent reality but rather a parenthetical bracketing of the question of its existence.

Now, we have already drawn attention to Janicaud's criticism of the 'theological turn' or 'theological swerve' in phenomenology in which 'phenomenology has been taken hostage by a theology that does not want to say its name'.[36] According to Janicaud, says Kosky, what this amounts to is 'a betrayal of the phenomenological reduction and the claim to a first philosophy'.[37] The rigour and discipline of phenomenology would be short-circuited by theology. But Levinas does not come to his conclusions by way of religion but by way of phenomenology. The 'theological' opening proceeds phenomenologically. Phenomenology may experience a certain discomfiture with this, as if theology were appropriating or usurping the place of phenomenology as first philosophy. The reality is more fundamental, however. Neither phenomenology nor theology are in conflict as mutual opponents. Rather both are placed in question and need to reconcile their differences, not so much in relation to each other, but by their common attentiveness to the ethical encounter with the other person. Ethics is not only first philosophy. It is also first theology.

Wright does not argue very much differently from this when she advocates an ethical or 'non-theological interpretation of Jewish texts and teaching' in Levinas.[38] Similarly when she writes that Levinas' key philosophical works are works of phenomenology rather than theology:

Neither *Totality and Infinity* nor *Otherwise than Being* should be interpreted as theological texts. On the contrary, these texts are explicitly critical of the theology of 'positive religions', and frequently emphasise that the Infinite is refractory to the thematising discourse of theology. The apparently theological claims in *Totality and Infinity* can be understood phenomenologically as belonging to the description of the relationship between the self and a transcendent other.[39]

Levinas, despite Janicaud's criticisms, does not have a 'theological intent' and does not undertake a theology which could in any way be considered as systematic or dogmatic. Yet, in reconsidering the subject in terms of ethics and as responsibility for the other person, there is in his philosophical undertakings something which is of fundamental theological significance.

How, then, does Levinas understand theology?

THEOLOGY AND THE TEMPTATION OF ATHEISM

Levinas mistrusts theology on three counts. First, theology has tended to be theory rather than practice, not only valuing *theoria* over *praxis*, but imposing theoretical frameworks to circumscribe and delimit practice. Secondly, it attempts to circumscribe God, and thus offends and does violence to God's absolute transcendence. Thirdly, in its attention to itself and the God whose mystery it endeavours to probe, it has – unlike the God whom it seeks to understand – been inattentive to the neighbour to whom God always inclines an ear.

Yet, Levinas is not wholly opposed to theology. Theology, however, will only ever be worthy of the name when it is attentive to the neighbour, that is, when it is ethically redeemed.

The temptation of atheism

For Levinas, the counterpart of theism is atheism, but atheism is given a positive signification. *Atheism* is of value precisely because it is not theism. To understand the value of atheism, it is important to understand the theism which Levinas refuses. Levinas finds theism problematical, and for a number of reasons.

First, belief in God is not a singular or individual enterprise, but is intersubjective and communitarian.

> *Believe* is not a verb to be employed in the first person singular . . . The existence of God is not a question of an individual's uttering logical syllogisms. It cannot be proved. The existence of God, the *Sein Gottes*, is sacred history itself, the sacredness of man's relation to man through which God may pass. God's existence is the story of his revelation in biblical history.[40]

In other words, God does not call individuals to himself, but calls a people to himself. The encounter with God is always by way of the encounter with other people. Said theologically, belief is an ecclesial event, and, as such, must necessarily have an ethical dimension.

Secondly, access to God is not gained by way of mystical encounter, by which a person might be removed from the social world and be caught up in singular rapture with the divine. For Levinas, a theology which tends towards the mystical approaches the divine by way of a neglect of the world.

Thirdly, neither negative nor apophatic theology provides any solution either, for, although it attempts to safeguard divine transcendence and unknowability, it again does so at the expense of ethical engagement with other people. It also acts as a foil to – and so is related to – positive or kataphatic theology which, for its part, attempts to put God on a leash, confining God within the abstract and the theoretical.

In short, the theism against which Levinas reacts and which he rejects, is forgetful of ethics and the human existential. Such a *theism* invites *a-theism*, not because 'there is no God' but because the God of theism, before whom thought fails, is not the God of Abraham, of Isaac and Jacob. It is only by way of the ethical encounter with the other person that access to God can be gained. Given the holiness and utter transcendence of God – the utter absolution of the divine – the sole point of contact with the divine is by way of the encounter with the holiness and transcendence of the other person.

The positive value of atheism is glimpsed in the experience of divine deafness, or the absent God. Prayer remains unanswered; God, who is silent, refuses to intervene, or perhaps withdraws, and one is thrown back on one's own solitariness. In such a situation, atheism 'is the simplest and most common reaction' (*DF*, 81) to the absent God. 'There is no God'. Such a reaction, however, is the reaction of 'those whose idea of God . . . was of some kind of kindergarten deity who distributed prizes, applied penalties, or forgave faults and in his goodness treated men as eternal children' (*DF*, 81). The refusal of such an image of God, who is more idol than icon, is the necessary prelude to a relationship with the true God of monotheism, for the way to the true God has 'a way station where there is no God . . . Genuine monotheism owes it to itself to respond to the legitimate demands of atheism' (*DF*, 82). To have no recourse to the divine is to be thrown back upon the resources of the human.

This point is argued in *Totality and Infinity* in a consideration of the emergence of the subject. The affirmation of the self demands separation. Always and already caught up in the world, one 'comes to oneself' by taking distance from the world, by affirming one's independence, and situating one's self *here*. As Levinas puts it, 'the soul [that is, the self] . . . being an accomplishment of separation is naturally atheist'. Again, '[o]ne lives outside of God, at home with oneself; one is an I, an egoism' (*TI*, 58).

Such an atheism, however, should not be understood as a denial of the divine. Rather this atheism is 'prior to both the negation and the affirmation of the divine' (*TI*, 58). Separation – the effort and process of self-affirmation – is the very condition of transcendence, the very possibility of a movement towards God and neighbour. Atheism, as the natural condition of the self, becomes the very possibility of response and responsibility towards the other than the self. Such an atheism, then, is essentially an *a-theism*. It is not so much the denial of the divine, but rather the refusal of a theism in which God is reduced to theory and abstraction, a God who could be approached other than by way of the detour of the other person. Levinas argues,

The atheism of the metaphysician means, positively, that our relation with the metaphysical is an ethical behaviour and not theology, not a thematisation, be it a knowledge by analogy, of the attributes of God. God rises to his supreme and ultimate presence as correlative to the justice rendered unto men. The direct comprehension of God is impossible for a look directed upon him, not because our intelligence is limited, but because the relation with infinity respects the total Transcendence of the other without being bewitched by it, and because our possibility of welcoming him in man goes further than the comprehension that thematises and encompasses its object. (*TI*, 78)

In other words, access to the true God is more to be achieved through engagement with other people rather than through any 'adventure of cognition'.

A God invisible means not only a God unimaginable, but a God accessible in justice. Ethics is the spiritual optics . . . The Other is the very locus of metaphysical truth, and is indispensable for my relation with God. (*TI*, 78)

It is in following through the arduous demands of responsibility for the other person which the ethical encounter puts in play that God is to be found. There can be no approach to God other than by way of the other person. Ethics alone gives access. Thus,

Metaphysics is enacted in ethical relations . . . Everything that cannot be reduced to an interhuman relation represents not the superior form but the forever primitive form of religion. (*TI*, 79)

Now, to stress the relation with the other person as the unique access to God is not to compromise the initiative and freedom of God with respect to his creation. Indeed, one can argue that it is precisely to maintain the utter freedom and transcendence of God with respect to creation that Levinas stresses the value and importance of atheism. For the atheist there is no interventionist God who will relieve the subject of his or her responsibilities for the other person. In this sense, God is freed of his responsibility for his creation. But further and positively, the affirmation of God's utter freedom and transcendence with respect to creation means that creation in its human form becomes the focal point of any theological reflection on the divine. A theology which seeks to be phenomenologically adequate is a theology whose point of departure must be shamelessly anthropological (and ultimately incarnational). The way to God can only start from a here which is wholly human.

But this can be usefully illustrated from Levinas' 'more religious writings', particularly, in this instance, a short article on 'Loving the Torah more than God' in which Yosl Rakover speaks to God.

GOD'S SELF-HIDING AND THE POSSIBILITY OF ETHICS

Levinas, in a way that is consonant with his *mitnagged* inheritance, mistrusts both theoretical and mystical approaches to God, since they attempt to gain access to divine presence other than through the detour of the human. In this regard, atheism is presented as a positive and responsible attitude, for, in providing a foil to positive theology, it draws attention to human responsibility as the locus of divine presence. God is forever inscrutable and inaccessible, not simply because of the finitude and incapacity of human thought, but because, positively, God is one who is utterly Transcendent. But further, God

purposively withdraws in order that the human creation can attain its
purpose, which is the coming to maturity of an ethical humanity, and
the emergence of an adult religion. An ethical humanity, working to
realise justice, is the fulfilment of the original creation, and opens the
way for the return of a God who arises as the counterpart of the justice
rendered to others. God withdraws in order to create a space wherein
ethics might be possible and so the creation reaches the fulfilment of
its original purpose. God's self-distancing, then, is the possibility of
an ethical humanity. Thus Levinas writes,

> God is real and concrete not through incarnation but through Law . . . To
> hide one's face so as to demand the superhuman of man, to create a man who
> can approach God and speak of Him without always being in His debt –
> that is truly a mark of divine greatness! (*DF*, 145)

It will be useful to explore the notion of the *Deus Absconditus* in
Levinas' thinking, since it gives a sense of his understanding of the
relationship between the divine and the human, and the demand of
the ethical. The problem is addressed in a short article, 'Loving the
Torah More than God'.

Levinas' reflection opens with the fictional Yosl Rakover addressing
God and struggling to understand why God should have hidden his
face in the final days of the Warsaw Ghetto during the Second World
War. The destruction of the ghetto seems evacuated of meaning. This
was a moment when the 'to be' or 'not to be' of the universe was yet
again being decided; Israel's original acceptance of the Torah was an
acceptance of the ethical intent of creation because, in accepting the
Law, even before understanding the extent of its demands, Israel was
committing itself to enactment in ethics and to a responsibility for a
future which was yet to come.[41] The fictional Yosl Rakover, refusing
to submit to the seeming meaninglessness of the events that surround
him, struggles to find an answer to the question, 'Why does God hide
his face?' The answer emerges in Yosl's reflection on *loving the Torah
more than God*.

Psalms of lament

God's self-hiding is a recurrent theme in the psalms, particularly the
psalms of lament. God has abandoned Israel and 'hides his face'. Thus

the cry, 'How much longer will you forget me, Yahweh? For ever? How much longer will you hide your face from me?' (Ps. 13:1). 'Why do you reject me? Why do you hide your face from me?' (Ps. 88:14). Yet such questions meet with no response. Indeed, such questions are not even questions since they find no respondent. God having departed, they rebound on the one who asks the question, and thus become a question for the one who questions. Lament 'serve[s] to bring to expression the plight of the worshipper in his struggle to understand his own situation in relation to God'.[42] The inability 'to perceive God at work' and the 'urgent need for God's intervention in an intolerable situation . . . has arisen because of God's lack of involvement'.[43] God is absent, and thus disaster has befallen the suppliant.

Now, the divine absence prompts two things. There is, first of all, an attempt to understand 'why' God should have hidden his face, and also 'how long' the situation will continue. Such questions, however, attempt to 'negotiate encounter' rather than response. In the midst of disaster, where is the place of an encounter with the divine? 'What is desired is not so much dialogue with God as . . . the confirmation of God's presence'.[44] The psalmody of lament 'has at its core an urgent appeal for confirmation of God's presence'.[45] Such is Yosl's situation in the final hours of the ghetto. Why has this happened? How long will it endure? And Yosl, hearing no response from God, is thrown back upon his own questions in search of his own answer.

A good example is Psalm 42, the 'Lament of a Levite in exile', which witnesses the turmoil of one who is abandoned and seeks the presence of God. The psalm opens with the experience of dereliction, so much in evidence that even others raise the taunt, 'Where is your God?' (Ps. 42:2–3). One can attempt to recall the divine presence by an initial retreat into past memories and mercies, but this is in vain (Ps. 42:4). The past remains past; it is immemorial and cannot be recuperated into the present. The future may hold promise, for with its own particular intentionality, hope is a possibility: 'Put your hope in God' (Ps. 42:5, 11). But this too remains unfulfilled. The intending is empty, for the future is yet to be known.[46] Presence cannot be commanded or engendered either through memory or hope, and remains elusive. It may be that the fool who says in his heart 'there is no God' is not so foolish after all, and that the atheist is the wisest of all. But, this

would be too simple an answer and Levinas is not so simple as to
suggest this. There is a *God* who is absent, and there is an *absence* of
that God which is not without meaning. In his intolerable situation,
Yosl struggles for this meaning.

Now, from the vantage point of biblical scholarship, Balentine
notes that the 'merit of lament simply as lament' has largely been
ignored. Lament has been viewed as a prelude to praise and an opening to thanksgiving,[47] and certainly, fidelity to the discipline of praise
and thanksgiving in the midst of adversity can be considered as an
attempt at restoring contact with the God who has hidden himself.
More earnest prayer is often an initial response in times of trouble
and distress. One ritually does in order that there might be an understanding in the wake of doing. The question is one of whether the
recovery of meaning in the midst of disaster needs to be expatriated
to a God who may or may not intervene, which is also the question
of the place of encounter with the divine.

Now, lamenting is solitary. One is thrown back on oneself. As
Levinas will say in *Existence and Existents*, the verb 'to be' (*être*) is a
reflexive verb (*s'être*). It is not so much that 'one is' (*on est*), but that
one is oneself (*on s'est*). Lament has no interlocutor, and there is no
response from an absent and silent God. To neglect the significance
of sheer lament, Balentine notes, 'is to misjudge the crucial function
of the God question which is so frequent in the psalms of lament',
and to be deaf to 'the real and present element of anxiety to which
the psalms of lament give expression'.[48] God has hidden his face, has
withdrawn his presence from the present, and the plaintive enters
into the experience of doubt and despair, an experience seemingly
devoid of meaning. In the 'the agony of the struggle'[49] what does one
do? How does one move from despair to meaning and purpose? God,
being withdrawn and silent, provides no answer, but recourse to the
divine may not, in itself, be the locus of meaning.

Yet, it is the 'crucial function of the God question' that needs to
be explored, for the question of God and the questioning of God
are intimately related to the question of the human and the quest for
meaning. It is the function and the meaning of the God-question that
Levinas raises, and answers in terms of an ethics of human responsibility for the other person, which, in turn, is the occasion of God's
return, and the locus of the encounter with the divine.

But, let us pursue this further. Lament casts the lamenter back upon himself, and provokes reflection as an attempt at discovering or creating meaning. This is not to suggest that lament is self-indulgent, wallowing in its own misfortune, nor that the lamentable situation finds its resolution in a self-enclosed subjectivity, endlessly haruspicating its own entrails, and entertaining its own grief; neither is it to suggest the tragic strategy of suicide as the only exit from a despair in which the subject, on the verge of meaninglessness and chaos, is overwhelmed to the extreme point of losing its very subjectivity. What is being suggested – and this is the extreme demand which comes to the fore in Levinas' extreme ethics of responsibility – is that, in situations of lamentation and desolation, the resolution is only ever by way of a turning to the neighbour. The singularity and solitariness of a lamentable situation in which a solitary self might find itself finds its egress and resolution not in recourse to a God who purposively elects to be absent, silent and unresponsive, but in the one who, lamenting, becomes aware of a responsibility which only s/he can bear. It is not catharsis but kenosis which is required.[50] But this is an extreme ethics, and not without difficulties for Christian theology.

Yosl Rakover talks to God (Yossel Rakover s'addresse à Dieu)[51]

Yosl finds himself in the midst of the disaster of the Holocaust. One thing which needs to be refused at the outset is the notion that the withdrawal of the divine is, in some way, punishment for past offences, by which 'Israel's accusations against God becomes God's accusations against Israel'.[52] God has not abandoned Israel; rather, Israel has abandoned God, and so 'the events of history appear to be out of control'.[53] Generally speaking, prophetic literature tends to present a God who

does not hide himself from Israel capriciously but angrily; he is not hidden from the beginning of time but rather during the course of history. Hence his hiddenness is an angry reaction against a guilty people at specific points in history.[54]

As Leora Batnitsky observes, the 'view of suffering as punishment for sin is the most pervasive view of the Hebrew Bible'.[55] It seems to me that such a notion of God hiding his face on account of the sin of his people should not and cannot be sustained in a post-Holocaust situation. Balentine notes,

God's hiddenness is not primarily related to his punishment for disobedience. It is not basically a reflection of man's inability to understand or even perceive God's presence in the world. It is manifest in both these ways, but it is not restricted to them. It is rather an integral part of the nature of God which is not to be explained away by theological exposition of human failures or human limitations. God is hidden just as he is present; he is far away just as he is near.[56]

The fictional Yosl, then, in addressing himself to God, struggles to find the reason for divine abandonment in his own conduct. A God who withdraws in a fit of pique because of the wrongdoings of his people is precisely a God who acts capriciously – one might even say irresponsibly.

Now, Levinas considers this point when he considers the notion of 'deserved' or 'merited' suffering, that is, the attempt to explain suffering either in terms of its being endured in view of some higher Good or 'a kingdom of transcendent ends' (*US*, 120) or in terms of some original and ongoing falling which acts as its cause. Such an original sinning, as found in the Christian tradition, is, according to Levinas,

in a certain sense implicit in the Old Testament, where the drama of the Diaspora reflects the sins of Israel. The wicked conduct of ancestors, still non-expiated by the sufferings of exile, would explain to the exiles themselves the duration and the harshness of the exile. (*US*, 161)

Yet, this does not necessarily 'make God innocent' nor 'make suffering bearable'. Indeed, being aware of situations of profound or extreme suffering – suffering *in extremis* – 'makes waiting for the saving actions of an all-powerful God impossible without degradation' (*US*, 159). The scandal of suffering cannot be resolved by referring it to a 'metaphysical order', whether as *arche* or *telos*. What, then, is the human response to divine unresponsiveness? For Levinas, since access to the divine is always by way of the human, suffering will only find some meaningful resolution in the 'ethical perspective of the interhuman' (*US*, 159). Here the fictional Yosl Rakover illustrates the response.

In trying to understand the divine *remotio*, Yosl himself is placed in question. 'To know God is to know what must be done' (*DF*, 17). In faithfully adhering to the demands of the Law in respect of one's neighbour – in 'loving the Torah more than God' – the God who has hidden himself arises as the counterpart of the justice which is rendered to others. 'The Justice rendered to the Other, my neighbour, gives me an unsurpassable proximity to God. It is as intimate as the prayer and liturgy which, without justice, are nothing' (*DF*, 18). But, to encounter 'the God who hides his face' and yet 'is recognised as being present and intimate' – 'is this really possible?' (*DF*, 144). How does Yosl resolve his dilemma?

Kolitz outlines the significant fiction, which is true as only fiction can be true. Yosl begins his address,

I, Yosl, son of David Rakover of Tarnapol, a follower of the Rabbi of Ger and descendent of the righteous, learned and holy ones of the families Rakover and Maysels, am writing these lines as the houses of the Warsaw Ghetto are in flames, and the house I am in is one of the last that have not yet caught fire. For several hours now we have been under raging artillery fire and all around me walls are exploding and shattering in the hail of shells. It will not be long before this house I'm in, like almost all the houses in the ghetto, will become the grave of its inhabitants and defenders.[57]

Now, Yosl refuses to see his present crisis, a present severely defined by God's absence, as the result of sin or failing on Yosl's own part. He is a faithful Jew.

I do not say, like Job, that God should lay his finger on my sins so that I may know how I have earned this. For greater and better men than I are convinced that it is no longer a question of punishment for sins and transgressions. On the contrary, something unique is happening in the world: *hastoras ponim* – God has hidden his face.[58]

Why has God hidden his face? In the relationship between God and Yosl, Yosl certainly does not consider himself the debtor. Rather it is God who is in debt to Yosl – 'greatly in debt' – and is to be admonished. So, too, Berkovits can say, 'Within time and history God remains indebted to his people'.[59] Yosl's situation is one of a fidelity which refuses to be extinguished, despite the absence of God. Humanity has been delivered over to its most savage instincts, yet Yosl can nonetheless continue to say, 'I believe in the God of Israel, even when he has done everything to make me cease to believe in him'.[60] Again, 'You have done everything to make me lose my faith in you, to make me cease to believe in you. But I die exactly as I have lived – an unshakeable believer in you'.[61] Yosl has faith, but it is a faith which seems to have no other foundation than that of its own fidelity, nor is there any supporting evidence to sustain it. One must 'love the Torah more than God' that, in doing, hearing and understanding may come.

Now, one of the significant aspects of faith is that it 'cannot be founded on anything else', nor does it 'depend on rational justification or on objective grounds'; it is 'invulnerable to external events that contradict them'.[62] With regard to Yosl's faith, this is severely – and one might say 'deliberately' – tested. The utter transcendence of God, implicated in God's self-concealing, is not a positive experience of a transcendence which could be interpreted as 'an experience of an inexhaustible richness in meaning', namely God's goodness, but rather, as Moyaert puts it, an experience which 'test[s] the belief in his goodness, such that in this world and in this life – at their very limit – we no longer see, possess, or receive any sign that could support that belief, and such that even the recollection of earlier signs disappears. God's transcendence is manifest in the suspension of any sign of his goodness, which is to say, his radical absence'.[63]

For Yosl, God's transcendence is something which is 'suffered' or undergone. But, Yosl indicates that the reason why he refuses to lose faith is not simply because 'I love him' but because 'I love his Torah more . . . God commands religion, but his Torah commands a way of life.'[64] Implicated here is the relation between religion and ethics, and the importance of fidelity to the ongoing ethical injunctions of the Torah.[65]

Levinas continues his reflection on Zvi Kolitz's story, a story 'true as only fiction can be', recognising in it 'a profound and authentic experience of spiritual life' (*DF*, 80). Does the suffering of the innocents not prove a world without God? In fact, does the death of God, which Nietzsche announced, not become a quasi-empirical fact in the events of the Holocaust?[66] Levinas refuses to acquiesce in such a conclusion. The atheism of the metaphysician that he speaks of in *Totality and Infinity* is not to be considered as a refusal of the divine but an affirmation of the ethical, in which the true God makes his return. The refusal of knowledge, that 'temptation of temptations', as an opening on to God, is an initial positive aspect of atheism, not a 'negation of the divine'. Despite the experience of 'life without God', Yosl does not yield to the temptation of atheism; he believes and refuses not to believe. Positively, God's withdrawal opens on to the possibility of encountering him in our opening on to the other person. Levinas comments,

Yosl experienced the certainty of God's existence with new force in an empty world. Because Yosl exists in his utter solitude, it is so that he can feel all God's responsibility resting on his shoulders. (*DF*, 81)

In other words, God withdraws in order to create a space wherein the individual can achieve the stature of humanity which is 'responsibility for-the-other'. Just as, in the creative act, God, as it were, removes himself or stands back in order to create a world of time and space, so now God withdraws in order that this world might become ethical. A like sentiment is expressed in *Totality and Infinity*: 'It is certainly a great glory for the creator to have set up a being capable of atheism, a being which without having been *causa sui*, has an independent view and word and is at home with itself' (*TI*, 58–9). The self-absenting move on the part of God enables an ethical humanity by its very otherness from God, and the heavy demands that this otherness brings. There is 'no external reprieve'; there is no institution to which one might take recourse and surrender this responsibility; there is no 'consolation of divine presence'. God 'renounces any manifestation of himself that would give succour, and calls on man in his maturity to recognise his full responsibility' (*DF*, 82–3). Again, 'His divine grandeur is shown when he veils his face in order to ask everything, to ask the superhuman of man; it is shown in his creation of a man capable of responding, capable of approaching God as a creditor, and not always as a debtor' (*DF*, 85–6).

This will inevitably entail suffering, for, in the absence of an interventionist God, the subject is thrown back on its own resources, and 'can triumph only in his own conscience, which necessarily means through suffering' (*DF*, 82) with and for the other person. For Levinas, 'responsibility-for-the-other' will become the defining moment of subjectivity. The mature stature of the person arises in the movement from self-consciousness to conscience, which is the response to the plight and the demands of the other person. And it is in this moment that God returns. But, '[t]his God, this distant God, who veils his face and abandons the just man to a justice in which there is no victory, springs immediately from within' (*DF*, 83).

Ethics is responsibility. God withdraws to create the *my* time and the space of responsibility and justice. Thus, theology and the question of God arise in the context of ethics, and God arises as the counterpart of the justice rendered to others.

CHAPTER 3

Incarnate existence

It could be argued that 'the true life is elsewhere', but Levinas deliber-ately reverses Rimbaud's words and states, 'but we are in the world'. There is a commitment to engagement with and involvement in the world. To be 'in-the-world' is to be incarnate and enfleshed. Life is terribly secular. What Levinas will draw attention to, from his earliest phenomenological reflections in *On Escape*, *Existence and Existents*, and *Time and the Other*, is the salvific significance of sec-ularity. Human fulfilment is not a withdrawal from the world, but a commitment to the world. God arises as the counterpart of the justice rendered to others. Thus there is a commitment to incarnate or enfleshed existence, for 'we are in the world'.

Incarnate, or enfleshed, existence is a significant object of both phe-nomenological and theological reflection, not least in France, where, from its very beginnings, phenomenology developed a more overtly existential stress. Heidegger, of course, assuming Husserl's chair in Freiburg-im-Breisgau, had already published *Sein und Zeit* (*Being and Time*) (1927), and Levinas had been influenced by the stature of this work, and the themes of human existence which it developed. In France, however, phenomenology developed a particularly existential thrust. Already mentioned is Janicaud's criticism of phenomenology's original falling in France with Sartre's abandonment of the work-place of French phenomenological investigations 'to turn resolutely towards politics and an ethics of engagement' since, for Sartre, phe-nomenology was altogether too abstract, 'too detached from concrete situations and sociopolitical struggles'.[1] However, Merleau-Ponty also turns to the question of enfleshed existence when, in his *Phenomenol-ogy of Perception*, he notes the phenomenological significance of the body. Theologically, the significance of incarnate existence is a theme which is taken up and developed by such thinkers as Michel Henry, Jean-Louis Chrétien, and Jean-Luc Marion.

How, then does Levinas understand incarnate existence, and what for him is the significance of the world? To appreciate Levinas' understanding of human existence, Heidegger's philosophy of human existence (*Dasein*) and the world which Heidegger inhabits needs first to be considered, for it is the climate of the particular philosophical world that Levinas wishes to escape and go beyond.

What this chapter argues is Levinas' positive appreciation of the world in which the self finds itself. It is my singular 'place in the sun' which I enjoy. It is an encounter with the elemental. Yet, such an existence can also be termed 'pagan' for it lacks positive transcendence. What Levinas advocates is an ethical existence in which subject emerges from its solitude and its enchainment to its own self-concerns. The defining characteristic of human existence is not the ontological condemnation to being '*pour-soi*', but rather the ethical liberation or redemption of a self-enclosed subjectivity by an other whose gracious prevenience enables the self to be radically '*pour-l'autre*', to be responsive and responsible, and this opens on to a transcendence provoked by the excess of the other. In short, what does it mean to be human? To be human is quite simply to be '*for*'. And thus does ontology find itself always and already in the service of ethics.

THE HEIDEGGERIAN CLIMATE FROM WHICH WE MUST
ESCAPE: *DASEIN*'S WORLD

Levinas' appreciation of Heidegger flows from *Being and Time* (*Sein und Zeit*) (1927, hereafter *BT*). He had gone to Freiburg to pursue studies on Husserl, and encountered there for the first time the thinking of Heidegger. The events of 1933 and Hitler's coming to power had not yet happened. Disastrously for Levinas, the existential phenomenology of *Being and Time*, which becomes an ontology of human existence, would lead almost inexorably to the commodification and utilisation, not only of things encountered within the world, but also of peoples and generations. Although, in Levinas' eyes, 'Heidegger has never been exculpated . . . from his participation in National-Socialism' (*EI*, 41),[2] he acknowledges, nevertheless, that 'I discovered in fact *Sein und Zeit* . . . Very early I had a great admiration for this book. It is one of the finest books in the history of philosophy' (*EI*, 37). In its 'analyses of anxiety, care and being-towards-death, we witness a sovereign exercise of phenomenology' (*EI*, 39). What Levinas appreciated in *Being and Time* was an 'awakening' to the 'verbality' of the word 'being', to 'being' as an event rather than a substantive. Heidegger's key concern was the question of the meaning of Being – the *Seinsfrage*; and, whereas Husserl still seemed to be proposing a transcendental philosophy, Heidegger clearly defined philosophy in relation to other forms of knowledge as 'fundamental ontology' (*EI*, 38). Ontology is the fundamental question since it enjoys not only an ontic priority, but also an ontological priority over all other questions. Not only is it the fundamental and more important question for the one who enquires (*Dasein*), but it is also the question whose answer gives foundation to all other sciences.[3] In Heidegger, human existence (*Dasein*) – outlined in 'the existential analytic of Dasein' in *Being and Time*, §9 – becomes 'the "place" of fundamental ontology' (*EI*, 40).

How, then, does Heidegger understand human existence? In brief: it is unique; it is uniquely 'mine', and it is 'in-the-world'. There is no doubt that, for Heidegger, existence (*Existenz*) – a signal and significant human characteristic – is incarnate. Further, *Dasein* alone exists (though Levinas will stress significantly that *Dasein* does not exist alone). Thus, Heidegger will point out in his *Introduction to Metaphysics* that 'Stones are, but they do not exist; angels are, but they do not exist; God is, but he does not exist; only *Dasein* exists.'

For Heidegger, beyond any hint of essentialism, *Dasein* is an existential project, a project charged with immense possibilities. '*Dasein* always understands itself in terms of its existence – in terms of a possibility of itself' (*BT*, 33) and 'comports itself towards its Being as its ownmost possibility' (*BT*, 68). To the extent that *Dasein* realises or fails to realise these possibilities, that existence (*Existenz*) will either be authentic (*eigentlich*) or inauthentic (*uneigentlich*), and Dasein will either win itself or lose itself. It can fulfil itself by its own active and unique engagement in the world, or it can fail to realise its own possibilities by contenting itself with the ordinary and average everyday behaviour and the aspirations of others.

But, possibility does not only implicate *Dasein*'s own existence. Since existence is a project – a work in progress – *Dasein* considers things encountered in the world in terms of its own possibilities. *Dasein* assigns meaning to things. Objects encountered within the world are interpreted in terms of possibility, but in terms of possibility *for Dasein*. *Dasein* is the centripetal point of significance, and the world is a referential totality which begins from, and returns to, *Dasein*. In short, the Heideggerian environment is instrumentalised. That instrumentalisation can also extend to others, the significance of whose existence becomes determined in terms of their usefulness to *Dasein*. Thus is the other reduced to the same. Thus, for Levinas, Heideggerian existential phenonomenology finds its conclusion in National Socialism. What Levinas will contest and reverse is the meaning and the significance of the '*for*'. What is other is not there '*for-Dasein*'. Rather, *Dasein* finds itself there '*for others*'.

Take, for example, a hand-sized stone lying on a beach which I pick up. It is a handy object, and it might be of some use. It is not simply something lying there which is, as MacQuarrie translates it, 'present-at-hand' (*vorhanden*). It is not 'just a stone'. In relation to me, it acquires significance and possibilities. It becomes something 'ready-to-hand' (*zuhanden*).[4] At times, because the stone is at hand, and of a hand-held size, it becomes handy as the heart-sized stone I can make illustrative use of when speaking about 'hearts of stone'; at times, it is handy as a doorstop; at times, it just sits insignificantly and unnoticed at the side of my fireplace among other stones, picked up elsewhere and at other times, until it is thrown once more into relief as one of the stones gathered up on another beach with other friends. Phenomenologically, the stone is never *just a stone*. It *is* what it is because of the meaning-structure in which it is situated, a meaning-structure which I assign.

One can pursue this in Heidegger's example of a hammer. What is a hammer? This may seem a facile question, for everyone seemingly and naively knows what a hammer is. A hammer is for hammering. The significant point is that what makes a hammer to be a hammer is that it is caught up within a world of possibility which finds its origin and fulfilment in terms of possibilities *for Dasein*. Heidegger distinguishes two ways in which things encountered in the world which *Dasein* inhabits and makes habitable are related and relevant to *Dasein*. For example, a stone lying on a beach is just there, without any particular significance. But my roof is leaking and I need to hammer a nail into a piece of wood, with no hammer in hand. The stone, which is 'at hand', becomes 'handy' as a tool. This stone, of all the other stones on the beach, is no longer 'just a stone'. In my hand, it can become useful as a tool. It acquires another significance in view of my concerns, and becomes not just a stone but a tool for hammering. It *is* no longer a stone, but a hammer. As Heidegger writes,

> *[W]ith* this thing, for instance, which is ready-to-hand, and which we accordingly call a 'hammer', there is an involvement in hammering; with hammering, there is an involvement in making something fast; with making something fast, there is an involvement in protection against bad weather; and this protection 'is' for the sake of providing shelter for *Dasein* – that is, for the sake of the possibility of *Dasein*'s Being. Whenever something ready-to-hand has an involvement with it, *what* involvement this is, has in each case been outlined in advance in terms of the totality of such involvements (*BT*, 116).

In other words, things *are* what they are in terms of their significance for *Dasein* and its possibilities. Thus is it that the task '*towards-which*' the hammer is directed (the securing of the roof), and '*for-the-sake-of-which*' it is used (protection against the elements) is ultimately '*for-the-sake-of*' *Dasein*, whose concern is for its own Being. Thus does Heideggerian phenomenology have ontological intent.

For Levinas, this concern with the privileging of the ontological over the ethical usurping the prevenience of the other over the same is evident in one of his most early writings. Nor is it phenomenologically adequate. In his *Reflections on Hitlerism*, first published in 1934, he draws attention to the awakening of the 'raw sentiments' (*sentiments élémentaires*) which predetermine or prefigure life in the world. As an adventure, the one both enjoys and triumphs over the other, a triumph of the same over any other, the privilege of totality over infinity. In a postscript to this article, written in 1990, Levinas notes that this early article flows from a conviction that the 'bloody barbarity' displayed by National Socialism is contingent neither on a rationality which was gone wayward, nor an 'accidental ideology', but rather on an 'elemental evil' (*Mal élémental*) which challenges western philosophy. The very possibility of this evil is 'inscribed in the ontology of Being' and its concern for itself. It is a possibility which threatens the individual, situating him or her within a dominating totality. In a sense, National Socialism became the ontology of Being pushed to its political limits.[5]

LEVINAS' CRITICISM OF HEIDEGGER

One cannot read Levinas without taking Heidegger into account. Heidegger is the climate from which one needs to escape. For Levinas, Heidegger developed Husserl's phenomenological insights along existential pathways. Things *are* what they are, and they *are* in the way that they are, in terms of their phenomenological significance. However, three related criticisms are directed by Levinas against Heidegger: first, the privileging of ontology in Heidegger; secondly, the ethical deficit which this engenders; thirdly, the significance of the world.

With regard to Heidegger's fundamental ontology, Levinas asks '*Is Ontology Fundamental?*' Heidegger's achievement was in developing an existential phenomenology and recognising the '*factual situation* of the mind that knows' (*IOF*, 2). Authentic ontology 'coincides with the facticity of temporal existence' (*IOF*, 3). There can be no understanding of human existence without acknowledging that that existence is always and already an existence in the world. For Heidegger, one never finds *Dasein* without also encountering a world; but the world which is encountered is a world which is already predetermined by *Dasein*'s understanding (*Verstehen*) of that world. *Dasein* is the meaning-bestower, the one who enables things to be what they are, but only what they are in terms of their possibilities for *Dasein*.[6] The world, in short, is a 'referential totality' with *Dasein* as the focal point of reference, and thus things become possible insofar as they can be part of *Dasein*'s own self-project. Thus, for Levinas, '[t]he whole human being is ontology' in Heidegger and his 'philosophy of human existence . . . is only the counterpart, albeit inevitable, of his ontology' (*IOF*, 3). The eventual and inexorable outcome is a totality. For Heidegger, '[w]e exist in a circuit of understanding with reality. Understanding is the very event that existence articulates' (*IOF*, 5). By reducing the world to 'that "*wherein*" a factical *Dasein* as such can be said to "live"' (*BT*, 93), an ethical deficit becomes apparent. Heidegger's ontology works well with things encountered within the world, but becomes problematical when one encounters other people.

Other people are not reducible to things which are useful – though it happens – and offer a certain resistance in being situated within structures and totalities which deprive them of a voice. The 'factual situation' in which *Dasein* finds itself is a situation in which there are other people.

Levinas argues, then, that it is not ontology but ethics which is fundamental. The ontological surplus evident in Heidegger is also an ethical deficit. This extreme ethical deficit in Heidegger provokes, in Levinas, a fundamental ethics of responsibility in Levinas. Ethics is not a derivative of ontology; but rather precedes it. The world may indeed be 'that "*wherein*" a factual Dasein can as such be said to "live" ' but 'consciousness of reality does not coincide with our habitation of the world' and 'our consciousness and our mastery of reality does not exhaust our relation with reality' (*IOF*, 4). In short, the world is not to be considered in terms of *Dasein's* existentiality. The fact of other people places in question *Dasein's* elemental enjoyment and happy habitation of the world. For Levinas, Heidegger's existential analysis of *Dasein* is *structurally* deficient and phenomenologically inadequate. Although Heidegger is phenomenologically faithful in pursuing the intentionality of human existence, there remains nonetheless 'a responsibility beyond our intentions' (*IOF*, 4) which defies *Dasein's* understanding of reality. Paradoxically, the phenomenological fidelity which Heidegger displays in affirming the factual situation in which *Dasein* finds itself cannot give an account of what Marion terms the excessive or saturated phenomenon which often gives itself strikingly in its phenomenality and, as striking, gives itself in a way which is excessive to understanding.[7] For Levinas, Heidegger's analysis cannot account for the excess of the other person who ethically interrupts ontology, and thereby displaces ontology as fundamental. Heidegger correctly argued that phenomenology cannot pass over the significance of the world; but, in making ontology fundamental, he does not simply bypass but paradoxically passes over the other person whose significance is other than that projected by understanding. The other person interrupts the 'circuit of understanding and reality'. Ethics, not ontology, is fundamental.

What then is the significance of the world? Heidegger emphasised that *Dasein* finds itself always and already 'in-the-world'. In Levinas, 'thought . . . is *here*'. Consciousness is not located outside of space. It is 'essentially, and not as a result of a fall or a degradation . . . here'

(*EE*, 68). '*Here*' is the point of departure for phenomenological, existential, or even theological thinking. The world neither represents a
fall from 'the immediacy of translucid and spontaneous consciousness'
into receptivity and finitude, and thereby a 'deficiency of representation' (*OB*, 78) – as a philosophical gnosticism might argue – nor is it
strange or foreign to a thought which is properly phenomenological
or theological. Instead, because consciousness finds itself always and
already *here in the world*, incarnate or embodied existence is the singular point of departure for both phenomenology and theology. The
subject as origin 'is also a subject of flesh and blood', and this body
of flesh and blood is not an obstacle to translucid thinking. Rather,
it is, like the neck which is able to turn on its own atlas and thus give
sight its perspectival possibilities, the 'hinge of salvation' (*caro cardo
salutis*).[8] In short, this body of flesh and blood, always and already in
the world, is the *sine qua non* of thought.

The body of course has always been taken to be more than a chunk of matter.
It was taken to house a soul, which it had the power of expressing. The body
might be more or less expressive, and had parts which were more or less
expressive. The face and the eyes, those mirrors of the soul, were especially
the organs of expression. *But the spirituality of the body does not lie in this
power to express what is inward. By its position it realises the condition necessary
for any inwardness. It does not express an event; it is itself this event.* (*EE*, 72).

Jean-Luc Marion expresses this well when he writes, 'my flesh fixes me
definitively to its *here*, which becomes my *here*, the only one possible
for me'.[9]

Levinas himself displays this commitment to the world when,
adapting Rimbaud, he writes that '[t]he true life is elsewhere, but
we are in the world' (*TI*, 33), and it is this incarnate life within the
world which is the locus of salvation. For Levinas, *here* is the point
of departure for thought; it is also the point to which thought must
also and always return in its constant attempt at phenomenological
and theological adequacy.

EMERGENCE INTO A WORLD

It may be quite simply stated that 'everyday life is the locus of salvation'. Said otherwise, the world which we inhabit is the world of lived

experience (*Lebenswelt, le monde-de-la-vie*); this life-world *gives itself* wholly and entirely, even though that givenness may not be wholly phenomenalised. It is both world exposed to phenomenological and theological interpretation. But, first and foremost, it is world which gives itself, or a world in which we always and already find ourselves. Marion's principle of the givenness of the given has already been noted. Givenness is 'the basic determination of every phenomenon. For even if all that which gives itself does not phenomenalise itself, all that which phenomenalises itself must first give itself – unfolding according to the fold of givenness'.[10] What is required, then, is a phenomenology of life, somewhat along the lines developed by Michel Henry, which acknowledges that the reality of the world – which is *life* – 'can no longer be reduced to what we see'; the world is an incomprehensible content that cannot be deduced from its external appearance, nor ever explained from its disclosure in the world.[11] The difficulty with Heidegger – 'this German philosopher' – is that he appeals 'to an ontological finality' in which ordinary and everyday existence is caught up in the wider ontological project of possibility, the origin of which is *Dasein* (human existence). The world is a referential totality whose reference is *Dasein*. Thus, ordinary objects encountered within the world and everyday actions are meaningful to the extent that they accord with *Dasein*'s own projection of itself as a possibility to be realised. Ordinary and everyday events acquire meaning within a larger project, and objects become tools to be used and abused. What Heidegger has 'failed to recognise [is] the essentially secular nature of being in the world and the sincerity of intentions' (*EE*, 42). For Heidegger, the pragmatics of being-in-the-world are in view of Dasein's own concern for its own being. Actions assume a finality, or a teleological signification, which overlooks the sincerity of the quotidian. Yet, as Levinas will have it, '[t]here is something other than naivety in the flat denial the masses oppose to the elites when they are worried more about bread than about anxiety' (*TO*, 60). To ask for one's 'daily bread' (*panem quotidianem, le pain de ce jour* which is also *le pain de séjour*) is to ask for those elemental things which sustain human life in the everyday world. The need and the demand for bread is an everyday concern, and for many the most pressing of everyday concerns. The world may be terribly 'profane and secular' (*EE*, 41) yet life in the world is characterised not primarily by naivety but by sincerity. Conscious life is nourished by the event and the events of ordinary incarnate existence, and these both precede and provoke thought. There is something other than naivety in quotidian secularity. Everyday life is the locus of salvation.

The salvific significance of everyday existence

Everyday life 'is a preoccupation with salvation' (*TO*, 58). Levinas does not intend here any understanding of salvation interpreted through peculiarly Christian theological motifs. Rather, what he draws attention to is the significance of the secular or the ordinary, and the inherent excess which the givenness of this given gives to phenomenology and theology, or leaves a remainder to which phenomenology and theology are challenged to respond. The extraordinary cannot be exiled from the ordinary; the ordinary already gives itself as excess or surplus.

Against Heidegger, Levinas remarks that to call things 'everyday' and condemn them as 'inauthentic' is to fail to recognise the salvific significance of the ordinary (*EE*, 45). Life is terribly ordinary. Why does one eat? One eats because one is hungry. Why does one drink? One drinks because one is thirsty. One gives to the beggar who solicits money on the street without calculating any economic equation, or even considering whether the gift is counterfeit. One feels horror at violence. One is provoked by injustice. Commitment to the work of justice and peace, and establishing the structures which can achieve this, finds its origin in the disgust and the discomfort which is felt in the face of injustices and violence. Before ever justice becomes a theory, it has been experienced or witnessed in a disquieting way. One is comforted by the touch of the hand of another at moments of tragedy and grief, and one weeps with others, not in view of some greater end, but because empathy and sympathy belong to the ordinary and everyday situation of sharing life with others.

Now, none of these human events are without significance, and all of them food for phenomenological and theological reflection.

What Levinas does is pull phenomenological thinking back to reflect on ordinary incarnate existence and its ability to disrupt the grander schemes of thought. For example, in *Time and the Other*, he argues, in 'Everyday Life and Salvation', that materiality and the body do not represent 'the misfortune [*malheur*] of hypostasis' (*TO*, 58). The ordinary and quotidian invite a 'phenomenology of life'. Manifestly against Heidegger, he writes,

However much the entirety of preoccupations that fill our days and tear us away from solitude to throw us into contact with our peers are called 'fall', 'everyday life', 'animality', 'degradation', or 'base materialism', these preoccupations are in no way frivolous. (*TO*, 59)

For example, one may attempt to interpret existence in terms of its various temporal ecstases, where time is gathered into the present, where the attempt is made to represent the past in the present and the future is a horizon of possibilities, as with Heidegger; or one may find oneself in the ridiculous situation of idealism where one finds oneself enquiring whether or not breakfast comes after lunch, as with McTaggart. Yet still, 'one buys oneself a watch' (*TO*, 60). But, why does one buy a watch? Quite simply, so that the time which I inhabit accords with the time of the other person. I do not buy a watch because I am hurtling towards death, or because my existence is a 'being-towards-death' (*Sein-zum-Tode*). I buy a watch because I need to make sure I am at the train station at the proper time or to be at a meeting with colleagues or friends. I need a watch, quite simply, because there are other people, and time is not my own.

Now, '[t]hese may seem like facile objections, recalling the ones certain realists address to idealists when they reproach them for breathing in an illusory world' (*TO*, 60). But, an adequate phenomenology – a 'phenomenology of life' – must facilitate the seemingly everyday and seemingly facile, for '[t]here is something other than naivety in the flat denial the masses oppose to the elites when they are worried more about bread than about anxiety'. The concern with the average and everyday is not a flight from the demand of phenomenological rigour; rather it demands that phenomenology take seriously what otherwise might seem trivial, and, as such, is an echo of Husserl's principle of 'back to the facts', where the fact is the life-world, or the 'phenomenology of life'. To speak of a phenomenology of the everyday and suggest that the most mundane of human encounters are significant might suggest that Levinas' thinking lacks rigour and is unscientific. To take as a possible phenomenological point of departure such ordinary events as consuming a piece of bread, the disruption of forgetting to put one's watch on before going to work in the morning, and the simple courtesies and discourtesies of daily living may seem frivolous. Yet, for Levinas, the ordinary and the everyday are not without significance. The intentionality of the ordinary and everyday is 'terribly sincere' (*EE*, 37). While Husserl suspended the 'natural attitude' and withheld 'his assent to the apparently conclusive results of everyday experience', the 'natural attitude', for Levinas, is not really natural at all for 'experience is questionable and strange before its settles into everydayness'.[12] Everyday experience is not necessarily naive experience, nor is it to be described as average and everyday. Phenomena are often saturated or excessive. Quite simply, there is most often 'more to things than meets the eye'.

The sincerity of intentions

Now, there is not first existence and thereafter the living out of that existence. Human life consists precisely in the living of life, and the world *is* its content. What Levinas argues is a 'phenomenology of life', as Michel Henry will later develop in his 'Philosophy of Christianity'.[13] The relationship with the world is sincere. In fact it is precisely *as* being-in-the-world, as Heidegger argues in *Being and Time*, that existence is lived. However, for Heidegger, *Care* is the basic mode of *Dasein*'s existence in the world such that everything is ultimately for the sake of *Dasein*. But this creates a kingdom of means and ends which displaces the initial sincerity of intentionality. For Levinas, intentionality is, from the first, sincere. Heideggerian *Care*, as a concern for self, does not offer an adequate understanding of human existence.

Nowhere in the phenomenal order does the object of action refer to the concern for existing; it makes up our existence. We breath for the sake of breathing, eat and drink for the sake of eating and drinking, we take shelter for the sake of taking shelter, we study to satisfy our curiosity, we take a walk for the walk. All that is not for the sake of living; it is living. Life is a sincerity. (*EE*, 44)

To describe such an existence as *inauthentic* is phenomenologically inadequate and is to fail to recognise the basic sincerity of our relation to objects which give themselves to us in the world, taking them for what they are. One eats because one is hungry. One drinks because one is thirsty. The desire for food and for water is immediate; its intentionality has no ulterior motive. Water quenches thirst, and there is satisfaction. We eat, not in order to live, but because we are hungry. The ordinary and the everyday does not display a 'care for existing'; rather, ordinary and everyday existence is being caught up with or absorbed with 'the desirable'. The phenomenological reduction will be needed to expose the wider and unsuspected horizons of these ordinary acts, and their further significance.

What Levinas is keen to draw attention to is the significance of the ordinary actions which comprise human existence. What is the significance of the simple handshake exchanged between friends? What is the significance of the simple act of opening a door for another and saying 'after you'? For Heidegger, the simple act of turning the door handle opens on to a totality whose singular point of reference is *Dasein*. For Levinas, one opens the door either to allow the other to go first, or in welcome. What is the significance of the crossing of the street to avoid the beggar whom we catch sight of ahead of us on this side of the street? What has provoked this in us? More negatively, what is the significance of the immediate horror we feel in the face of the slaughter of the innocent? It is the directness of such human encounters, both positive and negative, and the fact that such directedness is outwith or goes beyond any directedness or intentionality on my part, that Levinas wants to draw attention to and elicit its meaning, and further meanings. For Levinas, this will open to the priority of ethics, for the ordinary and the everyday is also the place where the ethical reality of the encounter with the other person takes place. When someone stumbles before us and falls to the ground, do we not, almost naturally, stretch forward to prevent their falling? When a parent is struggling to negotiate the stairs with a pushchair from the metro or the underground, do we not, almost naturally and without thinking, feel compelled to help? When we pass by the one who begs on the street, or even cross to the other side to avoid the confrontation, have we not already been confronted by a request or a demand which we have had to negotiate? We may do nothing, we may give nothing, but the question of whether we should have done something is already implicated in the very fact of the question and the hesitation before responding. Without our choosing and without our knowing, we are already in a prevenient ethical situation.

In short, the question is: what provokes subjectivity, not only as consciousness but also as moral consciousness, or conscience? We noted that, for Levinas, initially (phenomenologically speaking), 'everything in the subject is here' (*EE*, 93). Eventually the *here* of a self-enclosed subjectivity, at home with itself, provides no means of salvation. 'It can only come from elsewhere' (*EE*, 93), from an other whose approach is always gracefully prevenient.

Enjoyment and the elemental

Now, the sincerity of existence in the world is experienced as enjoyment (*jouissance*), and the primal source of enjoyment is the elemental world. It is the experience of lying on the beach where the water hits the shore and experiencing the surge of each wave as it washes over the body; it is the face turned to the sun, or the wind, or the rain; it is the satisfaction of teeth and mastication. This is the truth, says Levinas, of the Marxist analysis of the relationship one has with nature. The natural world becomes a human world. One occupies a world where one is at home, content, happy.

In affirming the enjoyment one has of the elemental, Levinas is also affirming the basic goodness of the world. Against Heidegger, for whom the world is understood in terms of its instrumentality, Levinas views the primary relationship with the world as enjoyment. The elemental world is satisfying and enjoyable; it is 'the very pulsation of the I' (*TI*, 113). The subject 'lives from', feeds on, and is nourished by a world which is at its disposal. The elemental is alimentary. It is to be consumed, and enjoyed in the consumption.

Nourishment, as a means of invigoration, is the transmutation of the other into the same, which is the essence of enjoyment: an energy that is other, recognised as other, recognised, we will see, as sustaining the very act that is directed upon it becomes, in enjoyment, my own energy, my strength, me. All enjoyment is in this sense alimentation. (*TI*, 111)

Elemental enjoyment is diving into the pool in the heat of the day, or feeling the waves breaking against one's body; elemental enjoyment is savouring the taste of a favourite food; elemental enjoyment is closing the curtains on a cold and wet winter evening and being surrounded by fire and light and warmth; elemental enjoyment is the feel and the security of the quilt being drawn around one's body in bed. Elemental enjoyment is sensual, immediate, direct, and sincere. It has 'no further intentions behind it' (*EE*, 37). 'Life is a sincerity' (*EE*, 44). In nourishment, restoration is accomplished in the actual restoring. Eating is its own satisfaction. Swimming is the simple delight of being at one with elemental water, an immediacy whose immediate restorative worth is negated by attributing to the task any instrumentality in respect of a greater purpose, such as 'health' or 'relief from stress', which would destroy the instant by the interposition of thought; it is, like breathing for the sake of breathing, simply swimming for the sake of swimming. 'One does not only exist one's pain or one's joy; one exists from pains and joys. Enjoyment is precisely this way the act nourishes itself with its own activity' (*TI*, 111).

Enjoyment is the satisfaction of needs. Levinas distinguishes pleasure (*plaisir*) and enjoyment (*jouissance*), and desire (*désir*) and need (*besoin*). Enjoyment results from the fulfilment of need in the subject, like filling an empty stomach; pleasure is associated with desire, and with other people. 'The human being thrives on his needs; he is happy for his needs' (*TI*, 114). Nonetheless, in 'living from something' we are dependent, but paradoxically, we are complacent about *what* we are dependent on, and we are able to master it. 'Living from . . . is the dependency that turns into sovereignty' (*TI*, 114). The world, then, presents itself as basically a happy place, my 'place under the sun', and enjoyment of what it has to offer is the first movement of subjectivity. 'In enjoyment throbs egoist being . . . To be separated is to be at home with oneself. But to be at home with oneself . . . is to live from . . . to enjoy the elemental' (*TI*, 147).[14]

Enjoyment of the elemental, however, is a solitary affair. It has its focal point in the self. Such a world is an *environment*, an *Um-Welt* which is constructed around the solitary self. The subject disperses meaning from its own point of departure, and creates its own happy environment. Yet this self-centred situation of the subject is threatened. The elemental world is not only to be enjoyed but overcome. The natural and material world resists. The coal which heats and lights my place in the sun is not delivered without effort and work. My place in the sun is dependent, but dependent upon others on whom I depend. Further, the place in the sun which I occupy usurps a place which others might also enjoy, and this is disturbing. Who has not been in the situation of engrossment in Dostoievsky's *Brothers Karamazov* by the side of the pool when, out of all the beaches and all the pools, and all the empty and wide space elsewhere, others interrupt and disturb the space which I have created and claimed as my *here*?

Subjectivity, which lapses and collapses into sheer enjoyment, finds itself to be not self-sufficient. Sheer enjoyment is never a solitary affair. It demands the elemental. However, my place in the sun is also an open invitation to the other than myself which invites invasion. The subjectivity which *I* enjoy as an ever open existential awaits the advent of a personal other, who gives the language of 'who' and 'whom', and breaks open self-enclosure. The subject as subjecting becomes now subjected as the one who is responsible for the other, where this 'responsibility for the other' becomes the mark of subjectivity.

Awakening to the world, and the temptation of sleep

Levinas uses the metaphor of sleep and awakening to illustrate the emergence of consciousness. Conscious existence is *here*, but the effecting of the *here* is not without effort and sustaining existence can be a burden. The notion of phenomenological awakening is an important one for Levinas as consciousness emerges and is summoned to be conscience, or moral consciousness. It enables a charting of the movement from subjectivity to intersubjectivity. Theologically, it will have significance in articulating a theology of graced existence, as well as implications for the requirements in sustaining the demands of an existence which is both responsible and just. What then is the significance of the phenomenon of sleep, and its counterpart, awakening? What of sleeplessness?

Sleep can be a welcome disburdening of the day. The work of the day being done, and fatigue and weariness being experienced, one lays oneself down to sleep; one assumes the posture of sleeping in order that sleep might overcome the burden of consciousness and conscience which is the measure of the day. Negatively, sleep is escape and evasion. Positively, it is a recollection of oneself. One divests oneself of the demands of the day until, with dawn, one is summoned to don the clothing of demand and responsibility once again.

But sleep also finds itself in bed with sleeplessness, for 'the night comes when no one may sleep'. But there are two kinds of sleeplessness. There is that sleeplessness in which consciousness has not lapsed, and the events of the day past and its concerns or the day to come and its projects remain. A subject maintains itself in the midst of its concerns. But there is another kind of sleeplessness, an insomnia, which is neither sleep nor awakening, and in which there is neither subject nor object. It is the phenomenon of the sleeplessness of insomnia which Levinas finds interesting, and it is helpful in charting the emergence of a subjectivity which, eventually, is summoned to be responsible and ethical, and bear the burden of responsibility in the heat of the day.

Insomnia and the 'il y a'

Insomnia, the sleeplessness which is not yet consciousness, is a *vigilance*, 'quite devoid of objects', a watching and listening for what can neither be seen nor heard, in which one is 'absorbed in the rustling of the unavoidable being' (*EE*, 65) of the *there is (il y a)*. The kind of situation which Levinas is attempting to lay hold of and describe is the experience (though one should not strictly call it experience for there is neither subject who experiences nor object which is experienced at this stage) of wakefulness in darkness. There is *no thing* there, but this is not *nothing*. It is the fact that *there is*.

Other situations abound, and often they occupy the twilight zone of vigilance. *There is* the walking home through the once familiar wooded path or familiar city street at twilight at that time when suddenly all the birds have stopped singing, and *there is* that silence which makes the ears listen all the more attentively. Trees have lost their form and shape to sight, and eyes struggle to identify and make sense of the sheer anonymity which *there is* and which is there as a threat. (It is not without significance that, in terms of film, psychological drama plays itself out often in terms of the *il y a*.) Or similarly, the awareness of the emptiness of wide open spaces – the threat of vastness – when there is no thing there, but one still looks around. A few points are worth drawing attention to here: first, the experience of the *there is* is not strictly an experience since it is not only 'quite devoid of objects' but also there is not yet a subject. Subject and object are not yet differentiated or distanced from each other. Thus, it is not so much that 'I am afraid' or 'I am vigilant' or 'I am threatened'. Rather, there is fear, there is vigilance, there is threat. Secondly, strictly speaking, there can be no phenomenology of the *there is*, since not being in the light, it is essentially nonphenomenal. The *there is* – being in its very anonymity – is not known in itself; it is only known rather in what it provokes. It is known *as* fear, *as* threat, *as* vigilance, all which can be subjected to phenomenological scrutiny.

How, then, does one escape the threat of anonymous being? Quite simply, by standing up and engaging with the day, or, as Levinas puts it, effecting the subject as a *hypostasis* of existence and existent. One emerges from anonymous Being by adopting a position, a stance, and coming into the light of day.

THE SUBJECT AS HYPOSTASIS

Now, if sleep can be a refuge and escape from the excessive demands of responsibility and the burdens of the day, so standing up from a state of sleepless vigilance and taking up a position is a refuge from the threat and the impersonal anonymity of the *there is* (*il y a*). Subjectivity is both an overcoming of anonymity and the struggle to exist, and the bearing of a responsibility to the point of excess. The subject, as it were, is suspended between anonymity and oblivion on the one hand, and extreme responsibility *in extremis*. But getting up is not a simple thing, either physically or phenomenologically. The time and the distance between waking up and putting one's foot on the floor is not without effort. Accounting for this phenomenon philosophically is also not without effort.

Philosophically, the process whereby a subject becomes a subject – that is, the subjectivising of the subject, or the emergence of subjectivity – involves forging a *hypostasis* of existence and existent.

Hypostasis, the apparition of a substantive, is not only the apparition of a new grammatical category; it signifies the suspension of the anonymous *there is*, the apparition of a private domain, of a noun. On the ground of the *there is* a being arises. (*EE*, 82–3)

One gathers one's existence to oneself after the matutinal alarm as one might gather one's clothes to oneself. Levinas speaks of this in terms of this emergence into the light of day in terms of a *contract* between existence and existent, a contract which is sustained by effort, and is often experienced as fatigue and indolence and weariness. But this weariness is a weariness of Being itself. Although the world may be a place of happy enjoyment in which the self can lose itself — though really, the self cannot really be lost in happy and elemental enjoyment, for it has, in Heidegger's language, neither found itself nor won itself — solitary existence is not salvific. Being, for Levinas, is not generous; it does not give itself (*es gibt*). It is threatening, and the forging of the contract between existence and existent is difficult to sustain in the solitude of the self. The escape from the threat and the terror of Being can only come from elsewhere. What is being suggested here is the ethical redemption of the solitariness of human existence. Levinas writes, 'There exists a weariness which is a weariness of everything and everyone, and above all a weariness of oneself . . . The weariness concerns existence itself . . . To be weary is to be weary of Being' (*EE*, 24).

Thus, the phenomenological analysis of fatigue as 'a numbness, a way of curling up into oneself . . . a condemnation to Being . . . the lag of an existent tarrying behind its existing' (*EE*, 35). One does get tired and would withdraw into oneself, disburdening oneself of existence. One would rather not get up in the morning and face the day and the inevitability of its demands. 'Effort is a condemnation because it takes up an instant as an inevitable present' (*EE*, 34). But one must exist, and existing is *travail*. One speaks of 'holding oneself together', of 'getting a grip on yourself', as if, in some way, the subject was not wholly at one with itself, as if, at the core of a subjectivity concerned for its self, there was a fissure, or a cleaving of existent and existence. But, this gap between the subject and its self – existent and existence – is not so much a transcendental divide which separates the transcendental from the categorial; rather it is existential. What Levinas indicates is that, at the very core of individual existence, there is a fissure, a division, a cleaving of the existent and its existence.

'To be' is a reflexive verb

This tension which is at the core of individual existence is described in terms of the reflexivity of the verb 'to be' (*être*). The verb 'to be' is a reflexive verb: 'it is not just that one is, one is oneself [*on n'est pas, on s'est*]' (*EE*, 28). In other words, individual existence is not simple, but a composite of me and my self, such that one is never quite at one with one's self. It is this alien nature of *my* existence as a self to which I must relate which is encountered in fatigue and lassitude, and which one seeks to escape from in lying down to sleep.

Now, this preoccupation with one's existence, a poring over the self, is a condemnation to being. Phenomenologically speaking, to undertake the phenomenological reduction in transcendental terms, as Husserl did, is to remain preoccupied with the ontology of the ego. Because the subject still has a foothold in existence, it

> finds itself again to be a solitude, in the definiteness of the bond with which the ego is chained to its self . . . The *I* always has one foot caught in its own existence . . . It is forever bound to the existence which it has taken up. This impossibility of the ego not to be a self constitutes the underlying tragic element in the ego, the fact that it is riveted to its own being. (*EE*, 84)

Again,

> The enchainment to oneself is the impossibility of getting rid of oneself . . . To be an ego is not only to be for oneself; it is also to be with oneself. (*EE*, 88)

Further, the preoccupation with one's own existence – or better, *my* existence as a preoccupation – is an act without transcendence. 'Transcendence is not the fundamental movement of the ontological adventure; it is founded in the non-transcendence of position' (*EE*, 100), a position from which I cannot make my own escape. As indicated previously, 'thought . . . is . . . here', and from the *here* one cannot effect one's own salvation, which can only come from elsewhere.

'ATTEMPTING TO ESCAPE FROM BEING'

In one of his earliest works *On Escape* (*De l'évasion*) (1935/36), which straddles *The Theory of Intuition in Husserl's Phenomenology* and prefigures much of *Existence and Existents*, Levinas speaks of the possibility of an escape from being, or 'getting out of being by a new path, at the risk of overturning certain notions that to common sense and the wisdom of the nations seemed the most evident' (*OE*, 73).

Certainly it is a rude and rudimentary work which Jacques Rolland, in his introductory essay, describes as 'youthful' and 'introductory' into the space of questioning of the ancient problem of being *qua* being and the possibility of an escape from being into an otherwise than being. This seminal work gives an insight into the particular phenomenological approach which Levinas will develop and employ in his later works.

It is worth drawing attention once again to the later criticisms of Levinas' work, particularly those of Janicaud. Levinas is criticised for abandoning the rigour of Husserl's phenomenology; he 'loftily and categorically' affirms 'the primacy of the idea of infinity, immediately dispossessing the *sameness* [*mêmeté*] of the I, or of being [*être*]'. Levinas 'takes liberties' with Husserl; he emphasises the 'overflowing [of] the intentional horizon', and wants to overcome 'the purely intentional sense of the notion of horizon'. Yet, it is perhaps precisely the phenomenological analyses which Levinas begins to undertake in *On Escape* which give an indication of the concern and development of his later thought, a thought which is not as undemanding and lacking in phenomenological rigour as Janicaud might suggest. What is also interesting is that Janicaud regards the errance from the scientific discipline and rigour of Husserl as beginning with Sartre's *Transcendence of the Ego* in which 'Sartre abandoned [the workplace of French phenomenological investigations] to turn resolutely towards politics and an ethics of engagement.' Phenomenology, for Sartre, was altogether too abstract, 'too detached from concrete situations and sociopolitical struggles'. *Transcendence of the Ego* appeared in 1937, the same period when Levinas was writing *On Escape*. As with Sartre, so with Levinas: it is the existential analyses of the human condition, pursued in a phenomenological manner, which are distinctive. The analyses of need, shame and nausea, against the backdrop of the question of being, give an insight into Levinas' later works, for one must 'get out of being' by another way, the final articulation of which will be *Otherwise than Being, or Beyond Essence*. Existence is both a philosophical and theological complex.

For Levinas, in *On Escape*, the main question is the question of being, and the naive presumption that things are what 'they are' and in the manner that they are. 'Being is: there is nothing to add to this assertion as long as we envision in a being only its existence'

(*OE*, 51). Here is the naive realism which Husserl contested, and the lack of phenomenological investigation. Often the question of being has been associated with the question of transcendence, which can be interpreted as an attempt to 'get out of being'. However, with the 'existential turn' which Heidegger inaugurated in phenomenology, the question of Being (*Sein*) is bound up with the one for whom his or her own being is a question. One feels oneself bound to being. The fact would seem to be that one cannot get out of it. One is 'chained to it'. Here one can see Levinas' insistence, which is developed in *Existents and Existence*, that human existence exhibits 'a type of duality' (*OE*, 55). Although being is thought to be ultimately identical and at one with itself, human existence has a self-referentiality which is not so much experienced as being at one with oneself, but rather as tension, effort, and burden, and it is this experience which needs to be phenomenologically exposed. Duality is the mark (*stigmate*) of existence. The question of escape becomes

the need to get out of oneself, that is, *to break that most radical and unalterably binding of chains, the fact that the I [moi] is oneself [moi-même]* . . . to break the chains of the I to the self [*du moi à soi*]. (*OE*, 55)

Jacques Rolland notes that key to unlocking the problem of being which Levinas addresses is the Heideggerian 'ontological difference' between Being (*Sein*) and beings (*das Seiendes*), which Levinas translates into the contract between existence and existent, a contract which is sustained through work and effort. We have seen how, in *Existence and Existents*, Levinas will describe this in terms of the reflexivity of the verb 'to be'. *Être* is always *S'Être*. Thus the conjugation of *être* as *je me suis* and *on s'est*. To sustain one's contract with existence – to maintain one's possession of being – by which anonymous being is humanised in the 'here' of consciousness is an effort and a struggle, which one both wants to evade and escape. For Rolland, this points to 'a defect or taint inscribed in [the] very fact of existence' (*OE*, 10). The emergence of the solitary 'I' – the result of a contract between existence and existent – is a work to be achieved, and not without effort, and perhaps impossible for the solitary self.

CHAPTER 4

Existence as transcendence, or the call of the infinite: towards a theology of grace

For Levinas, transcendence and excendence are linked. Transcendence is a transcendence towards the other person (a movement which does not take its origin in the self). Excendence is an excendence from being, a movement from being towards the good. One still has a 'foothold in being', and because being does not give itself generously and as good, there is the attempt to escape from the threat and the burden which being lays upon us. The guiding idea here is that there is no escape, other than the advent of the other. The solitary self, thrown back on itself, does not contain within itself the means of its salvation.

How does Levinas proceed? By a phenomenological analysis of those existential experiences which can be interpreted as an attempt to escape the burden of existence, experiences in which being, in its anonymity, indeterminacy, and ultimate friendlessness, can be recognised and determined. Already in *On Escape*, and subsequently in *Existence and Existents*, this is prefigured. Already, from the outset, the phenomenological paradox which Janicaud criticises in Levinas is evident: how can the indeterminate, which is strictly speaking non-phenomenological, be phenomenologically exposed? Thus, Levinas begins, like Heidegger, with an existential analytic of 'the structure of this pure being?' (*OE*, 56) but, unlike Heidegger, asks how an *excendence* from it might be accomplished. In charting the escape from being to the otherwise than being, which is a movement from the threat and horror of pure being (*il y a*) to the encounter with the *illeity* of the other person, the very indeterminacy of the other determines the self as response and responsibility. In a sense, the whole of Levinas' work can be charted as a movement from the *il y a* to

95

illeity,[1] from being towards the otherwise than being, from ontology to ethics.

How is this non-phenomenal *il y a* encountered? The 'there is' (*il y a*) is bare being which continues to bear itself upon an existent in an unbearable way. '*This is the very experience of pure being*, which we have promised from the beginning of this work' (*OE*, 67). Confronted with the *there is*, there is, Rolland comments, in his introduction to *On Escape*, 'the impossibility of being what one is' (*OE*, 34). It is the bare being of the *there is* that needs to be laid bare, through a phenomenology of the *il y a*. The question becomes, then, the question of the possibility of the reconciliation of the self, both threatened and divided, and how such a reconciliation might be accomplished. For Levinas, what makes the reconciled self possible is the advent of an other, whose approach or coming is most often unsuspected and interruptive, but always prevenient. The advent of the other breaks open a subjectivity which is self-enclosed; it releases the self from its enchainment to bare existence, and enables the emergence of ethical subjectivity.

TRANSCENDENCE AS AN ESCAPE FROM BEING

Now, the early and careful consideration which Levinas gives of need, pleasure, and shame gives a beginning to his later phenomenological analyses, as we will see later when considering the transcendence of desire.

What is the structure of need (*besoin*)? Need seems only to intend its own satisfaction and the pleasure and the restoration of a 'natural plenitude' (*OE*, 58). Need seems to respond to a deficiency in being which, like an empty stomach, when filled, is satisfied. Certainly, in *Existence and Existents*, Levinas adopts this position and describes this more graphically in terms of the model of mastication, consumption, and the alimentation of the elemental.[2] Need satisfies at the expense of what is other. The self, in its needfulness, feeds on what is other than the self to fulfil a void in itself and, since alimentation is normally masticatory, the nourishing of the solitary self involves certain destruction and violence towards what is other. The self, as it were, harvests alterity to make up for its own defects.[3]

Yet, paradoxically, need does not respond to a deficiency in being, as if some lack had to be made up; rather, by attempting to fix itself on the particular, need attempts to escape from the pervasive plenitude of being; it seeks 'release and escape' (*OE*, 69) from the *there is*. Although seemingly intending the particular, need is, in reality, a disoriented intentionality. It does not know what it intends; it does not know what it wants; and, rather than achieving satisfaction, it ends in dissatisfaction. But this dissatisfaction is a dissatisfaction with being itself, which no particular object can assuage. 'What gives the human condition all its importance is precisely this inadequacy of satisfaction to need' (*OE*, 60).

Allied to need is *pleasure*, which might be thought to be the satisfaction of need's emptiness. Certainly, misconstrued pleasure does involve 'a loss of oneself, a getting out of oneself' (*OE*, 60); ecstasy is precisely an *ek-stasis*, an escape from existence. 'Yet it is a deceptive escape. For it is an escape that fails' (*OE*, 62). Pleasure comes to an end and one is returned to oneself and its emptiness, and the fact that one must exist: 'pleasures are like poppies spread: You seize the flow'r, its bloom is shed; Or like the snow falls in the river, A moment white then melts for ever.'[4] It is this very failure of pleasure, which inevitably results in a 'return to the self' and the impossibility of escape, that guides the further phenomenological analyses of *shame and nausea*, and which will eventually lead Levinas to distinguish 'need' (*besoin*) and 'pleasure' (*plaisir*).

Shame's whole intensity, everything it contains that stings us, consists precisely in our inability not to identify with this being who is already foreign to us and whose motives for acting we can no longer comprehend. (*OE*, 63)

As 'primarily connected to our body', which is a nakedness of being, shame confronts us with something about us which seems alien, something with which we cannot identify. One is ashamed of something which, though we are attached to it, seems strange and distant. Similarly with *nausea*. It clings and 'sticks to us' like treacle. We are immersed, as it were, in a morass of molasses. To be nauseous is to want to be elsewhere, but to have no place to go. 'There is in nausea a refusal to remain there, an effort to get out', and 'this fact of being rivetted, constitutes all the anxiety of nausea' (*OE*, 66).[5] Rolland describes this in terms of the disorientation which accompanies 'seasickness', a disorientation in which 'the recoil of beings in all their aspects' is experienced, and there is the experience of nothing but the *there is*. Nausea 'manifests nothing' (*OE*, 19). In Heideggerian terms, nausea causes 'being as distinct from beings' to appear. The nauseous subject can identify no thing, yet remains exposed to the threat and the horror of the nothing which is there. Such a nothing, in which there is no thing, is the experience of the *il y a*. Rolland comments, 'Nausea manifests . . . being as the *there is* [*il y a*] of *there is* being [*il y a de l'être*] . . . the there is [*il y a*] that murmurs at the depth of nothingness itself' (*OE*, 24). It is '*the very experience of pure being*' (*OE*, 67).

Now, if one emerges or awakens from the horror of pure being – the threat of the *il y a* – only to find oneself bound to a self which seems alien and strange, from which there is no escape; and if one is always on the precipice of falling back into the nothingness of the *il y a*, how is this escape achieved? If the self does not contain within itself the possibility of its own salvation, how is the *I* to be saved from itself, from that self with which there is recurring dissatisfaction? How does one escape from the enchainment to being and its solitariness? For Levinas, this can only be by way of an ethical redemption in which the other person intervenes or, we might say, insinuates himself or herself into those fissures of our existence which render us vulnerable to being breached by alterity.[6] One might also say that the horror and the threat of the non-phenomenal *il y a* is displaced by the equally non-phenomenal *illeity* of the other person. The move from the anonymity of pure being towards the *otherwise than being* is a move from the *il y a* towards *illeity*. It is a movement from fear and horror to responsibility.[7]

THE STRUCTURE OF TRANSCENDENCE

The idea of movement can be allied with the notions of a 'tendency towards', a directedness or an intentionality. That human life is intentional – that is, characterised by movement – has already been noted. But, like concupiscence, which can be understood as inclination or tendency *as such*, before ever it is differentiated into an inclination towards good or evil, Levinas identifies two different movements or tendencies in the self, which can be polarised. There is the ontological tendency towards being, and the imprisonment it offers from which there is no escape, and there is the ethical tendency towards the good which is beyond and otherwise than being. These two movements can also be articulated as the tendency towards *Totality* and the tendency towards *Infinity*. These two movements are 'two vectors moving in contrary directions' (*EE*, 31). The first only leads back to the self, and the totality which the self constructs around itself. The second leads to an other than the self which enables escape from the totality, and the ethical redemption of the self alone with itself.

How, then, is transcendence structured? Paradoxically, Levinas notes that the first movement of subjectivity and the possibility of transcendence, which is the possibility of 'getting out of being by another way', is the movement of *separation*. The withdrawal of the subject into itself is the possibility of transcendence, for transcendence presupposes separation. Separation is the first move of subjectivity and is, as already indicated, essentially atheist, as Levinas understands the term. But this affirmation of a subject as separate also gives the possibility of relation and of movement towards what is other than the self, which becomes ultimately the possibility of responsibility and ethical existence.

Separation, however, only results in a solitary self, a self concerned and anxious for its own needs, a self which is *pour-soi*, a self which lacks transcendence, a self which, having established and affirmed and positioned its self in being – in the non-transcendence of position – is unable by itself and by its own devices to get beyond that self. Levinas terms this solitary existence, devoid of transcendence, a 'pagan' existence, where 'pagan' simply means an existence which does not go beyond its own concerns, an existence which is untouched and unaffected by the other person. As separate and interiorised, self-enclosed subjectivity engages with what is other (*autre*) than the self in terms of need and enjoyment. Yet, even this first movement and affirmation of the subject already implicates something other than the self on which the self feeds and nourishes itself. The happy possession and enjoyment of the world already presupposes subjectivity as openness to otherness. The dwelling that I build and which accommodates my self has doors and windows which open on to a world at my disposal but also are open to the incursion of the world. The roof and the doors which Heidegger's *Dasein* secures for its own sake and security offer protection against the violence of the elemental and the terror of the night which threatens. Yet, roofs and doors and windows are not simply *there 'for-the-sake-of Dasein'*; doors and windows also open inwards, not simply to keep being in its threatening anonymity at bay, but as the possibility of welcome and hospitality to the other person (*autrui*). My own place in the sun which I have established and perhaps usurped for myself is also the place of 'a first revelation of the other person' (*TI*, 151). My own place in the sun can open in hospitable welcome to the Other, like the hospitality of Abraham and Sarah at the Oak of Mamre (Gen. 18:1–2).[8]

The notion of separation, however, needs to be pushed further. For it is not so much the case that subjectivity is accomplished as a work undertaken by the self and its own efforts. Separation gives the possibility of transcendence and a relation with alterity. It is the first revelation of the other person, however, which confirms the self as separate; the first revelation of the other person, by requiring some response, reveals the separated self in its own insufficiency. In short, with the advent of the other person the self-enclosed subjectivity is placed in question and the self becomes a question for itself. At the same time, however, the other person offers an escape from impoverished solitary or 'pagan' existence. The threat and the horror of the night of the *il y a*, in which no one may sleep, is overcome by the advent of the other person who saves the self from itself and its enchainment to solitary existence. The simple, sincere enjoyment of the elemental world, then, is not yet a habitation which can be termed 'human', nor is it transcendence. In Levinas' words, 'the idea of infinity, revealed in the face, does not only *require* a separated being; the light of the face is necessary for separation' (*TI*, 151). The first movement of subjectivity, which is the affirmation of the self and the establishment of the self as a contract between existence and existent, is redeemed by the advent of the other person, and the dilemma of hospitality is put in play.[9]

THE ITINERARY OF PHILOSOPHY

Philosophy might be said to have two itineraries or orientations. The one, following Abraham's journey into an unknown strange and foreign land, is essentially outgoing. Abraham is called by God to 'leave your country, your family and your father's house, for a land that I will show you'. Responsive and obedient to that call, Abram 'went as the Lord told him' (Gen. 12). As the letter to the Hebrews puts it, 'It was by faith that Abraham obeyed the call and set out for a country that was the inheritance given to him and his descendants, and that he set out without knowing where he was going' (Heb. 11:8). The other journey, more Greek, is that of Odysseus whose Odyssey is one of return. Odysseus leaves his native Ithaca and his exploits are narrated in the context of his return to the familiar and familial. For Levinas, these are two differing journeys, two differing vectors. The Abrahamic itinerary is outgoing and responsive to what is other than the self; it is a movement of transcendence, an intentionality which intends exteriority. The Odyssean is circular, is marked by a constant return to the same; it remains locked within interiority and immanence; its point of departure is also the point to which one returns.

Philosophically speaking, the Odyssean itinerary is an ontological itinerary which intends a coherent totality; theologically speaking, this culminates in an ontotheology which intends dogmatic or doctrinal coherence. The Abrahamic itinerary is 'otherwise than being'. It is ethical, and escapes the circle and the cycle of violence which ontology commands by 'getting out of being by another way'. The ethical itinerary is always otherwise than being, and calls being, and the totality and system which it engenders, to give an account of itself. What is Levinas trying to draw attention to in contrasting these two itineraries? The simple answer is 'the unique significance of the other person' whose infinite value, beyond system and totality, calls systems and totalities into question. More difficult, and complex, will be the question of how infinity and totality relate, for it is not a question of *Totality* or *Infinity*, but of *Totality and Infinity*, which is also the question of how responsibility for the unique and incomparable other person relates to justice for the many, for one must attempt the impossible and compare the incomparable, and remain guilty for having done so.

The tendency towards totality

What is to be understood by 'Totality'? At the outset of *Totality and Infinity*, Levinas seems to separate politics and morality, totality and infinity. Associated with politics are such notions as economy and the technology which supports and develops the economy. Contemporary philosophies of modernity seem to be characterised by the dominance of a politics and economics of expediency. Economics and technology provide the categories of understanding by which human relations are governed, and the language in which human relations are expressed. Politics and technology emerge as the practical culmination of Heidegger's ontology, which is most often opposed to ethics, morality, and the working out of justice.[10]

To collect in a totality, that is, to express, that is, to make signification possible – this is the function of 'the objective cultural work or gesture'. And there a new function of *expression* is established with regard to the functions attributed to it: either to serve as a means of communication or to *transform the world according to our needs*. The novelty of this function lies also in the ontological level on which it is situated. (*HO*, 15, italics added)

In other words, culture and history are caught up in the tendency towards totality, and consort in compromising the singular significance of the other person. Insofar as culture and historicity determine signification, the significance of the other person is assigned by particular systems understandings. Thus do individuals become functions of, or players in, a particular historical, cultural, religious, and economic framework, with the consequent reduction of their own singular and unique meaning. Thus,

art is not the lovely madness of man who takes it into his head to make beauty. Culture and artistic creation are part of the ontological order itself. They are ontological par excellence; they make it possible to comprehend being. (*HO*, 17)

So things and people acquire an 'economic signification' within 'the fixed favoured signification that the world acquires according to man's needs. Need raises things to the ranks of values . . . Economy alone is truly oriented and signifying' (*HO*, 21).

Jürgen Habermas' distinction between 'instrumental reason' and 'communicative praxis' is helpful in understanding Levinas' critique. What Habermas draws attention to is 'the spread of instrumental reason to many areas of social life' and the 'rise of technocratic consciousness'[11] which reduces individuals to functions within economic and technological structures, and assigns significance within the context of social theory. The instrumentalisation of reason not only obscures the epistemic subject, divesting him or her of autonomy and responsibility but also disregards the singular significance which a unique individual has within any system or totality. To counter technocratic and instrumentalised consciousness, Habermas advocates a communicative praxis, which frees language from the systematic distortion it has experienced in purposive rationality. Language is ordered towards consensus, but needs to be emancipated through 'the transcendence of such systems of distorted communication'.[12] He writes,

> By 'work' or *purposive-rational action* I understand either instrumental action or rational choice or their conjunction. Instrumental action is governed by *technical rules* based on empirical knowledge . . . The conduct of rational choice is governed by *strategies* based on analytic knowledge.[13]

In contrast to *purposive-rational action*, in which the other person is reduced to a function within an economic or technological equation, 'interaction' responds to the reciprocal demands of intersubjectivity, and results in a consciousness which might be said to be ethical rather than instrumentalised.

> By 'interaction', on the other hand, I understand *communicative action*, symbolic interaction. It is governed by binding *consensual norms*, which define reciprocal expectations about behaviour . . . Their meaning is objectified in ordinary language communication.[14]

For Levinas, this will correspond to the originality and priority which *saying* (*le dire*) has over *what is said* (*le dit*), and the fact that the unique individual is its own signification, signifying with a signification irreducible to any cultural, historical, religious, or economic totality. Quite simply put, even idiots demand a hearing, despite the meaningless of what they say (*le dit*), because more to be respected than what is said is the one who is doing the saying (*le dire*). The uniqueness of each singular individual who is his or her own signification makes of us all *idiotes*, in its original Greek sense of a private or singular individual.

The call of the infinite

Now, the non-transcendence instrumentalised reason and its expression is pursued by Levinas in his own consideration of cultural meaning and value. Modern instrumentalised consciousness, in interpreting cultural meaning and value in terms of need, tends to privilege
particular cultural and historical forms of expression, and particular
economic and political systems, thereby extending the totality. This
amounts to the absorption of otherness into the politics and economics of the same, and a 'neutralisation of alterity'. Although life
precedes philosophical reflection, and existence is prior to essence,
philosophy tends to maintain an aversion to alterity, and develops
as 'a refusal of engagement in the other [*l'autre*]'. Instead of actively
engaging in commerce with otherness and difference, philosophy –
whose attentiveness and indifference to alterity is only latent – tends
to be characterised by that 'universal allergy of the first childhood of
philosophers', which, caught up in its own concerns, lacks any transcendent reference. It has not yet woken up to alterity, and remains
deaf to the other person (*autrui*) who disturbs its own particular
dogmatic slumbers and self-complacency. 'Philosophy's itinerary still
follows the path of Ulysses whose adventure in the world was but
a return to his native island – complacency in the Same, misunder-
standing of the Other',[15] an effort 'where the adventure pursued in
the world is but the accident of a return' (*TI*, 176–7). It remains also
the nostalgic mourning of Penelope, weeping for Odysseus, longing for his return and for unity with him once again. This Odyssey
which retraces its past, and seeks to recollect and incorporate into
the kingdom of the same whatever is outside and other, whether by
assimilation or removal and exclusion, has been the philosophical
agenda of western metaphysics which, maintains Levinas, 'has most
often been an ontology: a reduction of the other to the same' (*TI*,
47) and where 'to know amounts to grasping being out of nothing or
reducing it to nothing, removing from it its alterity' (*TI*, 44). Philosophy, as it were, bears the mark of Cain who, unable to comprehend
the alterity of Abel within his own system of values, removes him
absolutely in an original fratricide.[16]

In place of the ontological which intends a totality in which there is
no place for what is other, Levinas advocates *a non-allergic relation with*

alterity. Philosophy is summoned to be non-indifferent to difference, and such non-indifference to difference is negotiated by an infinite conversation. In a sense, the only generic aspect of humanity is each person's specific difference. Each person is his or her own species, beyond any genus.

Now, this is not to abandon the concerns of modernity, such as subjectivity, autonomy, freedom, knowledge, and truth. It is to push these notions phenomenologically further in the direction of an inter-subjective reduction. Thinking is not a solitary affair, as might be displayed in Rodin's sculpture of 'The Thinker', bearing the weight of his head upon his own hand. Nor is subjectivity a solitary undertaking. Philosophy is not original, but is provoked by something other than itself. In fact, Levinas notes that *Totality and Infinity* is 'a defence of subjectivity' (*TI*, 26). Philosophy is to be situated once again in the sincerity of intentionality, but the interiority of the subject is to be affirmed 'on the basis of exteriority'. Before ever one withdraws into the confines or circle of the self, we have already been engaged in commerce with alterity, and sincerely so. It is this ordinary and sincere encounter with the other person which is the point of departure for philosophy.

[T]he ethical relation, opposed to first philosophy which identifies freedom and power, is not contrary to truth; it goes unto being in its absolute exteriority, and accomplishes the very intention that animates the movement unto truth. (*TI*, 47)

In other words, philosophy depends on something other than itself and is essentially responsive. Its effort and work is provoked and inspired by the other person whose unique signification challenges thinking to think again, and constantly. Systems find themselves challenged and confounded and called into question – and always guilty – by questions of ethics and morality. The proper provocation and origin of philosophy is the ethical. The philosophical itinerary is not so much the Odyssean enterprise of philosophical modernity, but rather the Abrahamic journey which departs from the familial and familiar for a strange and alien place, in response to a call. But this is also the theological itinerary, for ethics is also first theology.

What does this mean for a philosophy and a theology? For both, it means a reconsideration of their origins. For Levinas, the encounter with the other person – which is immediately and before thinking – as an ethical situation is both 'first philosophy' and 'first theology'. Both philosophy and theology are essentially responsive. This further entails a re-consideration of the nature of subjectivity which is to be declined not in the nominative but in the accusative.

> The religious discourse that precedes all religious discourse is not dialogue. It is the 'here I am' [*me voici*] said to the neighbour to whom I am given over. (*CPP*, 141)

To say 'I' is to say '*me voici*'. The nominative self becomes the accusative: *me voici*! Levinas notes, 'the accusative [*me* voici] here is remarkable: here I am, under your eyes, at your service, your obedient servant' (*CPP*, 141). Ultimately, the appeal of the other which both accuses and invites response as 'me'. The 'I' is constituted as 'me'. Ultimately, the meaning of subjectivity becomes further declined in the dative. To be a subject is to be 'for' the other, where this 'for' is the responsibility I bear towards the other person.

TRANSCENDENCE AS DESIRE

Metaphysics is a transcendence towards a transcendent exteriority, but a movement which can only be travelled by way of the ethical encounter with the other person whose appeal to us summons us always to go further in responsibility and commitment, and in whose face we glimpse a trace of God. The movement towards an exteriority has always and already an ethical provocation, the ontological circle of totality is broken, and an excendence from the limits which being imposes becomes possible. Levinas articulates this movement as a desire for the infinite. Insofar as transcendence is an 'escape from being by another way', transcendence is also necessarily a transascendence.[17]

Levinas' consideration of transcendence takes its point of departure in Descartes' *Third Meditation*, where he writes

> I would not have . . . the idea of an infinite substance, I who am a finite being, if it had not been placed in me by some substance which was truly infinite. (*Meditations*, 45)

It is worth considering this in slightly more detail.

Descartes' *Third Meditation* concerns '*The Existence of God*' and seeks to present his 'principal argument for proving the existence of God' (*Meditations, 14*). The incontrovertible starting point is the affirmation of the subject as 'a thing which thinks', a *res cogitans*. But, *doubting* is also a characteristic of thinking. If everything that the thinking subject perceives can be doubted, how is it possible not to doubt that 'thing which thinks'? Perhaps there is a God who deceives us, all thinking is deceptive. In fact, it may be that God, whose truthfulness co-foundation what we can know clearly and distinctly may not exist at all. Descartes then proceeds by examining whether or not there is a God, and whether or not he could be a deceiver (*Meditations*, 36), and does so by classifying his thoughts to see if there might be a thought which did not take its point of departure within the subject itself, and the presence of which in thought would testify to something other than the self. For, if there is an idea in me whose objective reality is such that I cannot be its cause, then my solitary existence in the world is contested, and something other than my self needs to be posited.

Now, of all the ideas that I, as a thinking thing, have, it seems that only the idea of God could not have originated in myself, since to have the idea of God is to have the idea of the infinite, whereas I am finite. Further, it is not that I perceive the idea of the infinite 'merely by negating the finite'; the idea of the infinite is a true idea. Further, 'there is more reality in an infinite substance than in a finite one' and so 'my perception of the infinite, that is God, is in some way prior to my perception of the finite, that is myself' (*Meditations*, 45), 'for it is in the nature of the infinite not to be grasped by a finite being like myself' (*Meditations*, 46). Descartes concludes, therefore,

it is true that I have an idea of substance in me by virtue of that fact that I am a substance; but this would not account for my having the idea of an infinite substance, when I am finite, unless this idea proceeded from some substance which really was infinite. (*Meditations*, 45)

Levinas' re-working of Cartesian infinity

Levinas draws a number of conclusions from the Cartesian conclusion. First, one must discard any Socratic maieutics whereby the teacher simply elicits from the pupil what is already contained within. The idea of the infinite is a teaching which teaches by placing within us what would otherwise not be there.

The idea of infinity . . . has been *put* into us . . . The thinker who has the idea of infinity is *more than himself,* and this inflating, this surplus does not come from within, as in the celebrated *project* of modern philosophers, in which the subject surpasses himself by creating. (*CPP,* 54)

Socratic maieutics has a value in encouraging independent thinking against ideas and systems which captivate, violate, or seduce the mind. In this sense, it acted as a counter to totalities and totalitarianisms. But teaching is to be understood as a relationship with the 'whole infinity of exteriority'.

Teaching is not a species of a genus called domination, a hegemony at work within a totality, but is the presence of infinity breaking the closed circle of totality . . . a discourse in which the master can bring to the student what the student does not yet know. It does not operate as a maieutics, but continues the placing in me of the idea of infinity. (*TI,* 180)

The Cartesian order, in which infinity approaches, is prior to the Socratic.

Secondly, Descartes conceives of Infinite Being, or God, 'as an eminent being, or a being that *is* eminently'. Levinas, however, is not concerned with any proof for God's existence, but rather with the 'break up of consciousness' which the idea of infinity in us announces. The force of the idea of the infinite is that it 'breaks up the unity of the "I think"'. Such an insight is 'unsurpassable' and enables methodologically another way of 'getting out of being', an egress from totality, and excendence towards exteriority which is a true transcendence.

Now, the idea of the infinite places in question consciousness as the absolute and original point of departure. Phenomenologically, consciousness is the proper starting point, for consciousness can only ever be understood as 'consciousness of'. What the idea of the infinite introduces is the notion of an excessive or saturated phenomenon, the phenomenon which is described not simply as phenomenal because of its restriction to the phenomenal world, but rather is described as 'phenomenal' because in its very phenomenality it is excessive and overwhelming, and confounds the capacity of thought to contain or comprehend. The idea of the infinite disrupts consciousness for the idea of the infinite is earlier than the finite and precedes any thought that the *cogito* might actually think. Consciousness finds itself in a 'situation . . . in which the "I think" maintains with the Infinite it can nowise contain and from which it is separated by a relation called "idea of infinity"' (*TI*, 48). In short, what is being described by Descartes is the 'posteriority of the anterior'. What is thought to be founding and original finds itself, on reflection, to be founded and originated.

Thirdly, while Descartes considers a God 'that *is* eminently', Levinas would rather prefer a God 'that is *eminently*'. *Eminence* is not simply an indicator of a transcendence beyond finitude, but takes us beyond being itself; it is 'otherwise than being, or beyond essence', for 'we are outside the order in which one passes from an idea to a being' (*CPP*, 159–60). It is this notion of *eminence* which will find theological translation into the notion of the *excessive and saturated phenomenon* in Marion.

The idea of the infinite in us is exceptional, for what thinking thinks about (the *ideatum*) not only preveniently precedes thinking (the *idea*) but actually goes beyond and surpasses and exceeds the capacity of thought. But it is this excess which constantly awakens thought, and ultimately becomes its condition of possibility. To relate to the infinite is radically impossible for the subject. Paradoxically, it is the impossibility of the thinking subject to think the infinite as part of its own project, which enables the possibility of a subject that can think beyond itself.

The infinite – and, for Levinas, the singular other person whom thought cannot contain is in the realm of the infinite – provokes thought, and provokes thought preveniently.

> Infinity does not enter into the *idea* of infinity, is not grasped; this idea is not a concept. The infinite is the radically, absolutely, other. The transcendence of infinity with respect to the ego that is separated from it and thinks it constitutes the first mark of its infinitude. (*CPP*, 54)

CHAPTER 5

The economy and language of grace: grace, desire, and the awakening of the subject

For Levinas, the constitution of subjectivity as response and responsibility is a key concern. Subjectivity is phenomenologically reduced to intersubjectivity. The subject is both aroused and awoken by the other person who is discovered lately on reflection as always and already having been there. The advent of the other is disturbing, challenging, appealing. The advent of the other is the proximate and prevenient cause of my emergence into ethical humanity, and will become a summons to both responsibility and justice. But, this happens 'in-the-world'. Although the 'true life may be elsewhere', 'we are in the world'. For Levinas, the ethical redemption of humanity is situated *here* and *now*. Thus Levinas commits to enfleshment or incarnation, but understood as an individual responsibility which needs to be worked out justly. 'The flesh is the hinge of salvation [*Caro cardo salutis*]'. The world is a corporate undertaking which involves others.

The notion of incarnation is a key Christian doctrine, and its meaning much disputed in the development of theology. How do the divine and the human come together in concert and speak with one voice? Is it possible to begin to think of an incarnation which neither compromises the transcendence of God nor removes responsibility for the other person and a commitment to justice and a just society to another world yet to come, but rather returns responsibility and justice to the world in which 'we live and move and have our being'.

Irenaeus, the second-century bishop of Lyons, is a helpful interlocutor for he interprets history (and history is only ever interpreted events) and is committed to incarnation. In his writings, Irenaeus argues against those who would see the concordance of the divine and the human and merely apparent. Irenaeus is committed to enfleshment. History has meaning and a purpose – always interpreted – and it involves a world which is a life with others. Like Levinas, who is critical of philosophical *gnosis* and draws attention to existence as enfleshed, Irenaeus likewise opposes those who would argue that the 'true life is elsewhere' and commits himself to the reality that 'we are in the world'. Excluded is any notion of salvation as *gnosis*, and affirmed is salvation as necessarily incarnate. What Irenaeus argues is the benevolence of God towards creation and, particularly, created humanity which comes to life and awakens as response. God inclines towards humanity and humanity is thereby inclined towards God. For Irenaeus, this culminates in an enfleshment which both reveals God to humanity and returns humanity to God. The invisibility of God is preserved lest humanity should end up despising God by making God into an idol; yet, at the same time, drawing close so that humanity might possess something towards which it might also advance. For Levinas, ethical humanity requires unique incarnation: responsibility cannot be vicariously surrendered to another *me* without compromising my own *self* which is constituted as responsibility for the other person. I am *me* because of the *other person*. I am summoned to be 'ethics incarnate'. Humanity is already summoned towards divinity, and ethics achieves this. But, to return to Irenaeus,

For the glory of God is a living human being; and human life [consists in] the vision of God. [*Gloria enim Dei vivens homo, vita autem hominis visio Dei*]

Irenaeus' theology is incarnationally directed. Human salvation is achieved at those points of meeting of the divine and the human in a gradual and educational movement of recapitulation (*anakephalaiosis*). For Irenaeus, human life is incarnate; the inherent goodness of creation is affirmed; the invisibility, transcendence, and incomprehensibility of the Father is preserved; salvation is a result of the divine–human encounter, historically enacted; God draws ever closer to the human creation, and humanity, without bypassing the world, is drawn into closer communion with God, the ultimate vision of whom is life's fulfilment.

Now, some elements here would seemingly fit very comfortably with Levinas. For Levinas, the world is the locus of salvation, and there is no access to God other than through human relations; God remains transcendent and invisible, yet is to be found in the immanence and the visibility of the encounter with the other person who provokes responsibility and demands justice – God is the counterpart of the justice rendered to the other person. Humanity is divinised, and becomes fully alive as ethical humanity, in heeding and responding to the call of the infinite, yet that call is always by way of the world in which one always and already finds oneself.

Levinas' analyses are profoundly phenomenological; the human existential is the point of departure, and the human existential, in all its dimensions, is subject to phenomenological reflection to the point of the excessive. This is no less true of theology which can only ever ask the question of God from the starting point of the phenomenon of the human. Theologically, one can say that '[c]reatures, and more especially humans, are the grammar of God's potential Self-utterance'.[1]

A few problems arise in translating a theology of grace into a Levinas-inspired way of thinking. But these are only seemingly problematical, or quasi-problematical. Two approaches to a theology of graced existence seem possible. The first relates to the phenomenology and theology of desire which intends the excessive. The second can be articulated in terms of the phenomenology of awakening, whereby the glory of God is not only the human person fully alive (*gloria dei homo vivens*), but also the human person fully awake (*gloria dei homo vigilans*).

GRACE AND THE DESIRE FOR GOD

A first question within the context of a theology of grace is whether or not humanity is 'naturally' good. For Levinas, no one is 'naturally good', and no one can be good without another person. Goodness does not belong to the ontological order but to the ethical which is *otherwise than being, or beyond essence*. The solitary self cannot be 'naturally good' for goodness is something which arises as a provocation and as a responsibility for the other. There is no 'natural benevolence' for, prior to the advent of the other, the notion of benevolence as an intentionality towards an other would make no sense; nor is there any room for altruism, for altruism already presupposes an other who both appeals to and commands the self.

The recurrence of the self in responsibility for others, a persecuting obsession, goes against intentionality, such that responsibility for others could never mean altruistic will, instinct of 'natural benevolence', or love. (*OB*, 111–12)

But this problem has already been enacted and articulated in the development of the theology of grace. Theologically, one might say that Levinas is opposing an understanding of subjectivity which, essentially Pelagian, stresses the effort of the individual in both willing and enacting the good and attaining salvation; instead, Augustine, who recognised the entirety of an existence which was truly human, might be said to be the more natural interlocutor in the development of an adequate theological anthropology. The theological problem and the phenomenological challenge is the coming together of the divine and the human in a way that respects transcendence yet is committed to an incarnation which is both responsible and just.[2]

A second question concerns the transposition of an Augustinian theology of grace to the ontological framework which one finds in Aquinas, and which subsequently raised problems regarding a presumed distinction between the natural and the supernatural and how one might both be summoned to a fulfilment which was both natural and supernatural. Fierce debate about this took place in mid-twentieth-century Catholic circles, and this can provide a useful case study to achieve a further transposition of a theology of grace beyond the ontological to the ethical.

There is a third and more fundamental question, namely the dilemma of relating the good (which is always *otherwise than being* but not necessarily *other than being*) to being which is not so immured in itself as to be immune from the encroachment of the good. This *otherwise than* that is not *other than* puts in play both phenomenology and theology. Levinas sought an escape (*evasion*) from being by another way, or by a way which is *otherwise* (*autrement*). The encounter with the other person *immediately* places the acting subject in an ethical situation. Both phenomenologically and theologically, this *otherwise* becomes a question of phenomenological and theological adequacy, both with regard to object and method.

By way of proceeding, the controversy over the relationship between grace and human nature which preoccupied Catholic theology in the mid-twentieth century is a useful case study. The emergence of *la nouvelle Théologie* placed in question the bifurcation of human fulfilment into natural and supernatural orientations, and its implicated ontology. It continues the question of the structure of human subjectivity and human fulfilment. It gives an insight into the intricacies of theology and the problems which arise from its ontotheological commitments. But it also provides an opportunity to consider the structure and intentionality of desire, and the possibility of reconsidering graced existence *otherwise than being*.

'DESIRING THE INFINITE': A CASE STUDY

In the *Summa contra Gentiles*, Aquinas comments,

> Every intellect *desires naturally* to see the divine substance. Now the natural desire cannot be void. Therefore, every created intellect *can* arrive at the vision of the divine substance, the lowliness of its nature being no obstacle. (*Contra Gentiles*, III, 57; cf. *S. T.*, I, 12, 1 c)

This 'apparently minor thesis' in Aquinas which considers the human subject 'in the inmost heart of his being as "*desiderium naturale visionis beatificae*"'[3] sparked off extended theological polemic between Karl Rahner and Henri de Lubac on the relation between the 'natural' and the 'supernatural' and how, in terms of an ontology of human nature, there might be a calling to fulfilment and satisfaction beyond nature. The traditional Catholic theology of grace had tended to view grace as a 'superstructure' which was imposed upon nature, as if there were such a thing as 'pure nature' apart from the environment of grace; as if, one might say, there were pure subjectivity apart from the advent of alterity. Rahner correctly notes that the notion of 'pure nature' is a 'remainder concept' (*Restbegriff*) which is merely a philosophical and theological tool serving a particular framework of understanding – a framework which is perhaps not attentive to the actual human existential as always and already relational and intersubjective.

Joseph Maréchal

The fruitful point of departure is Joseph Maréchal's consideration of the supernatural destiny of humanity in *Cahier V* of *Le Point de départ de la métaphysique*.[4] In response to Kant's transcendental consideration of human subjectivity and its confinement of human knowledge to the realm of the categorical and phenomenal, Maréchal recognises an inherent dynamism within the intellect which intends something other than itself. Kant had focused on the transcendental conditions of knowing and the interiority of the subject. Yet such a constrained subjectivity constantly strains to go beyond such self-imposed limits. The intellect is dynamic, seeking and probing. The question will eventually become: 'what is its provocation?'

To follow the argument: human fulfilment rests in the vision of God (*vita hominis visio Dei*), and human existence has 'a natural desire for the beatific vision (*desiderium naturale visionis beatificae*)'. The link between phenomenology and theology needs also to 'come to mind', like *Dieu qui vient à l'idée*, and the incarnate nature of human existence by which the intersubjective world becomes the place wherein human salvation is enacted. The excessive and oppressive nature of the phenomenal, which is a challenge to both phenomenology and theology is also pressing thought to think further.

The problem which Maréchal identifies, which is pertinent to a theology of grace and an understanding of the structure of desire, is this: human fulfilment lies in the vision of God, but since God is infinite and absolute, the possibility of attaining this goal 'depends upon the free bestowal of supernatural grace'.[5] Although the human intellect desires the absolute as its ultimate end, being finite, its attainment is outwith 'our purely natural possibilities'. How is it possible to desire that which the finite human intellect is radically incapable of desiring? How can there be a '*natural* impulsion' which moves a being 'towards something which is *impossible in itself*'?[6]

For Maréchal, the starting point is Aquinas' affirmation that '[e]very intellect *desires naturally* to see the divine substance' and that 'the natural desire cannot be void' (*Contra Gentiles*, III, 57; cf. *S. T.*, I, 12, 1 c). From the fact of the 'radical disposition of our faculties' – that is, an intentionality towards the infinite – 'we deduce legitimately . . . *the absolute* (positive) *possibility* of this beatitude, that is, the *existence of the remote objective causes which render its realisation possible*'.[7] Now, such a natural dynamism cannot be the result of *blind and necessary* forces for then attaining the infinite would not only be possible but would be realised by finite subjectivity. Such natural dynamism must

therefore arise in the subject as a result of *free agency*. The human
subject may exist as a capacity for the infinite (*capax infiniti*), but the
satisfaction of this capacity depends upon grace freely given.

No *logical* incompatibility exists between the 'possibility in itself' of the
ultimate end, towards which our desire orients us, and the absence of every
proximate possibility of realising this rigorously supernatural end, without
an entirely free and gratuitous gift on the part of God. Further, there is
moreover no *moral* incompatibility.[8]

This necessarily implies, in other words, first, '*the existence of an absolute Being*, capable of communicating itself', and secondly, 'the *capa-
bility of our intelligence* for receiving this communication'.[9]

   Now, Aquinas distinguishes between the intrinsic dynamism of
the intellect whose satisfaction rests in the vision of God, and explicit
interpretations of this dynamism.

Beatitude can be considered in the abstract and in the concrete. Take it in
its *general* meaning, then everybody is bound to wish for happiness. For it
signifies, as we have said, *complete goodness*. Since the good is the object of
the will, the perfect good is that which satisfies it altogether. To desire to be
happy is nothing else than to wish for this satisfaction. *And each and everyone
wishes it.* Take it, however, to the point where happiness lies, *then all do not
recognise it*, for they are ignorant about the object which gathers all good
together. (*S. T.*, Ia, IIae, 5,8, c; cfr. Ibid., ad 2)

Maréchal, following Aquinas, concludes

the natural impulsion of our intellectual faculties drives them towards the
immediate intuition of the absolute Being. It is true that this intuition
exceeds the power and the exigencies of every finite intelligence, left to
its sole natural resources. Yet the radical impulsion which drives it to this
intuition is not conceivable without the objective, at least remote, possibility
of reaching it.[10]

Implicated here is the affirmation of an excessive exteriority which,
by a strange reversal, drives the intentionality of the will. Rahner gives
a summary of Maréchal's thought:

This desire is conditional and so there is no necessity for the actual call to the
vision by grace. But it is a real longing for the absolute being and one which
is present in every spiritual act as its *raison d'être*. Without being expressly
and conceptually present, it is the *a priori* condition of all knowledge where
a finite object is grasped.[11]

Karl Rahner

Rahner, however, develops his own kerygma on grace: 'God wishes to communicate himself, to pour forth the love which he himself is. This is the first and the last of his real plans and hence of his real world too'.[12] To achieve this, God creates a creature not only whom he can love but also who *can* receive this Love which is God himself, and who can and must accept it as 'the unexpected, unexacted gift'. In other words, the capacity for grace *as* grace in man is a hypothetical necessity of his nature. Put theologically, Rahner argues that a perduring ability and congeniality for grace belongs to man as an absolutely defining existential, but that grace can only be accepted *as* grace, that is *as* supernatural, when the existential itself is accepted as unexacted.

Where man knows of the *visio beatifica* by the word of revelation, and experiences it as a marvel of the free love of God in his longing for it, he has to say that it is not due to him (by nature), even as an existing nature – so that the gratuitousness of creation, as a free act of God, and grace as a free gift to the creature, as something already existing, are not one and the same gift of God's free act.[13]

In other words, although the human existence desires the vision of God, or intends the infinite, the fulfilment of this intention relies on the free and gracious advance of the infinite whose trace and taste are already inscribed within the arena of the phenomenal.

Following Aquinas, however, Rahner recognises that this intentionality towards the infinite is not always recognised as a dynamic towards the divine. It may be the case, as Aquinas says, that 'to desire to be happy is nothing else than to wish for this satisfaction' and that '*each and everyone wishes it*'. But taking it 'to the point where happiness lies, *then all do not recognise it*, for they are ignorant about the object which gathers all good together' (*S. T.*, Ia, IIae, 5,8, c). Phenomenologically and theologically, the experience of grace is necessarily incarnate and therefore in the realm of the phenomenal, but 'the possibility of experiencing grace and the possibility of experiencing grace *as* grace are not the same thing'.[14] To experience grace is to experience 'grace *as* . . .' Thus are phenomenology and theology co-implicated.

Rahner, however, raises the key problem which will orient the controversy between himself and Henri de Lubac concerning the

'natural desire for the beatific vision': it is one thing to say that the
human existential is a 'supernatural existential' and to affirm a natural
desire for the infinite; it is quite another thing altogether to say that
this natural desire exists as a demand for grace in order that it might
be fulfilled. 'To be ordained to grace, and to be so constituted that
there is an exigence for grace . . . would render the whole ordination
to grace futile if grace were not actually imparted'.[15] For grace to be
grace, it must be utterly gratuitous on the part of the giver; it must
be unexacted.

Henri de Lubac

De Lubac, like Rahner, is also sympathetic to Maréchal's interpretation of Aquinas. 'In the context of his time' Aquinas had to 'defend
the possibility of the beatific vision', and 'to explain above all else
how the order of grace envelops and completes the order of nature'.[16]
For de Lubac, however, Maréchal was 'a little too timid, founded on
a historical enquiry which is insufficient' and his adoption of Kant's
transcendental critique as a basis of enquiry means that this approach
was 'a little too dependent on conceptions or points of view which
are too modern'.[17] Thus,

it happens frequently that one reasons as if the whole mystery was on the side
of God, while nothing in man escaped being grasped in common experience
or natural reason. All our nature would be in us, at least in right, transparent,
and we would hold the key to all that manifests itself to us.[18]

What de Lubac intends then is study 'undertaken from a theological
point of view and on an enlarged base'[19] which can complete and
accomplish Maréchal's project. The deficit which de Lubac recognises in Maréchal is that the interpretation given to the Thomistic
axiom *desiderium naturae nequit esse inane* is 'only half exact' for, in
addressing the problem of the desire for the beatific vision, it sought
to situate the problem within the context of an intellectual dynamism
which would give a metaphysical and epistemological foundation to
knowledge rather than 'to place in relief and analyse directly the desire
of the spirit'.[20] While Maréchal could rightly argue that 'the Absolute
has placed its mark on the basic tendency of our intelligence' and
that 'the natural impulsion of our intellectual faculties orients them

towards the immediate intuition of absolute Being' since this intuition 'goes beyond the powers [*puissances*] and exceeds the demand of every finite intelligence given over to natural resources', nonetheless, such a transcendental perspective which deduces the need of an absolute from the radical disposition of our faculties 'considerably limits the plan of knowledge'.[21] More is needed.

De Lubac agrees with Maréchal that the human subjectivity is constituted by a natural desire for God which is not a mere velleity. But, because finite, the subject is radically incapable by itself of realising its own intention. The desire, then, must be not the work of the subject, but the work of God, and so can rightly be called supernatural. But, since it is a desire which is found in human nature, it can also rightly be termed 'natural'. God fulfils the desire which he has implanted in us, and in so doing, he responds to his own call. The problem of whether or not grace is exacted or unexacted is a pseudo-problem which rests on the false dilemma created by an extrinsicism of first positing a desire for God, and thereafter a supernatural calling.[22] The reality of concrete human experience is otherwise, however. A purely natural existence devoid of supernatural finality is an abstraction or, as Rahner terms it, a 'remainder-concept' (*Restebegriff*). One does not first of all live a natural existence and then uncover a desire for the supernatural. One already lives in the midst of this desire.

Rahner versus de Lubac

Rahner is critical of de Lubac's position, fearing that it compromises the teaching that 'grace is absolutely unexacted' and the theological value of the concept of pure nature.[23] For a gift to be a gift, and for grace to be grace, it cannot be demanded for whatever reason. De Lubac too readily interprets the experience of human transcendence as the experience of the supernatural, and does not pay sufficient regard to the fact that human experience has a transcendental dimension which can never be absolutely and exhaustively analysed or represented. For Rahner, such an excess is articulated in terms of the transcendentality of experience. The new theology which de Lubac espouses comprises the unexactedness of grace, and therefore its utter gratuity. To view a supernatural orientation 'as on the one hand an intrinsic, inadmissible constituent of man's nature, and on the other so conceived that the withholding of the end of this directedness was expounded as being incompatible with God's wisdom and goodness and in this sense unconditional' is inconsistent, and so, says Rahner, '[w]e hold that . . . grace and beatific vision can no longer be said to be unexacted'.[24] One cannot say both that the supernatural orientation is natural and that grace remains unexacted.

A 'desire' which is natural and at the same time, even if only objectively, inevitably attracts grace to itself (the desire itself, not just God's wisdom and his promise but the latter through the former!), is a desire which 'demands' grace, demands precisely because it would otherwise be meaningless. But this is incompatible with the unexactedness of grace.[25]

De Lubac versus Rahner

Rahner criticises de Lubac's 'ontological presuppositions and conceptions', but Rahner himself is not immune from his own 'ontological presuppositions and conceptions' which derive from his adoption of Maréchal's transcendental critique. First of all, De Lubac accuses Rahner of misrepresenting him.[26] However, more constructively, de Lubac points out that Rahner himself recognises the insufficiency of the world for the human spirit, which opens out onto the horizon of absolute being. By its very nature, the human spirit possesses an 'unlimited transcendence' towards an infinite horizon, and it is this orientation or intentionality towards the infinite which is the defining characteristic and goal of humanity. Rahner admits that the scholastic concept of 'nature' is modelled on 'what is less than human' and agrees that human nature cannot be assigned an end which is perfectly defined materially.

One has only to ask why a supernatural end can be set for man without annulling his nature, and why God cannot do this with the nature of something below man. Then it becomes apparent at once that however universally the formal ontology of nature, end etc. may extend, these concepts can only be pursued in a highly analogical way.[27]

In fact, de Lubac points out, 'the "scholastic" concept of nature, too much copied on the model of the infra-human, is more the concept of a modern scholasticism', and the analogical corrections desired by Rahner are already to be found in Aquinas, who did not content himself with the universal aptitude for knowledge, but, instructed by faith and the tradition, understood the human soul to possess 'a centre from which the spiritual faculties pour out, a tendency towards the whole of being and towards God, to the vision of which it is also wholly naturally incapable of attaining'.[28]

Now, if we adopt Aquinas' understanding of the human intellect *being drawn* or attracted towards its model, and if we place this alongside Rahner's claim that 'a "desire" which is natural and at the same time, even if only objectively, inevitably attracts grace to itself . . . is a desire which "demands" grace, demands precisely because it would otherwise be meaningless', and that 'this is incompatible with the unexactedness of grace'[29] then we can perhaps begin to see that the problem of the unexactedness of grace is caught up in the interpretation of desire. De Lubac argues that God creates in the creature a desire for its fulfilment in the beatific vision, a fulfilment which cannot be refused. Rahner maintains that this amounts to a demand for grace.

The dynamic and intentionality of desire, however, as Levinas will argue, is that desire is incapable of being quenched or satiated for the desirable is excessive to the intentionality that it inspires. Desire, in other words, unlike need, is not awoken by a lack in the one who experiences desire, but by the excess of the desirable which remains absolute and exterior. De Lubac provides an important theological insight into the structure of desire and subjectivity when he writes,

> As 'natural' and as 'serious' as it is, the desire for the divine vision is in no way something which would determine the effective gift on the part of God. God is not regulated by our desire! Between the two terms, the relationship can only be inverse: it is the free will of the giver which awakens the desire in the one who wants to attain it. This point is beyond contest. All question of demand on the part of the creature is banished. But it remains nonetheless, one might say, that such an existing desire in the creature becomes the sign, not only of a possible gift on the part of God, but of a certain gift. It is the attestation of a promise, inscribed and read in being itself. In the knowledge acquired of this desire, would it not be right to conclude to the effective reality of this gift?[30]

However – and this has phenomenological significance – along with Rahner who argues that the experience of grace is only ever the experience of 'grace *as* . . .', de Lubac notes that 'once the natural desire for the vision . . . has been able to be recognised, discerned, analysed, its term is never known other than "*aliquo modo*".[31] In other words, phenomenological and theological method require a methodological adequacy which is adequate to the excess of the object intended. In terms of desire: the desired is only ever grasped in the midst of the desire it excites, that is, in its desirability. Desire, as Levinas indicates, is awoken and sustained by the very insufficiency and inadequacy of desire to the desirable which sustains the desire – like the very positivity of love lying in the negativity of possession (*EE*, 43). As Levinas indicates, 'desire is an aspiration that the desirable animates; it originates from its "object"; it is revelation – whereas need is a void of the Soul; it proceeds from the subject' (*TI*, 62).

THE DYNAMIC OF DESIRE IN LEVINAS

For Levinas, an existence which has not undergone the advent of the other person is an existence devoid of transcendent reference. In 'Philosophy and the idea of Infinity', he notes 'an existence which takes itself to be natural, for whom its place in the sun, its ground, its *site*, orient all signification – a pagan *existing*' (*CPP*, 52). 'Transcendence is not the fundamental movement of the ontological adventure; it is founded in the non-transcendence of position' (*EE*, 100). The first hypostasis of the subject, whereby a contract between existence and existent is forged, has not yet become an ethical existence. 'Hypostasis, the apparition of a substantive, is not only the apparition of a new grammatical category; it signifies the suspension of the anonymous *there is*, the apparition of a private domain, of a noun. On the ground of the *there is* a being arises' (*EE*, 82–3). What is significant in this first hypostasis is the self-relationality of the subject to itself: 'it is not just that one is, one is oneself [*on n'est pas, on s'est*]' (*EE*, 28). The escape from the 'corybantic necessity' of existence, with its tragic riveting of the ego to its own being, can initially be achieved in the enjoyment of the elemental, for 'to be at home with oneself . . . is to live from . . . to enjoy the elemental' (*EE*, 147).

As enjoyment (*jouissance*) is to need (*besoin*), however, so is pleasure (*plaisir*) to desire (*désir*), and the movement from need and its enjoyable satisfactions to pleasure and delight depends upon the advent of an other than the self who excites a subjectivity which can properly be termed ethical, and the possibility of a second ethical hypostasis in which the subject is no longer simply for-itself, but is now constituted as 'for the other person'. The threat which the *il y a* poses the solitary self whose own place 'in the sun' is a fragile possession is displaced by the approach of the other whose *illeity* calls the subject forth from its own entombment to responsive, responsible, and ethical existence.[32] One might say that the other person brings about a *kenosis* of the self.

Desire

Desire is not need. Need is hungry and voracious, and demands satisfaction. Need has its origin in an emptiness or lack in the subject. Need is a privation. Voids need to be filled. Desire is otherwise, and its origin is elsewhere. If lack and privation results in the hunger for the satisfaction of need, it is excess which provokes and sustains desire. Desire is provoked by the utter surplus of the other person. It is insatiable, like the 'insatiable compassion' of Sonia Marmeladova when she gazes upon Raskolnikov, in Dostoievsky's *Crime and Punishment*. 'Let us note again the difference between need and Desire: in need I can sink my teeth into the real and satisfy myself in assimilating the other; in Desire there is no sinking one's teeth into being, no satiety, but an uncharted future before me' (*TI*, 117).

Now, although desire may seem to follow need as if there were a chronology at play, in reality it is desire which provides the time in which needs can be satisfied. 'Human need already rests on desire' (*TI*, 117). In other words, it is because the personal other has opened up a time ahead of me that the present time of need and enjoyment is possible; I work and labour in order that I may put food on my family's table. The *travails* I take upon myself and endure are situated in the context of the larger work (*œuvre*) of being liturgically oriented towards the service of the other person. Paradoxically, my attempt to create my own place in the sun and enclose the home as my own totality within which I can be happily shut up in my self, demands an openness to what is other which is also the possibility of an egress beyond the world towards the *real* infinity of the other person in his or her absolute otherness. But, it is the advent of the other person that gives this possibility of a subjectivity awakening beyond its own concerns. Thus again is the case that what is seemingly posterior (the other person) is actually anterior, and that the very possibility of a subjectivity rests on an implicit orientation towards the inter-subjective and life-with-others. The un-peopled environment does not satisfy: '*within this very interiority* hollowed out by enjoyment there must be produced a heteronomy that incites to another destiny than this animal complacency in oneself' (*TI*, 149). As mentioned previously, my existence as a separated being and the possibility of transcendence implies 'a first revelation of the other person ... [for] ... the idea of infinity, revealed in the face, does not only *require* a separated being; the light of the face is necessary for separation' (*TI*, 149).

Desire and the Infinite

Why is desire inexinguishable? Why, in the dynamic of desire, is the point of climax never reached? Quite simply, because the other person is excessive to my own capacity to comprehend and my own power to control or determine. The other person is 'unanticipatable alterity' (*TI*, 34), eminently *other*, ungraspable (*insaissible*) *and* infinite. The other person, to use the language of Marion, is the 'saturated phenomenon' *par excellence*; such a saturated phenomenon requires a 'phenomenology of the relation with the Other [which] suggests this structure of Desire analysed as an idea of the Infinite' (*DF*, 294) and whose structure is such that its 'movement proceeds from what is thought and not from the thinker' (*TI*, 61). In other words, the relationship with the other person is a relationship which I, by my own Pelagian efforts, cannot achieve.[33]

The Cartesian origin of this 'idea of the Infinite' has already been mentioned. This idea of the Infinite in Levinas is articulated in terms of desire. The Cartesian *cogito* thinks more than it is able to think, and struggles in vain to think it.

According to Descartes, the I who thinks possesses the idea of the infinite: the otherness of the infinite is not deadened in the idea, as is the otherness of finite things of which, according to Descartes, I can give an account through myself. The idea of the infinite consists in thinking more than one thinks. (*DF*, 294)

Levinas' reflection on the dynamic of desire and the inspiration of desire's orientation offers theological opportunities and phenomenological challenges.

The absolute exteriority or 'unanticipatable alterity' of the other person excites and sustains desire. This desire cannot be assuaged for the subject is not the origin of the desire; it is aroused and provoked. To have the idea of the infinite, which is experienced *as desire*, is not to possess the other person, who always remains yet to be discovered and explored; 'the infinite is not a correlative of the idea of the infinite as if this idea were an intentionality *accomplishing itself* in its "object"' (*HAH*, 54). The infinite 'is infinitely removed from its idea, that is, exterior, because it is infinite' (*TI*, 49). But this involves 'an overturning of intentionality' and its appetite (*HAH*, 54).

What is implicated in this overturning and strange reversal of intentionality is a recasting of subjectivity as 'for the other person'. The dynamic of desire which does not take its point of origin in the subject, but is always aroused and excited by the other person, nonetheless is incarnated as responsibility. The excessive phenomenon of the other person demands excessive responsibility. 'Before the other person [*Autrui*] the self is infinitely responsible' (*HAH*, 54). The significance of self is the excess of responsibility undergone in the presence of the excessiveness of the other; it is as if the whole of creation rested on my shoulders. Such a responsibility is humbling. Its weight bends me. 'In front of the face I always demand more of myself' (*HAH*, 54).

A key notion which we have been constantly stressing is that of the prevenience of the other person in the intersubjective relationship. It is the other who excites desire in the self. It is the other who draws the self from its own self-enclosure into an existence which can properly be termed ethical and human. It is the other who effects the subject as the ethical hypostasis (the-other-in-me) of responsibility. This phenomenological reversal and deepening of intentionality, which continues the phenomenological reduction undertaken by Husserl into the realm of the intersubjective, can also be articulated in terms of a phenomenology of awakening.

AWAKENING TO GRACE

The fundamental aspect of a theological anthropology which relies on an integral theology of grace is the theological conviction of Irenaeus that 'the glory of God is a living human being; and human life [consists in] the vision of God' (*Gloria enim Dei vivens homo, vita autem hominis visio Dei*). This can be more simply rendered: 'the glory of God is the human person fully alive [*gloria Dei, homo vivens*]'. This can also be expressed, in a language which is both theological and phenomenological, as 'the glory of God is the human person fully awake' (*gloria Dei, homo vigilans*). The notions of wakefulness, awakening, being awoken, are enduring phenomenological motifs in Levinas, as they are in any theological consideration of any advent of the alterity. In an essay on 'Philosophy and Awakening', Levinas writes,

the reduction reveals its true meaning and the meaning of the subjective which it signifies in its final phase – the intersubjective reduction. The subjectivity of the subject shows itself in the traumatism of awakening, despite the gnoseological interpretation which, for Husserl, finally characterises the element of the spirit. But this is no longer Husserl. (*EN*, 102–3)

Already noted is Levinas' distinction between a 'pagan existence' which is a self-enclosed subjectivity devoid of a transcendent reference, and 'ethical existence', or, life as transcendence. Already noted also is Levinas' commitment to the secular. Adapting Rimbaud, he notes that '"the true life is absent". But we are in the world' (*TI*, 33). The way of transcendence has no other route or halt (*way-station*) than that of enfleshed or incarnate encounter with an other person, who always demands more of *me* on account of his or her *excess*. Such an encounter is a phenomenological and theological challenge; the dynamic of intersubjectivity attempts to bring the extravagance of the '*who*' to the fore, but often this is masked by the reduction of the '*who*' to the '*what*'. Being attentive to what is being said, often the fact there is someone saying is overlooked. Quite simply, even idiots (*idiotes*) demand a hearing, for the fact of saying (*le dire*) is excessive to what is said (*le dit*). Levinas expresses it well in his resistance to the reduction of the *who* to a *what*:

The logos as said . . . lets the 'who?' get lost in the 'what?' It gets lost in it still more evidently in our questioning 'who is looking?', which does not ask about such a one or other, but about the essence of the 'who that is looking' in its generality. In the 'who is this *who*?' it asks 'what about this *who*?' to which the look turned on being is given. Thus on all sides the privilege of the question 'what?', or the ontological nature of the problem is affirmed. (*OB*, 27)[34]

Exclusion is a function of ontology, even to the point of absolute exclusion which is a final solution.

But this question becomes more radical in Levinas: 'each question about the question is more radical still' (*OB*, 24). What is placed in question is not the other person upon whom the meaning-bestowing subject visits significance, but the meaning-bestowing subject itself. The 'folding back of being upon itself, or subjectivity' (*OB*, 28) is confounded by the other person to whom thought is inadequate.

The other to whom the petition is addressed does not belong to the intelligible sphere to be explored . . . Subjectivity is structured as the other in the same, but in a way different from that of consciousness. Consciousness is always correlative with a theme, a present represented, a theme put before me, a being which is a phenomenon. (*OB*, 25)

In short, ethics is otherwise than ontology.

Awakening

'An existence which takes itself to be natural, for whom its place in the sun, its ground, its *site*, orients all signification' is a 'pagan *existing*' (*CPP*, 52). For Levinas, to be 'pagan' is to live a life which is both deaf and blind to the other person. Allied to the negativity of living out a pagan existence is the positive value of atheism, which is not so much a refusal or denial of God but a repatriation of responsibility to a subject, which 'conditions a veritable relationship with the true God *kath'auto*' (*TI*, 77). Life with others is the place in which subjectivity is summoned and enacted. Life with others redeems the subject from its own self-enclosure. Life with others is the time and the place in which a God is both revealed and discovered. Thus,

The atheism of the metaphysician means, positively, that our relation with the metaphysical is an ethical behaviour and not theology, not a thematisation, be it a knowledge by analogy, of the attributes of God. God rises to his supreme and ultimate presence as correlative to the justice rendered unto men. (*TI*, 78)

Again,

to hear a God not contaminated by Being is a human possibility no less important and no less precarious than to bring Being out of the oblivion in which it is said to have fallen in metaphysics and onto-theology. (*OB*, xlii).

How, then, is this awakening accomplished, both phenomenologically and theologically?

The emergence of an existent can be charted as follows: as if waking, a subject emerges into the light as consciousness and wrests itself from the anonymity of the *there is* (*il y a*), but the escape is never complete; existence is a weight to be carried, and the subject can always fall back into oblivion. This awakening from the anonymity of existence is to assume a position, which is the very 'subjectivisation of the subject' (*EE*, 69) as a first *hypostasis*. 'Through the taking of position in the anonymous *there is* a subject is affirmed. It is affirmation in the etymological sense of the term, taking a position on solid ground, on a base, fulfilling the conditions, foundation' (*EE*, 82). Such an existence, however, is solitary, and lacks transcendence. It is an 'enchainment to oneself' and is 'the impossibility of getting rid of oneself' for 'to be an ego is not only to be for oneself; it is also to be with oneself' (*EE*, 88). In short, 'everything in the subject is here' but *here* offers no redemption from self-enclosed subjectivity: 'it can only come from elsewhere' (*EE*, 93).

Phenomenological awakening

Levinas describes consciousness in terms of awakening. Initially this is pursued by considering Husserl's phenomenology and phenomeno-logical reduction of the subject. In his *Cartesian Meditations*, Husserl described the Ego – 'where subjectivity is most living its life', and which Levinas refers to (*DQVI*, 47) – in terms of sleep and waking. However, in Husserl, the intentionality of consciousness is described in terms of cognition where representation is the dominant model. Husserl gives considerable thought to the notions of the adequacy and inadequacy of the evidence presented to consciousness in pursuit of a rigorous and scientific phenomenology.

But Levinas wants to pursue Husserl's subjective reduction further in the direction of the intersubjective, and draws attention not only to the inadequacy of thought to the excess of its object (the *noematico-noetic* correlation) but also the inadequacy of an intentionality con-ceived solely on the basis of representation. Hence, the *Totality* is presented as a 'defence of interiority on the basis of exteriority'. The 'living present' is already excessive and the excess of exteriority cannot be fully or adequately articulated in a phenomenology which is alto-gether too reliant on the model of representation. Rather, 'the living present' disturbs the self-complacency of immanence and ruptures or

breaks open interiority, and this is awakening and life [*réveil et vie*]'
(*EN*, 102). Husserl may have seen the phenomenological reduction
as a perfecting of knowledge, but its true import is its recognition
that knowledge, rather than being a perfecting, is a petrification and
paralysation of life: the spirituality of thought has not been so much
an adventure of knowledge, but the drowsiness which is part and
parcel of wakefulness (*DQVI*, 53). Husserl, for Levinas, unnecessarily
restricts phenomenology to the domain of representation and cognition, and this diminishes the scope and interest of phenomenology
(*TIHP*, 94, 134). The 'noesis-noema structure is not the primordial
structure of intentionality' (*TI*, 294) for true significance of the phenomenological reduction is the reanimation or reactivation of the life
'forgotten or weakened in knowledge' (*DQVI*, 99). Again, for Levinas, the phenomenological reduction pursued by Husserl 'reveals its
true meaning as the meaning of the subjective which it allows to be
signified, in its final phase, which is the intersubjective reduction . . .
[for] . . . the subjectivity of the subject shows itself in the traumatism of wakening, despite the gnoseological interpretation which, for
Husserl, finally characterizes the element of spirit'. It is an awakening
'from dogmatic slumber'. Husserl's reduction 'describes the awakening, beyond knowledge, from insomnia or from wakefulness of which
knowledge is only one modality' (*DQVI*, 102–4). Husserl's reduction
recognises that 'access to the object makes up the being of the object'.
Husserl's phenomenology, then, has an ontological interest, for access
is constitutive of 'the essential event of being'.[35] But, the 'lived present'
is already excessive, and access demands intentionalities other than
the merely cognitive. It is not only the case that phenomenological
method gives access to the object intended, but also that the phenomenal excess of the object challenges phenomenological method
to be adequate, which, as authors such as Henry, Chrétien, and Marion argue, is about recognising the way in which exteriority gives or
phenomenalises itself to subjective interiority. For Levinas, such interiority is always challenged to emerge under the *aegis* of exteriority,
and this is always an ethical situation.

Ethical awakening

In pursuing Husserl's reduction to the level of the intersubjective, Levinas exposes the subject as always and already exposed and

vulnerable to the advent of the other person. The first *hypostasis* of *position* by which subjectivity overcomes the anonymity of bare being (the *il y a*) is already and always open to its *ex-positioning* and displacement by the other person. In terms of an ethical awakening, this ethical awakening is occasioned by the explosion of the other in the same, which provokes an absolute insomnia. The sleeplessness which is attentive to the horror and terror of the night is displaced by the overwhelming demand of the other person. The question of 'to be or not to be' is supplanted by the question, 'how does being justify itself?' In terms of an extreme ethic of responsibility, 'how can one sleep when one can still do more?' The *il y a* is redeemed by the *illeity* of the other person, and the emergence of an ethical subject is enabled. And within this *indefinable illeity* of the other person (indefinable because ultimately incomprehensive and excessive to assimilation by thought), there is 'the condition of possibility of ethics as the very possibility of the beyond',[36] which is also the possibility of the encounter with a God uncontaminated with being, and only available as the counterpart of the justice which is rendered to the other person.[37]

Now, Levinas describes this possibility of God in terms of a trace, which is akin to the effacing of tracks in the snow which are only known in their very effacement. The imprint of the divine is only known in the smudging of the prints left by the other person so that tracks become unidentifiable and incomparable.[38] To leave a trace is to absolve oneself. It is to have absented oneself in a transcendence of the ontology of the present. To relate to the other person is to relate to someone whose significance cannot be described or delimited in ontological categories, and who refuses any cultural or social identity which might be ascribed. In other words, it is to relate to someone whose unique identity lies in the non-identifiable enigma of the neutral '*il*' of *illeity*. The other person with whom I am fascinated and to whom I am attracted and drawn by grace is naked and formless. The other person – like the suffering servant in Isaiah 53 who in his very *disfigurement* of the other person by which he seems no longer human – is withdrawn from the structures and commerce of the world and reduces kings to speechlessness, much as 'the people remain silent at the end of *Boris Godunov* in the face of the crimes committed by those in power' (*DF*, 293). And, having withdrawn from the world absolutely, the other person is formless.[39] It is this lack of figure and form which is the *illeity* of the other person. The other person is beyond any possibility of a consciousness that would attempt to thematise, expose, and represent. The other person remains always somewhat strange and unfamiliar.

This is the basis of the difficulty which Levinas recognises in Buber. In addressing the other person as a 'Thou', the other is brought too close to me. *Tutoiement* is too familiar and compromises the sheer otherness of the other person. The other person cannot be a *tu*, but, as *il*, always withdraws into *illeity* and it is this constant withdrawal that sustains the possibility of any relationship. One cannot relate to the other person as an equal; I am always in debt for the other is neither in the time or the place of my world. 'If the relationship with illeity were a relationship of consciousness, "he" would designate a theme, as the "thou" of Buber's I–thou relation does' (*OB*, 12–13).

Now, this absolute withdrawal of the other person, however, is not to be interpreted in terms of some theological *via negativa* in which one might seek a *Deus absconditus* whose very hiddenness is signalled in the face of the Other who thereby becomes a means on the way to some theological end. In such a scheme, the trace would be transformed into a *sign* of a departure by representation and thematisation, and the face would be 'an appearance or sign of some reality . . . present as an invisible theme' imposed on me by this hidden God (*OB*, 93–4). The relationship with the other person is more positive than this. The absolute withdrawal of the other person finds its corollary in the infinite responsibility I bear towards him, a responsibility which can never be formally delimited because it responds to the other person through the detour of *illeity*, and thus more is always demanded of me. My inability to delimit the other person also means that I cannot delimit my responsibility for him or her. 'The exteriority of *illeity*, refractory to disclosure and manifestation, is a having-to-be in the face of another (*OB*, 193, n.35). This 'having-to-be' is a 'having-to-be-*responsible*'.

In the final paragraph of *Otherwise than Being*, we read that, 'after the death of a certain god inhabiting the world behind the scenes, the substitution of the hostage discovers the trace, the unpronounceable inscription of what, always already past, always "he" [*il*], does not enter into any present, to which are suited not the nouns designating beings, or the verbs in which their essence resounds, but that which, as a pronoun, marks with its seal all that a noun can convey' (*OB*, 185). In other words, 'illeity expresses its anachoresis, its holiness, the ab-straction of its unique name, more unpronounceable than any grammatical category would be able to contain'.[40] The other person to whom I am drawn in responsibility is beyond the nominalisation of the noun, that is, is pronominal, indicating without naming. Neither Jew nor Greek, slave nor free, male nor female, the other persona can be indicated only as *il*.

Now, if, on account of *illeity*, the other person is beyond comparison, then *this* other person could be *any* other person. 'The epiphany of the face qua face opens humanity . . . The epiphany of the face . . . attests the presence of the third party, the whole of humanity, in the eyes that look at me' (*TI*, 213). The *I* thus becomes uniquely responsible for the whole world; but this becomes unsustainable, and so arises the demand for justice and a co-operative society which derives from responsibility. The unique responsibility which each other person calls forth has to be translated into a justice for the many others, for not only must one be responsible; one must also be just. Responsibility requires justice, and justice must be responsible.

But, not only does my infinite responsibility for the one and the many require the moderation of justice; within this very justice there arises the possibility of God. 'The dimension of the divine opens forth from the human face . . . God rises to his supreme and ultimate presence as correlative of the justice rendered unto men' (*TI*, 78). In his reflection on God and Philosophy, Levinas considers the ethical relationship with otherness:

God is drawn out of objectivity, presence and being. He is neither an object nor an interlocutor. His absolute remoteness, his transcendence, turns into my responsibility – non-erotic par excellence – for the other. And this analysis implies that God is not simply the 'first other', the 'other par excellence', or the 'absolutely other', but other than the other [*autre qu'autrui*], other otherwise, other with an alterity prior to the alterity of the other, prior to the ethical bond with another and different from every neighbour, transcendent to the point of absence, to the point of possible confusion with the stirring of the *there is*. In this confusion the substitution for the neighbour gains in dis-inter*estedness*, that is, in nobility, and the transcendence of the Infinite arises in glory. (*CPP*, 165–6)

The *illeity* of the other person, opening on to a universal fraternity, also opens on to the universal parenthood of God. Picking up on the theme of the *imago Dei*, Levinas remarks that 'to be in the image of God does not signify being an icon of God, but being found in his trace. God . . . only shows himself by the trace, as in Exodus 33. To go towards him is not to follow this trace which is not a sign; it is to go towards Others who are maintained in the trace' (*DEHH*, 202).

Further, the pronominal '*il*' of *illeity* by which responsibility for the one becomes translated into justice for the many enables the name of God to be uttered divested of its divinity. Divinity, for Levinas, is an ontological term by which God becomes situation in being; it is the nominalisation of the noun insofar as it 'participates' in being. God, however, is otherwise than being, and accessible only as a trace in the responsible and just relationship with the other person. 'The name outside of essence or beyond essence, the individual prior to individuality, is named God. It precedes all divinity, that is, the divine essence which the false gods, individuals sheltered in their concept, lay claim to' (*OB*, 190, n.38).[41]

In other words, God is accessible as the counterpart of the justice I render to my neighbour because in the opening of illeity one finds the trace of God. My assignation as responsible-for-the other-person points to an anarchic anteriority of responsibility which is beyond the measure of finitude or presence as manifestation, and which,

neither being nor non-being, is the 'excluded third' of the beyond of being and of non-being, a third person which we have called 'illeity' and which perhaps also the word God says. Beyond being, refractory to thematisation and origin – pre-originary: beyond non-being – an authority which orders me to the neighbour as face . . . Illeity, in an extremely precise manner, is excluded from being, but orders it by relation to a responsibility, by relation to a pure passivity, to a pure 'susceptibility': an obligation to respond preceding every interrogation which would call for an anterior engagement, overflowing every question, every problem and representation, and in which obedience precedes the order which is furtively infiltrated into the soul which obeys.[42]

Illeity designates a 'detour from the face, the manner in which God concerns us without entering into conjunction with thematising consciousness and where the subject is obliged with an obligation which has not begun in him'.[43] God, as pre-originary, God as excluded third, 'assures the condition of possibility of ethics as the very possibility of the beyond'.[44] Thus again we see the posteriority of the anterior: that which one seemingly comes across last of all is shown through a successive reduction from the subjective to the intersubjective to the religious to be first.

The awakening to the intersubjective, then, is also an awakening to God; it is 'the very event of *transcendence* as life', a 'transcendence in which the distinction between transcendence towards the other person and transcendence towards God should not be made too quickly' (*EN*, 87). The Other 'is indispensable for my relation with God' (*TI*, 78) for there can be no 'knowledge' of God outwith the social relation; but, conversely, God is the indispensable other than the other [*autre qu'autrui*] who, as absolutely excluded third, makes possible the relationship with true alterity – the illeity of the Other – which is maintained in his trace.

At the outset of this chapter, the possibility of developing an understanding of grace as desire and awakening was suggested. The glory of God is not only the human person fully alive, as Irenaeus writes, but also the human person fully awake. *Gloria Dei, homo vigilans.* What provokes ethical awakening is the advent of the other person, always prevenient, who excites an insatiable desire for the other who is always excessive and unencompassable.

CHAPTER 6

The liturgical orientation of the self

The structure of human subjectivity is perhaps Levinas' key concern. How does a subject emerge into a world, and what governs and guides relations between subjects? For Levinas, to be a subject is not only to be always and already with others, but more importantly, it is to be *for* others in such a way that the relation between the self and the other is not played out on a plane of *inter*subjectivity where the other and the self would stand on level ground as equals. I am not the equal of the other, nor is the other person another similar to myself. Such a relation in which it is a matter of the mutuality and the reciprocity of the same, as found in Buber, is criticised by Levinas. The relation with the other person is a relation which lacks symmetry. There is no level playing field; the other person occupies a higher position than I do, even though he or she is often encountered in his or her destitution. Height is a moral quality before ever geometrical space comes into play.

What Levinas means by this is that the other person who faces me is experienced as command and responsibility, and thus occupies an ethical position which is higher than the position which I occupy, even though that higher ethical position often finds itself in a state of neglect and destitution. The other invokes and provokes a response in me. I am 'placed on the spot' by the appeal of the other person who displaces my happy possession and enjoyment of my 'place in the sun'. I am called to be responsible and to respond to the need and the plight of the other, and, even though I can walk away, nonetheless I am disturbed by this ethical challenge with which the other confronts me. For Levinas, liturgy is a work or intentionality that is oriented to another without any hope or desire of return. The liturgical relationship is an asymmetrical covenant between two interlocutors, one of whom is always inspired by, and indebted to, the other.

Levinas' reflection on the understanding of the 'I–Thou' (*Ich–Du*) relation in Buber is a useful propaedeutic for understanding a relationship which can properly be called *liturgical*. Levinas fundamentally disagrees with Buber. The relationship which Buber describes between the *I* and the *Thou* is reversible and mutual. But, two lovers can be so entwined in themselves that they remain deaf to the third who knocks on the door. A mutuality content in its own mutual satisfaction is a mutuality deaf to responsibility. Thus, in Levinas, the need for the constant instability of exclusive mutuality, and the disruption of mutual enjoyment by the appeal of the anonymity of a third.

With Buber, Levinas recognises that the relationship with the other person is a relationship which is characterised, not by cognitive intentionality, but by speaking. Speaking is provoked by a 'who' who enables anything to be said. The one to whom one is speaking enables what is said. The 'who' enables the 'what'. Thus, the relationship to a *Thou* is the prior condition of all objectifying thought, while the *Thou* remains beyond any thematisation. One does not 'think' the other person; one 'addresses that person as a *Thou* [*s'addresser à lui, de lui dire Tu*]' (*PN*, 22). The *I* is inconceivable without the *Thou*, but the *Thou* 'remains absolute despite the relation' (*PN*, 26). It is, then, the nature of the 'interval' between the *I* and the *Thou* – in fact, the very nature of the *between* (*l'entre-les-deux, le Zwischen*) – which needs to be understood. Positively, he argues that Buber maintains 'in its integrity the alterity of the *Thou*' (*PN*, 25), and recognises that the interval enables *dialogue*. 'The presence of the *Thou*, the other [*autre*], is *ipso facto* addressed to me, requiring a response' (*PN*, 25). Before the *Thou*, one cannot be a spectator; one must respond. For Buber, however, that response stops short of responsibility. Buber's relation has a formal, not an ethical, structure and this renders the relation reversible, a collectivity of *we* in which two stand side-by-side and 'where reciprocity remains the tie between two separated freedoms, and the ineluctable character of isolated subjectivity is underestimated' (*CPP*, 93–4). Buber's 'relation' thus compromises the absolute alterity of the other person, and, in fact, creates a totality of two.

Levinas, therefore, stresses the asymmetrical, or liturgical, nature of the relationship. The relation between the *I* and the other person can never be a conjunction established by an *and* which brings together into a mutual *ensemble*, but must also, disjunctively, maintain the absolute separation of the *Thou* from the *I*, or of the other from the same. What relates *I* and *Thou* is not the conjunction '*and*' but the preposition '*for*'. The *I* and the other person can only be related in terms of responsibility, and 'to be responsible' is to be responsible '*for-the-Other*'. Now, the relation between the two presupposes distance and separation, but the separation is not a separation of the *I* from the other person (for the *I* is always already subjected by the other person in terms of responsibility); rather, the separation which enables the relation is the separation of the other person from the *I*. In other words, the ethical relation is not reversible; the distance from *A* to *B* is not the same as the distance from *B* to *A*. It is the absolution of the other person *from* the *I*, without a corresponding absolution of the *I*'s responsibility, which renders the *I* radically *for*-the-other person. What Buber has neglected is the fact that 'man is not just the category of distance and meeting, he is also a separate being' (*PN*, 35). As separate, the other person cannot become a theme, nor does the other person coincide with any representation I attempt. It is not as the familiar *Thou* that the other person is approached but rather in terms of his or her *illeity*, that quality of absolute otherness which provokes responsibility *in me*. The absolution of the other person from the relation is an absolution which both effects and sustains the relation as *responsibility*. And to be responsible is to be '*for*-the-other-person.'

THE RESPONSIBLE RELATION AS A LITURGICAL RELATION

Responsibility can also be termed a 'religious relation'. Levinas often uses the term 'religious' to describe human relations. Jeff Bloechl notes that 'religious transcendence is a primary concern of Levinas' philosophy as a whole', and speaks himself of the relation with the other person as 'the Religion of Responsibility' or as a

'Liturgy of the Neighbour'.[1] How might a 'liturgy of the neighbour' be understood?

Liturgy has two aspects: worship and service, though these are not distinct but intimately related. For Levinas, the notion of liturgy is bound to the service rendered to the neighbour. The structure of liturgy might be said to be cruciform; that is, it has a movement outwards and upwards towards the transcendent, yet it is a movement outwards in service. The cruciform image of the movement upwards and the movement outwards remains useful as long as the two transcendences are not separated or disengaged. One might think that Christian theology articulates these two transcendences as a movement upwards towards the divine and a movement outwards towards the human, yet this would be to misrepresent any theological understanding of the liturgy. The theological structure of the liturgy is 'other-oriented' just as, for Levinas, the philosophical structure of liturgy is *'a movement of the Same towards the Other which never returns to the Same'*. The structure of liturgy is essentially *'for*-the-other', a structure which brings together the diaconal structure of liturgy as both worship and ethics.[2] For Levinas, as for theology, the intersection of the divine and the human can only ever arise in the ethical encounter with the other person. This does not negate the cruciform structure of liturgy for the other person commands from a position of ethical height, yet the summons to be responsible often strikes the subject from the other person's situation of debasement and destitution.

Now, to say the liturgy has a *'for*-structure' is to say that the structure of liturgy corresponds to the structure of responsibility, which is 'for-the-other'. In this orientation towards alterity, God is implicated. Liturgy, theologically understood, is both worship offered to God and achieves the sanctification of humanity. In short, the essential aspect of liturgy is *'a movement of the Same towards the Other which never returns to the Same'*. For Levinas, liturgy is an ethical reality, and the God who is worshipped arises as the counterpart of the justice we render to others.

Further, liturgy, theologically understood, is 'a pedagogy *of worship'*.[3] It is, as Levinas notes in his Talmudic writing, a pedagogy of doing in order to understand.

Liturgy as work

The word 'liturgy' originally meant a 'public work' [*œuvre*] or a 'service in the name of/on behalf of the people'. In the Christian tradition it means the participation of the People of God in the 'work of God'. Through the liturgy, Christ, our redeemer and high priest, continues the work of redemption in, with and through his Church.[4]

Liturgy is a work of the people. But, immediately liturgy is spoken of as ἔργον, a distinction needs to be made between *œuvre* and *travail*. The classical Greek origin of the term λειτουργία is 'public service, a function (ἔργον) undertaken on behalf of the people (λαός)'.[5] Liturgy is ἔργον – a work, a function, an activity.[6] The difficulty with understanding liturgy as *ergon* is that it tends towards an active understanding of liturgy as a task undertaken and fails to appreciate that any liturgical orientation is essentially passive and responsive, which finds its origin not so much in a subjective initiative but in the response elicited by an other-than-the-self. Liturgy is essentially *for-the-other*. As ἔργον, it is not so much the activity and expenditure of *travail* – though this is certainly part of it – but an *œuvre*, which involves a certain passivity. For Levinas, the meaning and direction (*sens*) of the liturgy is *œuvre*: '*Work [œuvre] thought radically is a movement of the Same towards the Other which never returns to the Same*' (*HAH*, 41). Liturgical intentionality is an intentionality which is provoked by and intends an other than the self. Liturgy is not so much something initiated by a subject, but is a work achieved and accomplished in the subject.

The philosophical sense of œuvre

To say that liturgy, as *œuvre*, is a movement of the Same towards the Other, a movement which has its origin not in the one who worships but in the one to whom worship is directed, is to assert the priority of alterity and the liturgical stance as one of response. Levinas uses the term 'liturgy' in a philosophical sense to express the non-allergic relationship of the same to the other. To be liturgical is to be responsive and drawn towards what is other than the self. The impetus of this movement is a pre-originary other who, like the work of grace in us,

preveniently precedes and enables the self to move beyond the self.
From the perspective of the self, the other has no origin, for as soon as
the self is there, the other has already been. The other person inhabits
a time and a space which the self cannot recuperate. The self and the
other person are never at the same time, and the self is always late or
delayed.

Now, Levinas describes the relation between the self and the other
person not only as asymmetrical but also in terms of diachrony. The
other person occupies a time which precedes my own in such a way
that my future is a constant attempt to recuperate the passing of the
other person. In this sense, the liturgical move is always a memorial
which gives a future.[7] My dealings with the other person are always
with goods which have already been provided – I know not whence
nor from whom – and what I give back is, in some sense, what
has already been given, an exchange of which I am not the author.
The core of the liturgical move is debt and indebtedness, a sense of
repayment, a sense of '*what return can I make?*' (Ps.116:12). What can
be given that has not already been given, where the very possibility of
giving presupposes the giving of the other to whom one might give?

It is this sense of indebtedness that provokes the movement of the
œuvre as liturgy. Its intentionality counters secular movement within
the world which is characterised by technics, instrumentality, and the
dominance of an economic, active model of understanding which
issues from the affirmation of the priority of the subject, and which
manifests 'an insurmountable allergy' to, and a horror of, the other. In
other words, the encounter with the other person offers a counter to
the self's tendency to enclose itself in its own secularity. Secularism is
not an egress from the subject but is a movement by which the other
is repatriated within the same. In this sense, it is opposed to liturgy. It
is also, in essence, an atheism, for, from the starting point of immanence and autonomy, it engineers 'a god adequate to reason, a god
comprehended who would not trouble the autonomy of conscience'
(*DEHH*, 188; *HAH*, 43).

Ann Smock, in her translator's introduction to Maurice Blanchot's
The Space of Literature, is helpful in pointing to the difference between
œuvre and *travail*. *Travail* has the sense of productive labour; it is *le
souci réalisateur*, 'the concern for real achievements', 'which implies
effective action'. 'This real purposefulness is the process by which

history unfolds, by which darkness is made to recede before the broad light of day' (*DEHH*, 188). *Travail* takes place in 'the world'. *Oeuvre*, on the other hand, 'has no place in the world'; it 'belongs neither to this world nor to any other, but to the "other of all worlds" in our own'. Work, as *œuvre*, 'excludes the complacent isolation of individualism, it has nothing to do with the quest for singularity'.[8] More specifically, just as desire provides the wider context for need, it is within the context of *œuvre* that *travail* is rendered possible. To affirm the liturgical sense of *œuvre* is as intending 'the "other of all worlds" in our own' is not to attempt to evade commitment and responsibility; rather it is to realise transcendence as commitment to and responsibility for the other person. It may be the case, as Levinas says, that 'the true life is elsewhere . . . But,' he adds, 'we are in the world',[9] and thus the salvific significance of secularity.

The recourse to liturgy reveals the true nature of subjectivity as a heteronomy, beyond the limits of the autonomy of the self and the freedom which rationality imposes. 'The heteronomous experience which we seek would be an attitude which cannot be converted into category and whose movement towards the other would not be recuperated in identification, nor return to its point of departure' (*DEHH*, 190). In opening on to heteronomy, *œuvre* ceases to be a transformative activity by a subject who, through technical skill and expertise, converts the foreign into the familiar, making it the objective counterpart of a subjective idea; such a project, fundamentally that of Heideggerian *Dasein*, extends a closed and categorial totality within which Being remains self-identical within the limits of its foresight (*Vorsicht*). Such a fabrication is *travail*, whereas the original structure of the relationship with the other is *œuvre*, which is the work of the other in me. 'The other is already inscribed in the same, the end in the beginning' (*HAH*, 41).

Expressed in terms of liturgical intentionality, the origin and term of subjective awakening is alterity. Liturgy, as *œuvre*, is '*a movement of the Same towards the Other which never returns to the Same*' (*DEHH*, 191; *HAH*, 41). It is an impetus beyond self towards an absolute other; it is a movement which is *free*, since it is a *movement* of the subject. But it is movement or a tendency which, though free, is conditioned by the advent of the other who enables a responsive movement beyond the confines of the same towards the other, the abandonment of the

same *for* the other person, without hope of return. Like the respir-
ation which always demands an initial inspiration, the freedom of
response is summoned and conditioned by a prior call to responsibility. Expressed scripturally, the work (*œuvre*) is an Abrahamic
movement of utter departure which is not the attempt to establish a
bridgehead towards alterity by which same and other would become
familiar, which would be the triumph of the same over the other;
rather the liturgical intentionality is a 'heteronomous experience', a
beckoned excendence into an unknown land. Liturgy is a pedagogy,
a doing in order to hear. It is exodus, a passage towards an unknown
future, without the possibility of return.

EUCHARISTIC EXISTENCE

The inspiration which provokes a liturgical intentionality translates
into a eucharistic subjectivity. Liturgy, as *œuvre*, is a movement whose
origin is not in the same but is provoked by the advent of the other,
and which is without return. This can be expressed eucharistically:
eucharistic existence is an existence which follows the structure of
responsibility as '*for-the-other*'. It also puts in place the logic of giving
as a constant *kenosis* and nourishment of the self, which follows the
dynamic of desire.

Now, just as need is phenomenologically reduced to expose desire
as its context, so is work as an overcoming labour (*travail*) exposed
as a work (*œuvre*) which is enabled by the other person. Subjectivity
is always and already in a situation of intersubjectivity, and only ever
realises itself as the *other-in-me*, a situation which realises the self as
'*for-the-other*'.

The displacement or usurping of the same by the other, which is
a re-designation of the nominative as accusative by which the *I* is
declined as *me*, is indicated by Maurice Blanchot when considering
writing and authorship. The work (*travail*) of writing is only accomplished when the work (*œuvre*) displaces and takes the place of the
subject, and gives the possibility of writing. Said otherwise, *travail*
only succeeds to the extent that it is under the auspices of *œuvre*;
travail must necessarily fail in order that the work (*œuvre*) may be
accomplished in me. In order that any writing may be accomplished,
subjectivity needs to be declined otherwise. Although the subject is

committed to the task of completing the work, nonetheless the work takes on a dimension of infinity and is beyond the power of the writer to complete. Blanchot writes,

The writer never knows whether the work is done . . . That the work [*œuvre*] is infinite means, for him, that the artist, though unable to finish it, can nevertheless make it the delimited site of an endless task [*travail*] whose incompleteness develops the mastery of the mind, expresses this mastery, expresses it by developing it in the form of power.[10]

In response to the demand that the work (*œuvre*) imposes, and the response which it summons as *travail*, the writer is thrown into the never-finished task of writing whose completion cannot be pronounced by himself. Writing, like responsibility, is a constant returning to what remains to be done, a constant; there is a constant returning to the work, yet what remains to be completed is interminable, a seemingly illusory labour. Thus, the writer 'only finishes his work at the moment he dies', with the corollary that 'the writer is dead as soon as the work exists',[11] which is to assert the displacement of the subject by, and in favour of, the *œuvre*. As Levinas says, '*Ecrire, c'est mourir*' (*SMB*, 16). Paradoxically, then, *œuvre* ends in the death of the subject. Its ultimate task is to defeat the power of subjectivity and affirm the primacy of alterity, which signifies by its own power and authority, and yet gives sense to subjectivity by exposing its liturgical nature as *for*-the-other. This is extreme *kenosis*, or *kenosis in extremis*.

The logic of giving

Liturgical existence culminates in eucharistic existence, which is an excoriation of the self by the other and on behalf of the other, and the declension of the subject as essentially 'for-the-other'. To be is 'to-be-*for*'. Liturgical intentionality is the intentionality of responsibility which is provoked and evoked, a moving beyond the self which does not return to the self, until and unless incarnated as justice. For Levinas, justice and responsibility are two sides of the same coinage, but the responsibility which the other provokes is already and always the foundation of justice.

The intentional movement from the liturgical to the eucharistic, without hope of return, puts in question the logic of gift, and giving and thanksgiving. Gifts are sheer expenditure without hope or promise of return. Such a movement of utter *kenosis* is addressed by Derrida in his consideration of the gift. The work, as eucharistic, is an orientation to what is other than the self without hope of return, but an orientation whose origin does not arise in the self. The character of thanksgiving is that it returns to the other what has always and already been given, and is evoked as responsibility. Thus, 'What return can I make, How can I repay the Lord for his goodness to me? . . . My *vows* to the Lord I will fulfill' (Ps. 116:12,18). Gift-giving is sheer expenditure, structured like responsibility which is always *for*-the-other. The liturgical *œuvre*, in terms of giving, is paradoxically itself problematical, for the very giving, if it is to be gift, demands what Derrida terms a double and radical forgetfulness on the part of the giver, a forgetfulness which is not only forgetful of giving but also a radical forgetfulness of having forgotten. Jean-Louis Chrétien relates this to the paradoxical incapacity of the finite to bear the infinite and the excessive. Phenomena are saturated.

Remembering does not conduct one to plenitude: it is not some kind of recapitulation, some complete grasp of my history, in full and definitive grasp such that my end would rejoin my founding principle . . . [T]he immemorial has for me something excessive about it, an excess that founds me, that sends me and destines me, and is known to me only obliquely, in the excess of being. It is not directly thematised.[12]

To remember the giving *as* giving, and the gift *as* gift, is to retain for oneself by way of recompense something of the gift, namely, the triumph of having given. So too, to look for the recipient to acknowledge the gift as gift is to await the return of the gift and to expect the completion of the economic cycle of giving and receiving, and so fall back into a self-assured subjectivity which not only annuls the gift as gift but thwarts the liturgical orientation of the gift as a movement of the same towards the other without hope of return. It is also to negate the gratuitous nature of grace, and the unmerited and unwarranted and unexacted nature of the gift being given.

Now, this strange structure of giving, as a movement provoked in the same with no promise or expectation of return – a liturgy of responsibility for the neighbour – is mapped out by Derrida in *Given Time*.[13] Usually, the logic of giving is understood according to the structure, 'A gives B to C', a compound logical structure which is indispensable if the gift is to be possible. '[S]ome "one" gives some "thing" to some "one other"'.[14] There is a movement from the same by way of the gift to the other. The gift negotiates the distance *between* the one who gives and the one to whom the gift is given. But, as Levinas points out in his consideration of the irreversibility of the relation between the self and the other person, a movement structured according to the accepted logic of giving would not be a liturgical movement absolved from the economy of giving, for economic giving implies the recognition of the gift as gift, and the consequent return of thanksgiving. In the logic of giving, Derrida explains, there is

a subject identical to itself and conscious of its identity, indeed seeking through the gesture of the gift to constitute its own unity and, precisely, to get its own identity recognised so that that identity comes back to it, so that it can reappropriate its identity: as its property.[15]

But further, not only does the 'economic odyssey' of giving constitute the identity of the giver; it also constitutes the one to whom the gift is given as identical. The economic cycle of giving appears 'as soon as there is a subject, as soon as donor and donee are constituted as identical identifiable subjects'.[16] Such an economic logic in which giving (*donner*) also implies giving back (*rendre*) destroys the gift as gift: 'these conditions of possibility define or produce the annulment, the annihilation, the destruction of the gift',[17] for within such a cycle, the logic of the gift is also the logic of the debt that the one to whom the gift is given owes the giver. The economy of giving argues: 'For there to be gift, *it is necessary* [*il faut*] that the donee not give back, amortize, reimburse, acquit himself, enter into a contract, and that he never have contracted a debt.'[18] The question of giving, then, is not so much 'What return can I make? How can I repay the Lord for his goodness to me?' (Ps. 116); rather it is the injunction that any giving must be done in secret. In almsgiving, the left hand must not know what the right hand is doing (Mt. 6:16–18).

Now, this is not without significance for a liturgical understanding of the subject as response and responsibility, the notion of the prevenience of grace, and the establishment of justice on the basis of responsibility (which is ontology on the basis of ethics). The truly significant gift is the gift whose origin and significance does not have a point of departure in the one who gives, but in the one who provokes and provides the possibility of giving. Gifts are given by way of response. Response, however, is provoked by the other person in the anonymity of *illeity*. The *illeity* which is at the core of *alterity* and is the excoriation of the subject is the prevenient and provocative origin of gift. Further, the significance of the gift is ordered not by the intention of the giver but by the one who provokes the giving and who, signifying *kath'auto*, orders intentionality and bestows meaning. As such, gifts are radically incapable of being memorialised, for their origin is other than the subject. Derrida raises the problem of the memorialisation of the gift:

It suffices therefore for the other to *perceive the gift* . . . to perceive its nature of gift, the meaning or intention, the *intentional meaning* of the gift, in order for this simple *recognition* of the gift *as* gift, *as such*, to annul the gift as gift even before the *recognition* becomes gratitude. The simple identification of the gift seems to destroy it.[19]

If recognition of the gift as gift becomes gratitude, it destroys the gift as gift; if the giving of the gift as gift is retained and memorialised, the gift is no longer gift; it is no longer utter gratuity or sheer grace. Recognising the symbolic significance of the gift as gift,

immediately engages one in restitution . . . From the moment the gift would appear as gift, as such, as what it is, in its phenomenon, its sense and its essence, it would be engaged in a symbolic, sacrificial, or economic structure that would annul the gift in the ritual circle of the debt. The simple intention to give, insofar as it carries the intentional meaning of the gift, suffices to make a return payment to oneself.[20]

To recognise the gift *as* gift is to enter into the obligation of debt, and maintain the economy of giving. If the one to whom the gift is given is obligated by the gift such that thanks is exacted or a gift in return is given, the gift is not truly a gift, but is a gift with strings attached, strings of obligation which can be retraced to the donor. Thus, says Derrida, 'the donee owes it *to himself* even not to give back, he *ought* not *owe* [*il a devoir de ne pas* devoir] and the donor ought not to count on restitution. It is thus necessary, at the limit, that he not *recognise* the gift as gift'.[21]

This demands, then, a radical forgetting, which is not only a forgetting of the having given, but a forgetting of the forgetting, an utter absolution. It is this necessity in giving which Jean-Louis Chrétien draws attention to: it is forgetfulness rather than remembrance which constitutes the gift as gift.[22] Derrida gives such a positive interpretation to this absolute forgetting; it is not simply a negative amnesiac non-experience but, as the affirmative condition of the gift, a happening which is outwith the economy of time, excessive to the grammar of ontology. The gift carries with it something excessive to itself which obscures its nature as a gift which might seek recompense, and this is not the impossibility but the very possibility of the gift. Gifts are, as Marion would say, excessive or saturated phenomena, the meaning of which cannot be recuperated by a meaning-bestowing subjectivity since the absolute significance of the gift is, one might say, not within the gift of the subject.

What, then, does '"to give" mean to say?'[23] What would a gift beyond signifying, an insignificant gift, a gift without intention to be gift, be? Levinas might pose the question: what is the significance of a gift whose signification is beyond the power of the subject to signify, since the significance of the gift is the one to whom the gift is offered? It would seem that, if gift is to be gift *as* gift, which is absolute gift, then it must be enacted outwith economy, and be conceived in the same way as the liturgical *œuvre* in which the same moves towards the other without hope of return. Liturgy is a return of the movement a self turning back on itself, 'the folding back of being upon itself' (*OB*, 28), in a self-affirming gesture of subjectivity. Expressed in the language of response and responsibility, the structure of giving follows the structure of responsibility: while I must be responsible *for*-the-other, I cannot expect that the other will be responsible for me. Responsibility, as a liturgical self-giving *for* the other person, is outwith the economic cycle of exchange. Expressed eucharistically, liturgy is absolute kenosis. But this is also to recognise that a liturgy of giving has the same structure as desire, and this, in turn, offers a response to Derrida's question of 'how to give time', for 'it so happens . . . that the structure of this impossible *gift* is also that of Being . . . and of time'.[24]

TIME AS A LITURGICAL PHENOMENON

When he considers giving, Derrida interestingly asks the question of how to give time'.[25] This has liturgical and eucharistic implications, for at the core of any consideration of eucharist is the notion of presence, recollection, and future orientation. For Levinas the liturgical is an egress without return which responds to sheer excess. It neither has an interest in being nor does its intentionality seek a return to a point of departure. Derrida exploits this economic background of interest and return, relating it to a subject-centred economy which is at odds with a religious and ethical *oikonomia*. The problem is that economy, like money, circulates.

> [T]he law of economy is the – circular – return to the point of departure, to the origin, also to the home. So one would have to follow the *odyssean* structure of the economic narrative. *Oikonomia* would always follow the path of Ulysses.[26]

The economic cycle of giving is that pursued by Odysseus who 'returns to the side of his loved ones or to himself; he goes away only in view of *repatriating* himself, in order to return to the home from which the signal for departure is given . . . [Economy] a *nostalgia*, a "homesickness", a provisional exile longing for reappropriation'.[27] It is precisely 'a folding back of being upon itself'. For Levinas, it the departure of Abraham from the familiar, 'without hope of return' which marks the structure of responsibility, of gift, of desire, and of time.

With regard to time, the asymmetry of the relation between the self and the other person is expressed in terms of *diachrony*. For Levinas, the self and the other person are not at the same moment. Yet, it is this very delay that gives the possibility of a self. Said otherwise, 'At this very moment in this work, here I am.'[28] With respect to the other person, the self always responds late and is always in arrears. There is always more that could have been given and there is always more that could have been done, for my unique responsibility for the other person cannot be delimited. This is an excessive ethics which responds to the excess of the other person *who* cannot be reduced to a *what*, for the significance of the other person lies in the realm of *illeity* which the self can neither define nor delimit but can only respond to. The other is its own signification, and opaque to any meaning-bestowing gaze which I might intend. In Marion's language, the other person in the *illeity* of his or her givenness to *me* is an icon, drawing me into responsive and responsible relationship which is the possibility of ethics, rather than an idol which simply reflects my looking, and returns my gaze to myself and confirms my identity in the realm of my being. (Icons gaze upon the subject, both disturbing the self and provoking response; idols are gazed upon by subjects who only can see their own reflection.)[29]

Now, in terms of the structure and nature of time, and how time is given, the notion of *delay* or being always *in arrears* or *indebted*, which is an indebtedness on the part of the one who gives the gift rather than one who receives the gift, is in play here. In his early phenomenological reflections, Levinas draws attention to the reflexivity of the verb 'to be'; it is not so much the case that one is; rather one is oneself (*on s'est*). *Être* is *s'être*. The solitary subject expends itself in holding itself together, but this is experienced as fatigue and indolence. To exist is always to carry the burden of existence which lags behind. This first *hypostasis* of existence and existent translate into labour and effort in the attempt to establish the *here* of subjectivity in which both existent and its existence are synchronised. But this *here* whereby a subject affirms itself in its own solitariness offers no possibility of escape from the enchainment of the subject to its *self*. Salvation from this situation is by way of the other person who intervenes. But this provokes a more profound delay; one is always late in responding to the other who has always been preveniently and provocatively there as the origin and possibility of a self. Thus, one comes across lately what has always and already been there earlier – the anteriority of the posterior, both phenomenologically and ethically.

Time is not within *my* gift. But it is this very impossibility of *my* giving time which hints at the possibility of giving, for if time is precisely that which I cannot give, then one must ask 'how to give time?' Or more precisely perhaps, 'how is time given?' As Derrida writes, 'if giving implies in all rigour that one gives nothing that is and that appears as such – determined thing, object, symbol – if the gift is the gift of the giving itself and nothing else, then how to give time?'.[30] The diachronic nature of the relation between the self and the other person gives further focus. I do not occupy the same time as the other person. I cannot recuperate the other person into a time which would be *for me*, a time in which *I give*. Hence 'the indispensable logic of the gift' in which 'A gives B to C', and which presupposes a common time, fails. The same and the other have no time in common, for the other person inhabits a past which I cannot recuperate, yet which on account of the failure of my recuperative attempts, actually gives me a future. The I, always being out of step, comes upon the other tardily.

Blanchot makes this point similarly when, following Levinas, he draws attention to the asymmetry in the relation between the self and the other person. The relation

is such that the relations, if they could be unfolded, would be those of a non-isomorphic field in which point A would be distant from point B by a distance other than point B's distance from point A; a distance excluding reciprocity and presenting a curvature whose irregularity extends to the point of discontinuity.[31]

Quoting Levinas, Blanchot notes that 'the curvature of space expresses the relation between human beings'.[32] Again, '[t]he form in which this [speech] relation is realised must in one way or another have an index of "curvature" such that the relations of A to B will never be direct, symmetrical, or reversible, will not form a whole, and will not take place in the same time; they will be, then, neither contemporaneous nor commensurable'.[33]

How, then, can the question of the impossibility of giving time, which Derrida asks, be answered? Perhaps by understanding that time itself is a gift and that time is realised as a giving which is a responsibility for the other person who, always excessive and thereby always appealing for more, continually unfolds a time wherein I may give. For Levinas, time is given in the unfolding in the infinite distance opened up by the absolute difference between the other and the same. As Levinas asks, 'How indeed could time arise in a solitary subject?' (*EE*, 93). Time is sociality. It 'is constituted by my relationship with the other' (*EE*, 93). Again, the

relationship with the future, the presence of the future in the present, seems all the same accomplished in the face-to-face-with the other [person] [*autrui*]. The situation of the face-to-face would be the very accomplishment of time; the encroachment of the present on the future is not the feat of the subject alone, but the intersubjective relationship. (*TO*, 79)

In other words, time is my impossibility. It is impossible for me. It is that which I cannot give. However, my impossibility is rendered possible in the relationship with the other who, in giving time, makes possible my impossibility. It is in this sense that time is essentially a *sacred* time for it unfolds as the relationship with the utter exteriority – the *holiness* – of the other. The absolute separation of the other from the self gives a distance which can be traversed in time. It is in this sense that the other, although he or she inhabits a past which, for me, is irrecuperable, gives a future which is yet-to-come. The immemorial becomes the possibility of eschatology, the possibility of a time of giving in which justice, borne of responsibility, may be realised. Derrida explains it thus: the economic logic of giving does not give access to exteriority and the possibility of a relationship beyond economic calculation; on the contrary, 'it is this exteriority that sets the circle going, it is this exteriority that puts the economy in motion. It is this exteriority that *engages* in the circle and makes it turn'.[34] On account of the relationship with an other (*autrui*), one is obliged by 'the law that obligates one to give even as one renders an account of the gift . . . to *answer* [*répondre*] still for a gift that calls one beyond all responsibility'.[35] In the face of the other, one must give an account and is held accountable. '*Il aura obligé.*'[36]

The dynamic of desire

The logic of giving, which is also the diachrony of time, is also the logic of desire. But this is a logic which is *otherwise than being*, and outwith ontology. There can be no correspondence between desire and the desired, otherwise desire would find itself satiated and extinguished. The desired is only ever known as desirable, and yet to be more fully discovered. The desired is excessive to the desire which it provokes and is only known in its desirability. Desire finds its satisfaction not in the possession of the desired – which would amount to the annulment of desire – but in the fact that, in its desirability, the desired thwarts desire's incursion upon itself, and so sustains desire as desire. In other words, desire, as an intentionality, is an unfulfilled intending that awaits a fulfilment which is always yet to come, and which, in fact, may never come, for the desired, always provocative and prevenient, is excessive to the desire which it excites, and desire is inadequate to its object.

But this is also the structure of liturgy. The work involved in liturgy, as movement beyond the self towards the other than the self, is inadequate to that other, for the other maintains itself beyond the economic cycle of satisfaction, and so sustains and provokes the work as a constant expenditure without hope of return.

Eucharistic time

Now, the diachrony between the self and the other person opens up a future. The immemorial gives itself eschatologically. Thus labour becomes productive in favour of what is yet to come. 'To renounce being the contemporary of the triumph of the work, is to have this triumph in a time *without me*, to intend this world here without me, to intend a time beyond the horizon of my time' (*DEHH*, 192). The liturgical orientation of the work is a self-sacrifice for a time in which I have no place, a time moreover, which is indifferent to me and my death; with respect to the future I am *a-topical* and an anachronism; the work as liturgy is an obligation to 'an eschatology without hope for the self or liberation in respect of my time' (*HAH*, 42).

Such a seemingly utter kenosis of the self in favour of the other person is not to be understood as the annihilation of the self, but rather as the constitution of the self. 'To be' is to be 'for-the-other-person'. This, for Levinas, in an extreme movement of responsibility without substitution, is the sole meaning of subjectivity. *Kenosis* is a displacement of the self in favour of the other person, a yielding of my place in the sun to make way for the other who has prior claim. Such a kenotic self-displacement is the transfiguring movement of the self from its signification as '*pour-soi*' to its signification as for-the-other-person. No longer is it the case, as with Heidegger, that human existence is to be interpreted as a 'being-towards-death' but rather as a 'being-towards-after-my-death' (*DEHH*, 192). It is '*l'être-pour-au-delà-de-ma mort*' (*HAH*, 42) which is to be for the one who is after me. The indifference of the future towards my death, then, opens on to my own non-indifference towards the other. Thus the liturgical sense of the work as *for*: *for* a time without me, *for* a time after my time, *for* the time of the other, *for* the other. 'We work *in* the present, not *for* the present' (*HAH*, 43). This work which has been begun in

us as a relationship with a *beyond* is not an illusory relationship that
negatively opens on to nothingness (*néant*) but rather is a positive
relationship with the other 'who is attained without showing himself
touched' (*DEHH*, 191). Such a positive relationship, as commitment
to a future, is eschatological, and 'such a work can be termed liturgy'.
God has not yet shown his face, for his face is invisible and can neither
be shown nor intended (*viser*) apart from justice, and only ever as a
trace; the notion of God is 'yet-to-come' like a 'God who comes to
mind'. Liturgy is not necessarily to be taken in its religious sense, 'even
if a certain idea of God should show itself as a trace at the end of our
analysis' (*DEHH*, 192). Thus does the phenomenological reduction
proceed.

Diachrony and diakonia

Now, as service of the people, liturgy is not only a generous impetus
towards the other without thought of return to the same, but also
involves the loss of one's base (*HAH*, 43). This unsettling loss of the
firm ground on which the solitary subject stands, however, which is
a de-basement and dis-placement of the self, does not result in the
annihilation of the self or its vertiginous fall into an abyss where the
self is lost; rather, the self is re-placed. The first, ontological, hypostasis
which was the basis of subjectivity as the relation of the self to its own
existence is not transformed by a second, ethical, hypostasis in which
the self is no longer simply *for-itself* but is, rather, *for-the-other*. In
short the prevenient advent of the other person draws self-enclosed
subjectivity beyond its own self-enclosure into ethical, or liturgical,
existence. The 'sovereign co-incidence' of the self with itself – the self
as for-itself – is overthrown.

Liturgy, precisely as a pedagogy of worship in which one is related
to the 'glory' and the 'holiness' of the other, is ultimately a work of
substitution in which the relationship with the other is experienced
positively not as subjection but as service, as *diakonia*: 'the wisdom
of love in the service of love'. It is not that liturgy is worship and
cult and thereafter and distinctly also ethics. As an action which
is absolutely patient and responsive to the advent of an other than
the self, liturgy does not range itself 'as a cult besides "works" of
ethics. It is ethics itself' (*DEHH*, 192; *HAH*, 43). Hence the truth of

the term 'divine *service*'. From the first, liturgy, as a transcendence towards an other than the self, is ethical. Further, as we have already said, it is a transcendendence in which the distinction between the other person and transcendence towards God must not be made too quickly (*EN*, 87), as we shall see when considering the nature of justice.

CHAPTER 7

Eucharistic responsibility and working for justice

In what has been presented previously, Levinas' mistrust of theology as a discipline which tends towards the theoretical, compromises the transcendence of the divine by seeking to make it accessible to thought, and bypasses the demands of responsible and ethical involvement with the other person, has been a constant caution. To conceptualise the divine often involves a forgetfulness of the human economy, which is the economy of salvation. For Levinas, there can be no access to the divine other than by way of the human. This is why ethics is fundamental. It is not only 'first philosophy' but also 'first theology'.

This is the reason why Levinas stresses the positive value of *a-theism*, which is a prelude to an adult religion which has no place for 'some kind of kindergarten deity who distributed prizes, applied penalties, or forgave faults and in his goodness treated men as eternal children' (*DF*, 81). The way to a relationship with the true God of monotheism has 'a way station where there is no God' (*DF*, 82). But such a halt on the way always, for Levinas, involves an essential and necessary detour along the way of the human. There is no recourse to the divine other than by way of the human. Levinas' ethical metaphysics is terribly incarnational. It may be argued that 'the true life is elsewhere' but, for Levinas, 'we are in the world', and it is within the world of responsibility and justice that one finds salvation. Salvation is a terribly secular affair, as long as the significance of the secular in its excess is grasped. To be 'in-the-world' is to find oneself in the midst of phenomenal excess and saturation.

One could express this in terms of a fundamental theology by quite simply saying that one cannot begin to ask the question about God until one has first asked the question about the one who is able to ask the question about God. The human existential is fundamental to the theological enquiry. Hence the stress throughout on 'fundamental theology' which is, at its most basic, a theological anthropology. Thus do phenomenology and theology occupy the same existential and ethical terrain.

But now, in the present, two main themes need to be associated: responsibility 'for-the-other' which opens on to justice 'for-the-many', and also the notion of eucharist which is a focal and foundational aspect of Christian theology. What will need to be resisted is doing violence to Levinas and recasting him as a theologian. Perhaps, it is the countermovement which is suggested: that Christian theology needs to revisit its more Jewish origins. But, since theology is a thoughtful discipline which speaks of significance, and since the ethical encounter with the other person, and the many other persons, is provocative and challenging, there is the mutual demand for theology and phenomenology to be equally rigorous in their attention to the phenomenological and theological reduction of the human, intersubjective, existential. The key point is that if, following Levinas, ethics is both first philosophy and first theology, phenomenology and theology cannot be otherwise than dialogical partners in service of the human: 'the wisdom of love in the service of love'.

LITURGICAL AND EUCHARISTIC SUBJECTIVITY

For Levinas, the human and the divine are entwined. God, as he stresses often, arises as the 'counterpart of the justice we render to others'. Responsibility and justice are related. The singular other person, who is unique, summons me to responsibility and affirms me as unique. But this unique other opens on to many others who also call upon my responsible response. In the face of the other person, the whole of humanity appeals to me. And so, responsibility opens on to justice which involves *me* in embarking on an exercise of attempting to compare incomparables. Now this can be expressed in terms of liturgy, for the work of liturgy intends not only the person but also God who is other than the other, and whose universal paternity is the basis of justice. Liturgy is a work begun in the self by an other than the self which does not seek to return to the self. Thus is ethical subjectivity constituted by the prevenience of the other person *as response and responsibility*. This is basically the thrust of Levinas' entire argument as is indicated when he presents *Totality and Infinity* as a defence of interiority on the basis of exteriority.

But one can also express the structure of subjectivity eucharistically. Eucharistic responsibility is a responsibility which intends justice. The liturgical and eucharistic orientation of the self intends a world other than it is, a world in which justice can be realised on the basis of responsibility for the other. Such a world may only be given as hope and as promise in a time which is not our own and in which we may not share. The nature of temporality has already been indicated in Levinas' *Time and the Other*. Time is given by the other person. Jean-Louis Chrétien has expressed this in terms of the immemoriality of the past which, in the attempt at constant recuperation in the present, opens on to an eschatological future. Thus are eschatology and working for justice brought together. But such is also the structure of eucharist which is also an essentially temporal event undertaken in the present as an attempt to memorialise an immemorial past, and which attempt at memorialising gives a future yet to come. The *unforgettable* is the *unhoped for*. The Good, which is that which is yet to come, 'is that which escapes all anamnesis'.[1] Aquinas, who should not be read as a Heideggerian at this point, indicates as much when he writes of the eucharist: '*O Sacred banquet in which Christ is our food: the memory of his passion is recalled, grace fills our lives, and a pledge of future glory is given.*'[2] The attempt to recuperate a past gives a present as a working towards a future given as pledge, promise, and hope.

Now, within the Christian narrative, the eucharist is focal. Paul writes:

For this is what I received from the Lord, and in turn passed on to you: that on the same night that he was betrayed, the Lord Jesus took some bread, and thanked God for it and broke it, and he said: 'This is my body, which is for you; do this as a memorial of me.' In the same way, he took the cup after supper, and said, 'This cup is the new covenant in my blood. Whenever you drink this, do this as a memorial of me'. Until the Lord comes, therefore, every time you eat this bread and drink this cup, you are proclaiming his death. (1 Cor. 11:23–26)

Eucharist, which is both a liturgy of responsibility and a liturgy of justice and which, in looking to the past opens up a future, finds clear expression in its central narrative which intimates that the attempt at the memorial which gives a future is both '*for-you*' and '*for-many*'. It attempts both responsibility for the singular other and justice for the many others. These two related moments of responsibility and justice are intimately connected in the words of the institution narrative which can, and should, be read ethically. First,

On the night he was betrayed, he took bread, said the blessing, broke the bread and gave it to his disciples, saying: 'Take this, all of you and eat it. This is my body which will be given *for you*.'

Responsibility, as 'for-the-other', has the same 'for-structure' of the eucharist. 'This is my body' which is 'for-you'. Then,

In the same way he took the cup filled with wine. Again he gave you thanks, gave the cup to his disciples and said: 'Take this all of you and drink from it. This is the cup of my blood, the blood of the new and everlasting covenant. It will be shed for you and for many (*pro multis*) so that sins may be forgiven. Do this in memory of me.'

Eucharist, as responsibility, is also a work of justice, even to the point of being subjected to death 'for-the-other'.

One hesitates here, for this is going further than Levinas might go. But, this particular 'halt' or theological 'way station' can be reflected on further with Levinas.

A QUASI-CHRISTOLOGICAL PAUSE: 'A MAN-GOD (*UN HOMME-DIEU*)'[3]

It is important to be aware of the scope and limits of doing theology with Levinas. Levinas is not a theologian, nor does he claim that what he attempts is theology. In fact, he admits that he has often been criticised for ignoring theology. Yet, ethics is both first philosophy and first theology. As such, what Levinas argues becomes a propaedeutic for theology whose point of departure, fundamentally, is in the human, intersubjective, existential. *Le point de départ de la métaphysique* is the ethical encounter with the other person, and ethics of responsibility and justice which opens on to the God who arises as the counterpart of the justice which the *I* renders to the other person. For Levinas, with his exacting phenomenological method, the human is the starting point of any theology. As he notes, 'one may wonder whether the first word of revelation must not come from man, as in the ancient prayer of the Jewish liturgy in which the faithful gives thanks not for what he receives, but for the very fact of giving thanks' (*EN*, 56).

Levinas' article, 'A Man-God' – an interesting reversal of the Christian preference for the 'God-Man' – is worth considering. This short article draws together many of the main themes, hints, and suggestions which have been presented in this work, often only by way of allusion. He begins with the notion of Incarnation, 'the mystery of mysteries' of Christian theology, both a scandal to Jewish thinking and folly to the Greeks. Yet, Levinas' thought is terribly incarnational. Its focus, however, is on the 'Man-God' rather than on the 'God-Man'. A brief outline and comment on this article will help draw together Levinas' thinking from a fundamentally theological perspective.

'Philosophy is a bringing to light'. From the start, philosophy is phenomenological in intent, yet the 'mystery of mysteries' is an excessive or saturated phenomenon which is a phenomenological and theological provocation. The common tradition, and the tendency towards the good, as well as the recollection of the 'tragic years' of holocaust is recalled – a past that cannot be forgotten but can never be memorialised as a past. Two dimensions are brought together: on the one hand, the notion of the 'God-Man', a God-incarnate, compromises the transcendence of God. It is a scandal. It involves the 'idea of a self-inflicted humiliation of the part of the Supreme Being, of a descent of the Creator to the level of the Creature' (*EN*, 53). The most 'active activity' becomes the most 'passive passivity'. Yet, the compromising of the transcendence of God in the notion of the 'God-Man' is not the focus; rather it is the reconsideration of the human in its orientation towards the divine, or its divine intentionality, in terms of 'expiation for others' or 'substitution' whereby 'to be' is 'to be for-the-other-person', and unique identity arises as singular responsibility for the other person. The significance of the 'Man-God' is the transfiguration of a subjectivity as responsibility, where 'to be' is to be 'for-the-other-person'.

Now, also implicated here is the notion of the excessive phenomenon which strikes, often forcibly like a blow against the cheek, and forces phenomenology further. This is the world that writers such as Marion, Henry, and Chrétien visit. Levinas writes,

These ideas, at first blush theological, overturn the categories of our representation. So I want to ask myself to what extent these ideas, which have unconditional value for Christian faith, have philosophical value, and to what extent they can appear in phenomenology. True, it is a phenomenology that is already the beneficiary of Judeo-Christian wisdom, That is no doubt the case – but consciousness does not assimilate everything in the various wisdoms. It supplies phenomenology only with what has been able to nourish it. Hence I ask myself to what extent the new categories we have just described are philosophical. I am certain that this extent will be judged insufficient by the believing Christian. But it may not be a waste of time to show the points beyond which nothing can replace religion.

I think that the humility of God, up to a certain point, allows for conceiving of the relationship with transcendence in terms other than those of naiveté or pantheism; and that the idea of substitution – in a certain modality – is indispensable to the comprehension of subjectivity. (*EN*, 54)

The force of transcendence, in human terms, appears in humility. What is placed in question here is the adequacy of phenomenological method when faced with the excess of religious exteriority; the phenomenological model of representation does not give access to reality. Phenomenological access finds itself confounded by the excess of its intended object. There is also the reconsideration of subjectivity in terms of responsibility, where the *I* is to be understood as *for-the-other* to the point of substitution – *usque ad mortem*. What Levinas substitutes for divine condescension and compromise are the notions of passivity and expiation which become the language and the voice with which subjectivity can give an account of itself. Subjectivity is a liturgical movement of responsibility which has eucharistic implications, for the work that has no hope of return to the self is a work that intends, and is provoked by, the other.

Thought, as representation, may be inclined to keep gods at a distance such that humanity no longer stands before the presence of God; but more significantly thought is disturbed by the fact that 'infinity manifests itself in the finite, but does not manifest itself *to* the finite', and this is an 'extra-ordinary surplus' *(EN*, 54). How then does one begin to appreciate 'a Man-God'? It can only be in terms of responsibility which is always 'for-the-other' which, though always otherwise than being, is also a being otherwise. The humiliation of God, which could be interpreted as the humility of a God who subjects himself to being humbled, is disturbing. Humility is a particular '*way of being* which is perhaps the source of its moral value' (*EN*, 55), an exilic way of appearing in the world without being of the world. Humility has ontological import. It disturbs the structures which order existence in the world by introducing the ethical.

> Humility disturbs absolutely; it is not of the world. Humility and poverty are a bearing within being – an ontological (or meontological) mode – and not a social condition. To present oneself in this poverty of the exile is to interrupt the coherence of the universe. To pierce immanence without thereby taking one's place in it. (*EN*, 55)

In short, ethics interrupts ontology, and forces it to think otherwise. Justice is constantly knocking on ontology's door, demanding more. Confronted with the other person, ontology as the context of understanding is usurped. The other person is 'an extirpation from the context of the world, from the world signifying as a context' (*EN*, 57).

But this has theological implications. God may no longer be the ontological support of the universe, the 'transcendent signified' who supports an ontological narrative of meaning, as Derrida would say. However, the divine withdrawal is not without significance. God withdraws, and even becomes silent, to give place to the human. This was the insight of Yosl Rakover when he spoke to God in the Warsaw ghetto (*Yossel Rakover s'adresse à Dieu*), and realised that the unresponsive God surrendered proximity to enable human responsibility. The retreat of God enables the advance of the human; atheism, as Levinas understands it, is the prelude to an ethics of responsibility and a commitment to justice. Humility's first move is a distancing, a *remotio*. Alterity, or otherness, challenges from the *outside*, and refuses both system and ontology by the very fact of its non-participation or incorporation.

> In order that the extirpation from the order be not ipso facto a participation in the order, this extirpation – by a supreme anachronism – must precede its entrance into the order. It requires the inscription of a retreat in the advance and, as it were a past that was never present . . . [T]his anachronism in which an entrance follows the withdrawal and which, consequently, has never been contained in my time and is thus immemorial – is what we call trace. But the trace is not just one more word: it is the proximity of God the countenance of my fellowman. (*EN*, 57)

It is in terms of responsibility for the other person that there is 'the transubstantiation of the Creator into the creature'; 'the notion of the Man-God affirms the idea of substitution' (*EN*, 58), a substitution which rehabilitates subjectivity as responsibility for-the-other and unlimited passivity before the other.

This is perhaps as far as we can go with Levinas. The person of Jesus serves as an example of what the human is and is called to be; the proximity and presence of God in the world can only be articulated in terms of the neighbour and the responsibility and justice which this provokes. Thus,

I alone can, without cruelty, be designated as victim. The *I* is the one who, before all decision, is elected to bear all the responsibility for the World. Messianism is that apogee in Being – a reversal of being 'persevering in his being' – which begins in me. (*EN*, 60)

THE PROXIMITY OF GOD IN THE WORKINGS OF JUSTICE

Responsibility and justice are two sides of the same coin: to be is not only to be *for* the singular other but for the many others. The work of justice, however, needs to be articulated eschatologically: the time which is yet-to-come gives a present in which justice begins to be realised. To work for justice is to live and work for a time beyond myself. It is an expiation.

Now, liturgy, both philosophically and eucharistically, can be said to intend justice. Liturgy, as a work which is begun in me but not by me (though often the commitment to liturgical living is sheer effort and expenditure by the self), is a movement beyond myself, and its fulfilment is service of an other than the self. Liturgy is egress towards a provocative excess. '*The work thought radically is a movement of the Same toward the Other that never returns to the Same*' (*HO*, 26). Liturgy is *provoked*, and because the reality by which it is provoked is always 'yet-to-come', it is a constant provocation, and a provocation that is also a constant *travail*. The *liturgy of the neighbour* is a work without end, for its demands, though imposed in the present, are always yet-to-come.

It could also be said that liturgy is akin to being on a constant pilgrimage. To be is always to be *in statu viatoris* with a provocative pebble in my shoe, a constant irritation from which there is no respite. Recalled here is the Abrahamic journey which Levinas refers to in contrast to the Odyssean itinerary: Abraham, in response to a call, leaves the familiar for an unknown land. Like liturgy, there is a departure towards an unknown time and place with no hope of return. Similarly, the Exodus experience: Israel moves from a situation of slavery and injustice in Egypt and wanders in the wilderness for forty years – not without murmuring – towards a land of promise, which Moses has sight of, but to which he is refused entry. It is given to him only as hope and promise yet, despite this, the movement towards it continues. 'The Work is then a relationship with the other, who is reached without showing itself touched' (*'L'Oeuvre est donc une relation avec l'Autre, lequel est atteint sans montrer touché'*). It is 'to act without entering into the Promised Land' (*HO*, 27).

The structure of liturgy is also the structure of justice: its orientation is eschatological, its incarnation is a present demand. The time of justice is yet to come, but hope for justice which the plight of the other person provokes gives a time in which justice might be realised. Time is 'patience'. Working for justice is a *passion* borne of the *passivity* of the self confronted by the plight of the other and the many, and is an *impatience* for that which is yet-to-come but which *might never come.* The justice yet-to-come is an unknown future, but as 'yet-to-come' it presents a future in which justice might be realised.

Now, Levinas considers the time in which justice might happen when he reflects on Heidegger's understanding of human existence as a 'being-towards-death [*Sein zum Tode*]'. Death marks the end of time as we know it. In his course of lectures on 'Death and Time' (7 November 1975), Levinas begins by saying that death – as an unknown future – gives time as patience: 'death is a point from which time takes all its patience, this expectation that escapes its own intentionality *qua* expectation' (*GDT*, 7). In other words, as expectation, *time* is given *as hope* for a future, but a future which is uncertain and unknown, and certainly not guaranteed. Implicated here is the question of whether, as a particular intentionality, hope has an object; and indicated is the breakdown of the Husserlian correlation of *noesis* and *noema*, and its privileging of cognition and representation. Against Heidegger, Levinas continues,

If the *Sein zum Tode* . . . does not exactly seem to posit death within time, this refusal to treat time and death in relation to being does not reserve us the facility of a recourse to eternal life . . . For the reduction of death to this dilemma [of being or nothingness] is a reverse dogmatism, whatever the feelings of an entire generation suspicious of the immortality of the soul, considered as the sweetest 'opium of the people'. (*GDT*, 8)

In other words, death does not so much open on to a time beyond the grave which is a hope which might be vain; rather, one is committed to a time beyond my own death, a time which I will not inhabit, but a time which is repatriated in the here and now as the responsibility of working for justice for the one and the many.

To be *for* a time that would be without me, *for* a time after my time, over and beyond the famous 'being for death', is not an ordinary thought which is extrapolating my own duration; it is the passage to the time of the other. (*BPW*, 50)

The notion of sacrifice is implicated here. Work, insofar as it is oriented towards the other, is an enabling of a generosity on my part by the other for the other. It is 'liturgy' – a work without remuneration. It is a responsibility which intends an ethical world other than it is; it is 'an action for a world to come, of going beyond one's epoch' on the basis of 'the epiphany of the other' (*BPW*, 50). The liturgical orientation of the self is a 'working-towards' what is unknown, not-yet-present, and yet-to-come. Levinas quotes Léon Blum who, writing from prison in 1941, said, 'We are working in the present, *not for the present* . . . "Let the future and the things most remote be the rule of all the present days" (Nietzsche)' (*BPW*, 50–1).

ETHICS AND JUSTICE, AND THE LIFE OF THE
WORLD-TO-COME

The danger of a theological approach to Levinas is that it runs the risk of becoming theory which is devoid of ethical inspiration or impetus. The question can be asked whether Levinas simply offers another good idea, albeit an ethically inspired good idea, which offers another interpretation of the world rather than seeking to change it. In short, to raise Marx's objection to philosophical idealism: is Levinas one of those philosophers who 'have only *interpreted* the world' or does his thought have the power 'to *change it*' (*Theses on Feuerbach*, XI)? Is Levinas' ethical metaphysics, with its interest in and emphasis on the ethical, merely an ethical idealism, or does it also display a '*categoric imperative to overthrow all relations* in which man is a debased, enslaved, abandoned, despicable essence'.[4] Is Levinas' ethics interpretative or transformative? Does Levinas only present a vision of a world to come, or supply the means for its realisation?

Totality and Infinity begins by saying that 'it is of the highest importance to know whether or not we are duped by morality' (*TI*, 21). Does morality fool us into thinking that things can be otherwise than they are at this moment? Does morality hold out the possibility of a new humanism, or are we consigned to be forever held within the realm of the political which is opposed to morality?

Morality will oppose politics in history and will have gone beyond the functions of prudence or the canons of the beautiful to proclaim itself unconditional and universal when the eschatology of messianic peace will have come to superimpose itself upon the ontology of war. (*TI*, 22)

Is this simply a messianic vision, or does a commitment to a future make a difference in the present? The answer must be that the commitment to a future without me does make a difference in the present. The summons to be responsible for the other person translates into the demand of justice, and the ethics places ontology in question.

Giving a responsible account of the self

'To be is to be responsible for'. '*For*' is the meaning of subjectivity. The work of justice finds its impetus in responsibility for the other person, and is experienced as an imposed obligation. The self is no longer to be declined as *I* but as *me*, both in the accusative and accused. No longer is the subject 'for-itself' (*pour-soi*), but is summoned and challenged to be 'for-the-other' (*pour-l'autrui*). Subjectivity is a subjection by the other which results in the ethical demand to be *for* the other, such that the self is constituted as 'for-the-other', where this 'for' is the 'for' of responsibility. In fact, *my* uniqueness as a subject is quite simply that it is *me*, and no one else, who is responsible. My responsibility cannot ever be vicariously surrendered to another. I am constituted, or individuated, *as responsibility*. Levinas writes,

[R]esponsibility is inalienable. A responsibility you yield to someone is no longer a responsibility . . . I have always thought that election is definitely not a privilege; it is the fundamental characteristic of the human person as morally responsible. Responsibility is an individuation, a principle of individuation. On the famous problem: 'Is man individuated by matter, or individuated by form', I support individuation by responsibility for the other. It is also hard; I leave the whole consoling side of this ethics to religion. (*EN*, 108)

Ethical existence is the hypostasis of the 'other-in-me'. It is the turgescence of responsibility.

Responsibility opens on to justice. But, such an excessive responsibility which extends to a responsibility for the entire world would suggest that the subject is summoned to be the 'ethical Atlas' bearing the burden of the whole of humanity. Certainly, this is the sense that one can draw from Levinas' frequent quoting of Markel's words from Dostoievsky's *Brothers Karamazov*: 'everyone of us is responsible for everyone else in every way, and I most of all'. Responsibility for the entire world becomes an exponentially increasing excessive demand. This is perhaps why Levinas has been accused of subjecting the responsible subject to such violence. 'The problematical theory of justice' is linked to 'the problem of absolute commitment to the Other', but is this commitment to the Other (which is 'a disturbing form of idolatry') not a form of violence? Should the Other, either as a single person, or . . . as representative of all humanity, ever be the object of unlimited commitments?' 'Is not a person under such conditions threatened with an oppression, a violence just as great as any Levinas wishes to avoid by constructing his attack against "totality"?'[5]

Yet, Levinas himself moderates this unlimited commitment. This very 'unlimited initial responsibility' which 'justifies this concern for justice' for all 'has to manifest itself also in limiting itself' (*OB*, 128).

It will be good to end with Maurice Blanchot whose time is 'yet-to-come'. In *The Writing of the Disaster*, Blanchot writes of responsibility:

Responsible: this word generally qualifies – in a prosaic, bourgeois manner – a mature, lucid, conscientious man, who acts with circumspection, who takes into account all elements of a given situation, calculates and decides. The word 'responsible' qualifies the successful man of action. But now responsibility – my responsibility for the other, for everyone, without reciprocity – is displaced. No longer does it belong to consciousness; it is not an activating thought process put into practice, not is it even a duty that would impose itself from without and from within. *My* responsibility for the Other [*Autrui*] presupposes an overturning such that it can only be marked by a change in the status of 'me', a change in time and perhaps in language. Responsibility, which withdraws me from my order – perhaps from all orders and from order itself – responsibility, which separates me from myself (from the 'me' that is mastery and power, from the free, speaking subject) and reveals the other [*autre*] *in place* of me, requires that I answer for absence, for passivity. It requires, that is to say, that I answer for the impossibility of being responsible – to which it has always been consigned me by holding me accountable and also discounting me altogether.[6]

And, what of justice? Justice becomes an issue with the appearance of the third. '[T]he word "justice" applies much more to the relationship with the third party than to the relationship with the other.'[7] 'If there were no order of Justice, there would be no limit to my responsibility' (*EN*, 108). Again, 'the order of justice of individuals responsible for one another does not arise in order to restore that reciprocity between the *I* and its other; it arises in the fact of the third who, next to the one who is an other to me, is "another other" to me'(*EN*, 229).

Justice provides the ground for the appearance and the legitimation of the state, and its institutional framework. 'The entire recovery of Institutions . . . is done . . . starting from the third party.'[8] 'Justice requires and establishes the state' (*EN*, 195). And what is the state? None other than the community of those who seek not only to do justice, but to be just, because first and foremost each is called to be responsible for the other person, no matter the guise or the disguise in which he or she comes towards us. The advent of the other person opens a time of response and responsibility – a liturgical and eucharistic time – in view of a future which is also yet-to-come. The end is inscribed in the beginning.

Notes

INTRODUCTION

1. J. Derrida, *The Work of Mourning* (Chicago: University of Chicago Press, 2001), 201, quoting E. Levinas, *Four Talmudic Readings* (Bloomington: Indiana University Press, 1990), 48.
2. Derrida, *The Work of Mourning*, 202.
3. E. Levinas, *Of God who Comes to Mind*, 2nd edn. (Stanford: Stanford University Press, 1998), ix.

1. LEVINAS, PHENOMENOLOGY, AND THEOLOGY

1. See M. A. Lescourret, *Emmanuel Levinas* (Paris: Flammarion, 1997), 72. Herbert Spiegelberg notes the influence of these early works of translation, remarking that '[t]here can be little question that after the early thirties the centre of gravity of the Phenomenological movement has moved to the French Philosophical world' (H. Spiegelberg, *The Phenomenological Movement* (The Hague: M. Nijhoff, 1984), 425). Similarly, Dermot Moran writes, 'Phenomenology also translated into different philosophical climates, most notably in France, where Emmanuel Levinas began a tradition of exploration of phenomenology' (D. Moran, *Introduction to Phenomenology* (London: Routledge, 2000), xiv). Mohanty also implicates Levinas among those belonging to 'a distinctive line of Husserl interpretation in Belgium and France', particularly 'Levinas's critique of Husserl's prejudice in favour of the theoretical' (J. N. Mohanty, *Phenomenology: Between Essentialism and Transcendental Philosophy* (Evanston: Northwestern University Press, 1997), 163).
2. E. Levinas, *Existence and Existents* (The Hague: M. Nijhoff, 1978), 44 (hereafter *EE*).
3. S. de Beauvoir, *La Force de l'âge*, 141–2, in Spiegelberg, *The Phenomenological Movement*, 485. Levinas himself comments on this in a dialogue with Richard Kearney: '[I]t was Sartre who guaranteed my place in eternity by stating in his famous obituary essay on Merleau-Ponty that

he, Sartre, "was introduced to phenomenology by Levinas". Simone de Beauvoir tells how it happened, in one of her autobiographical works. One day in the early thirties, Sartre chanced upon a copy of my book on Husserl in the Picard bookshop just opposite the Sorbonne. He picked it up, read it, and declared to de Beauvoir, "This is the philosophy I wanted to write"' (in R. Cohen, *Face to Face with Levinas* (Albany: State University of New York, 1986), 16–17).

4. Jean-Luc Marion, *In Excess: Studies of Saturated Phenomena* (New York: Fordham University Press, 2002), 16–17. Michel Henry similarly draws attention to these three principles enunciated by Husserlian phenomenology (see M. Henry, 'Le Christianisme: Un approche phénoménologique', in P. Cappelle (ed.), *Phénoménologie et Christianisme chez Michel Henry* (Paris: Éditions du CERF, 2004). With regard to the first 'as much appearance [*apparence*], as much being', the notion of appearance is equivocal, referring, as it can, to *what appears* and its appearing; thus, he prefers 'as much appearing [*apparâitre*], as much being'. The decisive significance of this principle is that it subordinates ontology to a prior phenomenology. But, what pure phenomenology fails to clarify is the fact of the appearing itself, leaving it wholly undetermined. The second principle – 'to the things themselves' – also implicates the appearing of what appears. But what, asks Henry, gives access to things? 'It is pure phenomenality insofar as it phenomenalises itself which constitutes the mode of access to any conceivable phenomenon' (17). But the way in which phenomenality phenomenalises itself also remains wholly undetermined by phenomenology. The third principle of intentionality indicates that the object (*ob-jet*) is placed at a distance (*en-dehors*) – in other words, a phenomenological epoché – and so exceeds the scope of intentionality. But, argues Henry, it is this very excess, or going beyond (*dépassement*) which constitutes phenomenality in its purity. Like Marion, Henry argues that what appearing designates is the self-giving (*autodonation*) of what gives itself in its entirety, without remainder.

5. R. Bernet, I. Kern, and E. Marbach, *An Introduction to Husserlian Phenomenology* (Evanston: Northwestern University Press, 1999), 52.

6. Husserl, *Logical Investigations*, quoted in Bernet et al., *An Introduction*, 53.

7. Edmund Mussem, *Ideas Pertaining to a Pure Phenomenology and to a Phenomenological Philosophy*, trans. F. Kersten (Dordrecht: Kluwer Academic Publishers, 1983), 216.

8. Ibid., 91.

9. Ibid., 86–7.

10. Ibid., 212.

11. Ibid., 214.

12. Ibid., 214–15.
13. Ibid., 215.
14. Ibid., 34.
15. James Mackey's comment on Cartesianism is helpful here (*The Critique of Theological Reason* (Cambridge: Cambridge University Press, 2000)). Recognising that the two main philosophical streams of phenomenology and materialism have been 'commonly fathered upon Descartes' (Ibid., 11), Mackey reminds us that Descartes did not operate with the two primitive notions of *res cogitans* and *res extensa*, but with the more original notion of 'the one united human being, *une seule personne, qui a ensemble un corps et une pensée*' (Ibid., 11), a unity most clearly seen in the operations of the passions in the human soul as it encounters the world. In other words, the *integrity* of the human person is to the fore. '[T]he process by which we know the world of which we are so integral a part, is a process in which our embodied spiritual presence is active in engagement with it and passive with respect to its active engagement with us' (Ibid., 13). What Husserl manages is an initial reconsidering of the *Cartesian self* by which, in distinction to the 'kind of philosophising which resolutely begins from the material realm . . . [a]n alternative appears', 'a kind of philosophising which begins with the phenomenon' (Ibid., 50–1).
16. My own *italics*. I stress the notion of the *between* since this is of particular significance in Levinas' thinking.
17. See R. Sokolowski, *Introduction to Phenomenology* (Cambridge: Cambridge University Press, 2000), 17–21.
18. Levinas uses '*être kath'auto (kath hauto)*' often. Its rendering is often misspelt. See A. T. Peperzak, *To The Other* (Purdue: Purdue University Press, 1993), 159, n.26. Yet the term has settled itself in a basic Levinas' lexicon. Within Levinas' context, the principal idea is that otherness or alterity signifies in and from itself. The other person is his or her own meaning. What an other person *is* is not in the gift of a meaning-bestowing subjectivity, for the other person is always a 'who' and never a 'what', pronominal before ever nominal. Said otherwise, *kath'auto* affirms the exteriority of the other.
19. Marion, *In Excess*, 23.
20. Ibid., 19.
21. Jean-Luc Marion will develop this point when he remarks that '[a]ccording to phenomenology, absolute certitude resides in the affectedness of consciousness by lived experiences from every origin, not only or even entirely, by thought of self, on the express condition, nevertheless that these lived experiences accomplish a givenness'. Marion continues, 'every lived experience (and possibly the intentional object) . . . is confirmed absolutely' for phenomenology 'does not support the *ego* alone

and to itself, it certifies a whole world, because it no longer bases it on thought (thinking itself), but on the given as it gives itself (to consciousness)' (*In Excess*, 20). In other words, phenomenology takes as its point of departure the correlation between noesis and noema, and already implicates a world. Thereafter, subject and object can be derived.

22. In the works of Husserl published at the time of Levinas' writing of *The Theory of Intuition in Husserl's Phenomenology*.

23. The three theologians suggested are Bernard Lonergan, Karl Rahner, and, more recently, Jean-Luc Marion. Later others such as Michel Henry and Jean-Louis Chrétien will add their voices, mainly because they tend to develop Levinas' phenomenological insights more explicitly in a theological direction. However, interesting work has also been done on links between Levinas and Barth. See, for example, Johan F. Goud, *Emmanuel Levinas und Karl Barth: Ein religionsphilosophischer und ethischer Vergleich* (Bonn: Bouvier Verlag, 1992), and Dorothee C. von Tippelskirch, *Liebe von fremd zu fremd: Menschlichkeith des Menschen und Göttlichkeith Gottes bei Emmanuel Levinas und Karl Barth* (Freiburg/München: Verlag Karl Alber, 2002).

24. B. Lonergan, *Method in Theology* (London: Darton, Longman and Todd, 1975), 238. For a comparison of Levinas and Lonergan, see Michele Saracino, *On Being Human: A Conversation with Lonergan and Levinas* (Milwaukee: Marquette University Press, 2003). Saracino argues the need in Levinas of greater attention to method and suggests that 'Lonergan, with his refined strategy for moving towards authentic progress and realising the human good' advances Levinas along the methodological way (207). Certainly, Lonergan is more explicitly committed to phenomenology than is Rahner.

25. Lonergan, *Method*, 3.

26. Ibid., 4.

27. Ibid., 212.

28. Ibid., 23.

29. Ibid., 29.

30. Ibid., 57–60.

31. Ibid., 81.

32. K. Rahner, *Spirit in the World* (London: Sheed and Ward, 1994).

33. See J. Maréchal, *Le Point de la départ de la métaphysique, I* (Brussels: Editions Universelles, 1944), 12.

34. Rohner, *Spirit*, 75.

35. Marion, *In Excess*, 27.

36. Ibid., 29.

37. Ibid.

38. Dominique Janicaud (1937–2002) was a key interpreter and critic of Heidegger in France. Faithful to a rigorous and scientific

phenomenology, he was critical of the theological turn in French Phenomenology, a critique which forces both phenomenology and theology to think further. Simon Critchley draws attention to the significance of *The Theological Turn in French Phenomenology*, 'which initiated a whole series of debates and polemics among French philosophers. Essentially, the book was a polemic against the theologizing tendency towards a phenomenology of the inapparent or the invisible that can be found in the work of Jean-Luc Marion, Jean-Louis Chrétien and Michel Henry, but whose ancestry can be traced to the influence of Levinas' *Totality and Infinity*' (*Radical Philosophy*, Jan/Feb 2003).

39. S. Smith, 'Reason as One for Another: Moral and Theoretical Argument', in *Face to Face with Levinas*, ed. R. Cohen (Albany: State University of New York Press, 1986), 53.

40. J. Derrida, *Violence and Metaphysics* (Chicago: Chicago University Press, 1978), 312, n.7.

41. Cf. R. J. Bernstein, 'Evil and the Temptation to Theodicy', in *The Cambridge Companion to Levinas*, ed. S. Critchley and R. Bernasconi (Cambridge: Cambridge University Press, 2002), 252.

42. E. Levinas, *Éthique comme philosophie première* (Paris: Éditions Payot et Rivages, 1998), 107–9.

43. Dominique Janicaud, *The Theological Turn in French Phenomenology* (New York: Fordham University Press, 2000).

44. Ibid., 28.

45. Ibid., 27.

46. Ibid., 16.

47. Ibid., 22.

48. Ibid., 25.

49. Ibid., 25–6.

50. Ibid., 50.

51. Marion, *In Excess*, 28.

52. Ibid., 27.

53. Ibid., 28.

54. Ibid., 29. Michel Henry will argue that the 'relation between ethics and religion offers a privileged theme in which more is discovered in the essential coming together of a phenomenology of life and of Christianity' (Henry, *Le Christianisme*, 32).

55. J. Bloechl, *Liturgy of the Neighbor* (Pittsburgh: Duquesne University Press, 2000), 7–8.

56. L.-M. Chrétien, *L'Appel et la réponse* (Paris: Éditions de Minuit, 1992), 11.

57. See K. Rahner, *Hearer of the Word* (New York: Continuum, 1994). Following Aquinas, Rahner understands subjectivity in terms of 'an obediential potency', that is, as 'receptivity'.

58. Ibid., 60.
59. Ibid., 16.
60. A. Carr, *The Theological Method of Karl Rahner* (Missoula: Scholars Press, 1977), 92.
61. Janicaud, *Theological Turn*, 39.
62. Levinas, *Is it Righteous to be? Interviews with Emmanuel Levinas*, ed. Jill Robbins (Stanford: Stanford University Press, 2001). The interview was given in 1992.
63. R. Burggraeve, 'The Bible gives to Thought: Levinas on the Possibility and Proper Nature of Biblical Thinking', in J. Bloechl (ed.), *The Face of the Other and the Trace of God: Essays on the Philosophy of Emmanuel Levinas* (New York: Fordham University Press, 2000), 166.
64. S. Carmy and D. Shatz, 'The Bible as a Source for Philosophical Reflection', in Frank and Leaman (eds.), *History of Jewish Philosophy*, 16.
65. See, R. Burggraeve and A. Anckaert, *De Vele Gezichten van het Kwaad: Meedenken in het spoor van Emmanuel Levinas* (Leuven: Acco, 1996), 181–2, 187.
66. R. A. Cohen, *Ethics Exegesis, and Philosophy* (Cambridge: Cambridge University Press, 2001), 124, n.5.
67. See Cohen's chapter on 'Post-Modern Jewish Philosophy' in Frank and Leaman, *History of Jewish Philosophy*, 880. See also R. Burggraeve, *The Wisdom of Love in the Service of Love: Emmanuel Levinas on Justice, Peace, and Human Rights* (Marquette: Marquette University Press, 2002).
68. Cohen, *Ethics and Exegesis*, 125.
69. Levinas draws attention to Buber's 'ingenious' interpretation of 'we will do *and* (*vav*) we will understand' as 'we will do *in order* to understand', arguing that what is at issue 'is not to transform action into a mode of understanding but to praise a mode of knowing which reveals the deep structure of subjectivity (*Temimut*).' By saying 'we will do and we will hear' before it understands, Israel maintains its adherence to the good which comes before understanding and 'is not the result of a choice between good and evil'. (See *NTR*, 42.)

2. ETHICS, THEOLOGY, AND THE QUESTION OF GOD

1. R. Kearney, 'Interview with Emmanuel Levinas', in Cohen, *Face to Face with Levinas* (Albany: State University of New York, 1986), 18.
2. Cohen suggests that Levinas' writings can be broadly placed in four categories. The first two are more philosophical; the latter two might be considered 'religious' or 'Jewish writings'. First, there are those works which develop and deepen Levinas' 'own philosophical thought, his

ethical and dialogical metaphysics'. These would be early works and articles on Husserl's phenomenology such as *The Theory of Intuition in Husserl's Phenomenology*, articles gathered together in various philosophical collections which address strictly phenomenological themes, such as *Discovering Existence with Husserl and Heidegger*, *Existence and Existents*, *Time and the Other*, as well as major works such as *Totality and Infinity* and *Otherwise than Being or Beyond Essence*. Secondly, essays and articles that 'analyse and comment on the work of various modern and contemporary philosophers, critics, writers and poets' insofar as their concerns approximate to his own; many of these are gathered together in *Proper Names* and *Outside the Subject*. Thirdly, there are the 'Talmudic Readings', commentaries on various texts from the Talmud delivered to mainly Jewish audiences; these are gathered together in *Four Talmudic Readings*, *From the Sacred to the Holy*, and *New Talmudic Readings*. Fourthly, there are 'many brief and occasional pieces of general Jewish and religious interest', such as those in *Difficult Freedom* and *In the Time of the Nations*. (See R. A. Cohen, *Elevations: The Height of the Good in Rosenzweig and Levinas* (Chicago: Chicago University Press, 1994), 120.)

3. M.-A. Lescourret, *Emmanuel Levinas* (Paris: Flammarion, 1994), 92. This extensive biography of Levinas, not yet published in English translation, provides a detailed account of his life and work.

4. J. Kosky, *Levinas and the Philosophy of Religion* (Bloomington: Indiana University Press, 2001), xiv.

5. Kosky, *Levinas*, xix.

6. Ibid., xix–xx.

7. R. Gibb, *Correlations in Rosenzweig and Levinas* (Princeton: Princeton University Press, 1992), 10.

8. For a fuller and detailed treatment of this, see F. Ciaramelli, 'The Posteriority of the Anterior', *Graduate Faculty Philosophy Journal*, 20/2–21/1, (1997): 409 ff. Similar is evident in *Existence and Existents* where Levinas indicates that 'Thought . . . is . . . here' (68). Consciousness instantiates a subject. One 'comes to oneself' as consciousness. But consciousness, as we have seen, is always, '*consciousness of* '. Consciousness is characterised by intentionality, and intentionality is transcendence. The 'coming to oneself' implies an 'already having departed from'; consciousness, as a point of departure, already marks a point of having arrived.

9. See Tamra Wright, *The Twilight of Jewish Philosophy* (Amsterdam: Harwood Academic Publishers, 1999).

10. Ibid., xiv.

11. Ibid., 41.

12. Levinas' distinction between ethics and morality is important here. Morality is 'a series of rules relating to social behaviour and civic duty'

(Kearney, in Cohen, *Face to Face with Levinas*, 29); it is about 'the world of government, institutions, tribunals, prisons, schools, committees, and so on' (Ibid., 30). What is constantly evident in Levinas is that the moral and the political draw their impetus from the ethical encounter with the singular other person, who, in turn, challenges the moral and the political to rethink themselves. '[T]he norm that must continue to inspire and direct the moral order is the ethical norm of the inter-human. If the moral political order totally relinquishes its ethical foundation, it must accept all forms of society, including the fascist or totalitarian, for it can no longer evaluate or discriminate between them' (Ibid., 30).

13. Wright, *Twilight of Jewish Philosophy*, 41. Carmy and Shatz express the same ideas in the questions: 'Is an action right because God commands it, or does God command it because it is right? Is an action wrong because God prohibits it, or does God prohibit it because it is wrong?' (Carmy and Shatz, 'The Bible as a Source for Philosophical Reflection', in Frank and Leaman, *History of Jewish Philosophy* (London: Routledge, 1996), 16).

14. R. Burggraeve, 'The Bible Gives to Thought', in Jeffrey Boechl, *The Face of the Other and the Trace of God: Essays on the Philosophy of Emmanuel Levinas* (New York: Fordham University Press, 2000), 16.

15. Ibid., 155.

16. Ibid., 158–9.

17. Ibid., 164.

18. Ibid., 161.

19. Ibid., 165.

20. Ibid., 168.

21. Ibid., 180–1.

22. Carmy and Shatz, 'The Bible as a Source', 13–37; see also David Novak, 'The Talmud as a Source for Philosophical Reflection', in Frank and Leaman, *History of Jewish Philosophy*, 62–80.

23. Carmy and Shatz, 'The Bible as a Source', 13–14.

24. Ibid., 31–2.

25. I deliberately use the term 'describe' on account of its ambiguity. 'Description' is about trying to give an accurate account, as in 'describing an image or a picture or an event'. But one also 'describes a curve' as in the admonition of the geometry teacher, 'Let us describe a curve'. Certainly, Levinas intends a careful and accurate description of the phenomenon of the human which approximates to adequacy. But, more than this, Levinas' description is not simple reporting. It describes ethics as one might describe a curve. Here *describing* and *circumscribing* come together, and in conflict. Levinas, in describing, is not attempting to circumscribe the area of the ethical. To describe a curve is not to draw

a circle. The domain of ethical activity can be described; it cannot be circumscribed, for the other person is always an exception. Maurice Blanchot notes, 'Let me recall that Emmanuel Levinas gave this turn of speech its determinant signification: "The curvature of space expresses the relation between human beings"' (*The Infinite Conversation* (Minneapolis: The University of Minnesota Press, 1993), 441, c VII, n.1).

26. Marion, *In Excess*, 24.
27. Kosky, *Levinas*, xiii.
28. Ibid., xiii, xiv.
29. Ibid., xvii.
30. Ibid., xviii.
31. Ibid., xix.
32. Ibid., 149.
33. Ibid., xix.
34. Ibid., 155.
35. Ibid., xxi.
36. Janicaud, *Theological Turn*, 43.
37. Kosky, *Levinas*, xx.
38. Wright, *Twilight of Jewish Philosophy*, 71.
39. Ibid., 93.
40. Cohen, *Face to Face with Levinas*, 18. In interview with R. Kearney. One sees this in the Roman Liturgy where one reads in the fourth Eucharistic Prayer, 'from age to age you gather a people to yourself'.
41. Levinas speaks of this in 'The Temptation of Temptation' in *Nine Talmudic Readings*. Jewish thinking – even from the ashes of the Holocaust – embraces a creation which is meaningful and purposeful. Levinas affirms that reality is meaningful; but this meaning, coinciding with the meaning of creation, 'is to realise the Torah' (Ibid., 41); and, to realise the Torah is to usher in and establish the ethical order. In other words, beyond ontology, reality is ethical. 'The act by which the Israelites accept the Torah is the act which gives meaning to reality' (Ibid., 41). Ethics orders ontology. The question of the meaning of Being – Heidegger's *Seinsfrage* – 'finds its answer in the description of the way in which Israel receives the Torah' (Ibid., 41), for Mount Sinai was the moment when the 'to be' or the 'not to be' of the universe was being decided. Indeed, to have refused to accept the Torah, to have refused the ethical intent of creation, 'would have been the signal for the annihilation of the entire universe' (Ibid., 41), for the Torah, in its ordering of creation, subordinates creation to the ethical order. The acceptance of the Torah is the establishment of the ethical order, and its eventual fulfilment is the establishment of social justice. From the beginning the end is implicated. Creation and eschaton come together in the ethical purposefulness of the divine act: 'fruits come before leaves. Marvel of marvels: a history whose

conclusion precedes its development. All is there from the beginning'
(Ibid., 45). Israel refused the 'temptation of temptation' – the temptation
of knowing before doing – and did not refuse to accept the Torah.
42. S. E. Balentine, *The Hidden God* (Oxford: Oxford University Press,
    1984), 120. I follow Balentine's instructive study of lament in what
    follows.
43. Ibid., 120.
44. Ibid., 153.
45. Ibid., 155.
46. The nature of hope is worth considering further. Paul Moyaert draws
    attention to the necessarily unfulfilled or empty nature of hope when he
    writes that
       'Hope will inevitably shape certain expectations and expressions, even
    though it cannot give them definitive content. Hope is an orientation
    towards a future without genuine or ultimate content: it maintains a
    minimal distance or discrepancy with regard to the facts and events that
    contradict expectations. It shatters the atemporal eternity of the present.'
    (Paul Moyaert, 'On Faith and the Experience of Transcendence', in I. L.
    Bulhof and L. ten Kate (eds.), *Flight of the Gods* (New York: Fordham
    University Press, 2000), 381.)
       The very condition of hope is that its hoped-for object defies pres-
    ence. Something similar can be seen both in Karl Rahner and Maurice
    Blanchot. Hope is most hope when it has no object, when what is hoped
    for is not only improbable but may well be impossible. Rahner notes
    that hope 'is an act in which we base ourselves in the concrete, upon
    that which cannot be pointed to in any adequate sense at the theoretical
    level, that which ultimately speaking is absolutely beyond our power to
    control' (K. Rahner, 'Theology of Hope', in *Theological Investigations*,
    X (London: Darton, Longman and Todd, 1973), 254). Hope, in other
    words, is an empty and unfulfilled intending. Blanchot indicates that
    hope is radically and truly hope when what is hoped for might never
    be realised. 'Hope bespeaks the possibility of what escapes the realm of
    the possible; at the limit, it is relation recaptured where relation is lost.'
    (M. Blanchot, *The Infinite Conversation*, trans. S. Hanson (Minneapolis:
    University of Minnesota Press, 1993), 41.)
47. Balentine, *The Hidden God*, 123. Balentine refers to C. Westermann, 'The
    Role of Lament in the Theology of the Old Testament' (*Interpretation*,
    28 (1974): 26), and W. Brueggemann, 'From Hurt to Joy, From Death
    to Life' (*Interpretation*, 28 (1974): 7).
48. Balentine, *The Hidden God*, 124.
49. Ibid.
50. Bloechl indicates this when he notes that this extreme ethics culminates
    in dying for the other. 'Levinas the protector of the other is also Levinas

the purveyor of an infinite and relentless burden.' Who can resist Levinas' argument, and on what basis, for 'not only the ground, but also the landscape belong to Levinas' (J. Bloechl, *Liturgy of the Neighbour* (Pittsburgh: Duquesne University Press, 2000), 4).

51. The translation loses it somewhat. *Yossel Rakover s'addresse à Dieu (Jossel Rakovers Wendung zu Gott)*. In 'talking to God' there is no direct object. Reflexive verbs take no direct object. *On s'addresse à . . .* One addresses oneself to . . . It is as if the one who speaks becomes the one who is placed in question by that very speaking to an other. The address to God is always indirect, or by way of the ethical encounter with the other person. Thus does theology arise by way of the ethical.

52. Balentine, *The Hidden God*, 135.

53. Ibid., 165.

54. Ibid., 164.

55. Leora Batnitzky, 'On the Suffering of God's Chosen', in T. Frymer-Kensky et al. (eds.), *Christianity in Jewish Terms* (Boulder: Westview Press, 2000), 205.

56. Balentine, *The Hidden God*, 175.

57. Zvi Kolitz, *Yosl Rakover Talks to God* (London: Jonathan Cape, 1999), 3–4. Levinas comments,

'The text presents itself as a document written during the last hours of fighting in the Warsaw Ghetto. The narrator has apparently witnessed all the horrors; he has lost his young children in horrific circumstances. The last surviving member of his family, but only for a brief interval, he leaves us his last thoughts. Literary fiction, to be sure; but fiction in which all of us who survive recognise ourselves with a sense of vertigo.

'I am not going to tell the whole story, although the world has learned nothing and forgotten everything. I refuse to offer up the ultimate Passion as a spectacle and to use these inhuman screams to create a halo for myself as either author or director. The cries are inextinguishable . . . What we must do it listen to the thought that they contain' ('Loving the Torah more than God', in *Yosl Rakover Talks to God*, 80–1).

The refusal 'to offer up the ultimate Passion as a spectacle' is important. That which becomes a spectacle runs the risk of supposing meaning to be transparent to the one who looks. The question is whether the Holocaust as the 'ultimate passion' of innocent suffering has any meaning which might be grasped, or even whether it has any meaning at all. One recognises here the significance of Giorgio Agamben's consideration of the Mosselman in *Remnants of Auschwitz*, and the impossibility of giving witness to the witness. Martyrdom cannot be explained or represented. It can only be undergone (see G. Agamben, *Remnants of Auschwitz* (New York: Zone Books, 1999)). Elizier Berkovits notes that 'the sacrificial way of the innocent through history is not to be vindicated or justified!

It remains unforgivable' (E. Berkovits, *Faith after the Holocaust* (New York: Ktav, 1973), 136). Howard Wettstein, in his recent article, 'Against Theodicy', gives a worthwhile outline of the difficulties attendant on theodocies. See *Judaism*, no. 199, vol. 50/3 (Summer 2001): 341–50. In the face of suffering and the horror of the Holocaust, none can play the part of Job's companions.

58. Kolitz, *Yosl Rakover Talks to God*, 9–10.
59. Berkovits, *Faith after the Holocaust*, 136.
60. Kolitz, *Yosl Rakover Talks to God*, 18.
61. Ibid., 24.
62. See Moyaert, 'On Faith', 381–2.
63. Ibid., 383.
64. Kolitz, *Yosl Rakover Talks to God*, 18.
65. Levinas draws attention to the importance of Yosl's faithfulness when, in 'Useless Suffering', he refers to Emil Fackenheim: 'To renounce after Auschwitz this God absent from Auschwitz – no longer to assure the continuation of Israel – would amount to finishing the criminal enterprise of National Socialism . . . and the forgetting of the ethical message of the Bible' (*Difficult Freedom*, 163).
66. The Holocaust and the meaning of innocent suffering is a perduring question. 'What', asks Levinas, 'is the meaning of the suffering of the innocents?' ('Loving the Torah More than God', 81). For Levinas, innocent suffering has no intrinsic meaning. The attempt to specify and interpret suffering is a specious endeavour; suffering can only be undergone. So, too, the attempt to value and evaluate suffering is an unworthy enterprise. There is a sense in which sufferings are incomparable. As Batnitzky notes, 'The tension between recognising the ethical and theological value of suffering without assigning it an intrinsic value is important for post-Holocaust Jewish thinkers' (Batnitzky, 'On the Suffering of God's Chosen', 215). The Holocaust cannot be theologically justified. 'My neighbour's suffering is beyond justification; it is, in a word, meaningless' (Ibid., 218).

'How can Jews believe in an omnipotent, beneficent God after Auschwitz? Traditional Jewish theology maintains that God is the ultimate, omnipotent actor in historical drama . . . To see any purpose in the death camps, the traditional believer is forced to regard the most demonic, anti-human explosion of all history as a meaningful expression of God's purposes' (216, quoting R. Rubenstein, *After Auschwitz: Radical Theology and Contemporary Judaism* (New York: Bobbs-Merrill, 1966), 153).

With specific reference to Levinas, Batnitzky writes that '[t]he Jewish tradition often maintains a difficult balancing act when it affirms both the theological and ethical value of suffering for others, while denying

the necessity of suffering itself' ('On the Suffering of God's Chosen',
218). One cannot justify suffering. Thus an end to all theodicy, and 'to
all attempts, theological or otherwise, to justify suffering' (Ibid., 218).

3. INCARNATE EXISTENCE

1. Dominique Janicaud, *The Theological Turn in French Phenomenology*
   (New York: Fordham University Press, 2000), 22.
2. It is difficult to read the positive inscription at the start of *Otherwise
   than Being*, which is dedicated to the victims of the Holocaust and also
   lists the members of his own family who died as a result, without calling
   to mind the deliberate removal of the original inscription of Heidegger's *Being and Time* (London: Harper and Row, 1962 – hereafter *BT*)
   which was '*Dedicated to Edmund Husserl in friendship and admiration,
   at Todtnauberg in Baden, Black Forest, 8 April, 1926*'.
3. For a useful commentary on Heidegger's *Being and Time*, see M. Gelven,
   A Commentary on Heidegger's 'Being and Time' (New York: Harper and
   Row, 1970).
4. Cf. Heidegger, *Sein und Zeit*, §69. Heidegger's term is *Zuhanden-
   heit*. McQuarrie and Robinson translate this as 'readiness-to-hand';
   Stambaugh opts for 'handiness' (Heidegger, *Being and Time*, trans. J.
   Stambaugh (New York: SUNY, 1996)). What is implicated is *Dasein's
   pragmatic* relation to things encountered in the world. Things are
   encountered as *ta pragmata*, that is, in terms of their usefulness to *Dasein*.
   See Heidegger, *Sein und Zeit*, §68.
5. E. Levinas, *Quelques réflexions sur la philosophie de l'hitlérisme* (Paris:
   Éditions Payot et Rivages, 1997), 25–6.
6. As Heidegger writes, '*Dasein*, in its familiarity with significance, is the
   ontical condition for the possibility of discovering entities which are
   encountered in a world with involvement (readiness-to-hand) as their
   kind of being, and which can thus make themselves known as they are
   in themselves [*in seinem An-sich*]' (*Being and Time*, 120).
7. Marion writes, in relation to flesh and incarnation, 'flesh becomes immediately the most simple and most constraining case of what I name
   elsewhere a saturated phenomenon or paradox' (*In Excess*, 99).
8. The phrase comes from Tertullian who writes, 'The flesh is the hinge of
   salvation – *caro cardo salutis* (*De Carn. resurr.* VIII (CSL47), 36; CCL3
   931, 6–7). Merleau-Ponty argues the significance of the body in his own
   phenomenology.
9. Marion, *In Excess*, 89. Marion quotes Didier Franck: 'Flesh is the condition of possibility of the thing, better, the constitution of flesh is
   presupposed by all constitution of thing[s], that is to say, by all constitution of worldly transcendence in general' (D. Franck, *Chair et corps:
   Sur la phénomenologie de Husserl* (Paris: Éditions de Minuit, 1981), 95).

For a fuller discussion of the significance of the givenness of flesh for thought, see Marion, *In Excess*, 82–103.

10. Marion, *In Excess*, 99.

11. See Michel Henry, 'Le Christianisme: une approche phénomeno-logique', 30–1, in Philippe Capelle (ed.), *Phénoménologie et Christianist chez Michel Henry*, Paris: Editions du Cerf, 2004). Henry writes, 'In its radical transcendence to each being and in its Difference from it, the world frees that which reveals itself in the horizon of this Difference. Being [*étant*] is the content of this "world" in such a way that the content can never be explained from its revelation [*dévoilement*] in the world . . . This reality of the content of the world, of this content which is incomprehensible and non-deducible from its external appearance, is life' (31). Henry develops these themes in *C'est moi la Verité. Pour une philosophie de christianisme* (Paris: Éditions du Seuil, 1996), and *Incarnation. Une philosophie de la Chair* (Paris: Éditions du Seuil, 2000).

12. C. Reed, *The Problem of Method in the Philosophy of Emmanuel Levinas*, Ph.D. Dissertation, Yale University, 1983 (Ann Arbor: University Microfilms International), v–vi.

13. Michel Henry, *I am the Truth: Toward a Philosophy of Christianity* (Stanford: Stanford University Press, 2003).

14. I think that Levinas, here, could be read as affirming creation as 'good' – but a 'good' which can be subjected to becoming 'goods' by a subjecting subject. Thus, the notion of the mastery of the elemental. But the elemental is also resistant and hard, and involves work and effort.

4. EXISTENCE AS TRANSCENDENCE, OR THE CALL OF THE INFINITE: TOWARDS A THEOLOGY OF GRACE

1. *Illeity* is a 'neologism formed with *il* (he) or *ille*' (*Otherwise than Being*, 12–13) which is 'the origin of alterity' (*Otherwise than Being*, 150). The relation between the *il y a* and *illeity* – both non-phenomenological – is complex, but at the crux of the phenomenological and theological, and to be articulated in terms of the differing responses which both evoke in a subjectivity declined as response.

2. In *Existence and Existents*, Levinas has not yet fully developed the distinction between need (*besoin*) and desire (*désir*) which will emerge in *Totality and Infinity*. Similarly, the distinction between enjoyment (*jouissance*) and pleasure (*plaisir*) which is found in *Totality and Infinity* is yet to be developed. Enjoyment comes from the satisfaction of need, like hunger being assuaged by a good meal, or thirst being quenched by cool water; pleasure is the delight which the company of other people brings to us.

3. A useful (if perhaps distasteful) illustrative image of what Levinas is pointing to is the violence and destruction which the act of eating visits on food before its eventual incorporation and assimilation into the self. The example can be extrapolated further in a number of directions: (1) to the relation of the needful subject to the wider environment (Heidegger's *Umwelt*) and the destruction of habitats and forests to satisfy voracious consumptive demands for farming and furniture; (2) corporate subjectivities which consider the environment as a commodity in the project of globalisation (*mondialisation*), where things (and people) become 'tools' or 'useful', and here tastes of the Heidegger of *Being and Time* echo; (3) the reduction of the other person to a factor in an economic equation – other people can often be reduced to commodities or useful tools in the economic cycle of need and its satisfaction. Levinas' own reflection on his internment in Stalag 1492 in 'The Name of a Dog', in *Difficult Freedom* and the process of exclusion and de-humanisation is worth reading again. In terms of the economics and politics of justice, Roger Burggraeve has done much on this.

4. Robert Burns, *Tam o'Shanter*, in J. A. Mackay, *Complete Works of Robert Burns* (Alloway: Alloway Publishing Ltd, 1986), 411.

5. Sartre's extended consideration of Nausea in *Being and Nothingness* is worth calling to mind.

6. In this regard see David Ford, *Self and Salvation* (Cambridge: Cambridge University Press, 1999).

7. The non-phenomenality of both *il y a* and *illeity* is nonetheless a phenomenological challenge. It would argue that the phenomenological distinction between them is precisely in the responses which each provokes in the self. While the *il y a* provokes 'the horror and terror of the night, *illeity* opens the self as responsibility for the other. For further reading on the phenomenology of responsibility, see Jean-Louis Chrétien, *Call and Response* (New York: Fordham University Press, 2004).

8. 'Yahweh appeared to [Abraham] at the Oak of Mamre while he was sitting by the entrance to the tent during the hottest part of the day. He looked up, and there saw three mean standing near him. As soon as he saw them, he ran from the entrance of the tent to meet them and bowed down' (Gen. 18:1–2). The story continues with a meal being prepared for the three strangers, and the promise that barren Sarah will conceive. Allegorically, in Christian theology this has been taken as prefiguring the Trinity, as famously depicted in Andrei Rublev's icon, 'The Trinity of the Old Testament'. Levinas argues, however, that the significance of the encounter is ethical rather than theological. Hospitality is the key theme. See Levinas, *Difficult Freedom*, 121. Also, M. Purcell, 'Leashing God with Levinas: Tracing a Trinity with Levinas', *Heythrop Journal*, 40 (1999): 301–18.

9. Derrida expresses this dilemma with his neologism 'hostipitality', where the host who offers hospitality is also a hostage and subject to the possible hostility of the guest.

10. See Levinas, 'Introduction' to *Totality and Infinity*. Levinas argues that it is important to know whether we are duped by morality, to which politics seems to be in opposition. It is not so much that Levinas dismisses the need for politics, and the structures of justice which need to be in place to safeguard the many; rather, the politics of expediency can often be exercised to the neglect of the unique singularity of the other person whom politics often inserts within a system.

11. David Held, *Introduction to Critical Theory: Horkheimer to Habermas* (London: Hutchinson, 1987), 254.

12. Ibid., 256.

13. Habermas, 'Technology and Science as "Ideology"', in *Towards a Rational Society* (London: Heinemann, 1980), 91.

14. Ibid., 92.

15. See Levinas, *HO*, 25–6. The same is found in 'Meaning and Sense', in *Collected Philosophical Papers*, 91. It is precisely this notion of the precedence of life over consciousness, and as that to which thought must (phenomenologically) respond which Henry will exploit in his notion of the 'phenomenology of life'. 'Life is understood from the start as phenomenological' (*I am the Truth: Toward a Philosophy of Christianity*, 33).

16. The two notions of assimilation or exclusion – exclusion to the point of absolute exclusion – are put quite aptly by Maurice Blanchot in *The Infinite Conversation* when, in a reflection on Cain and Abel, he notes that when faced with the other person the only alternative is 'to speak or to kill'. Levinas' own reflection in 'The Name of a Dog' in *Difficult Freedom* which recounts his own experience of Stalag 1492 picks up on the notion of camps as places of exclusion where prisoners were deprived of language. What do you do with those whose culture or values cannot be assimilated or incorporated? You exclude them, to the point of an absolute solution. Speaking (*le Dire*) is the antidote to violence. Each conversation is a conversation with the other person whose infinity cannot be circumscribed whether culturally, historically, or religiously. Its current manifestations are manifold in the various occurrences of genocide, the exclusion of refugees and other groups. To exclude is to deprive the other person of a voice, and when conversation is excluded the violence of ultimate and absolute exclusion is not more than a short step away.

17. Transascendence as a particular transcendence has to be understood in contrast to transdescendence. According to B. Forthomme (*Une Philosophie de la Transcendence: La métaphysique d'Emmanuel Levinas* (Paris: J.

Vrin, 1979), the term was first employed by Jean Wahl in 'Subjectivité et transcendance', *Bulletin de la Societé Française de Philosophie 1937*: 162, who wanted to contrast the two directions which transcendence could take – the upward movement of *transascendence* towards a transcendent superior, or the descent towards some demoniacal force (*transdescendence*), which could either be something elementary and elemental or the deep forces at play in being. For Levinas, however, transcendence always has the positive connotation of an ascent to the summons of the excessive. While for Wahl, transdescendence is always opposed to the metaphysical movement of transascendence, for Levinas, 'Transcendence is not Negativity'; in negation, 'negator and negated are posited together, form a system, that is, a totality. The doctor who missed an engineering career, the poor man who longs for wealth, the patient who suffers, the melancholic who is bored for nothing oppose their condition while remaining attached to its horizons. The "otherwise" and the "elsewhere" they wish still belong to the here below they refuse' (*TI*, 41).

5. THE ECONOMY AND LANGUAGE OF GRACE: GRACE, DESIRE, AND THE AWAKENING OF THE SUBJECT

1. Stephen J. Duffy, *The Graced Horizon: Nature and Grace in Modern Catholic Thought* (Collegeville: Liturgical Press, 1992), 98.
2. Pelagius argued that, whereas the ability to do the good (*posse*) came from God, the actual willing of the good (*velle*) and the doing of the good (*esse*) remained within the sphere of the subject. Against this, Augustine argued that not only the *posse*, but also the *velle* and the *esse* depended upon God, and the prevenience of grace.
3. K. Rahner, 'Nature and Grace', in *Theological Investigations, IV* (London: Darton, Longman, and Todd, 1966), 169. See also, 'Concerning the Relationship between Nature and Grace', in *Theological Investigations, I* (London: Darton, Longman and Todd, 1961).
4. J. Maréchal, *Le Point de départ de la métaphysique: leçons sur le développement historique et théorique du problème de la connaissance, V: Le Thomisme devant la philosophie critique* (Brussels: Éditions Universelles, 1949).
5. Maréchal, *Le Point de départ*, 419.
6. Ibid., 421.
7. Ibid.
8. Ibid., 422.
9. Ibid., 424.
10. Ibid., 423–4.
11. Rahner, 'Nature and Grace', 169.

12. Rahner, 'Concerning the Relationship between Nature and Grace', 310.
13. Rahner, 'Nature and Grace', 185.
14. Rahner, 'Concerning Nature and Grace', 300.
15. Rahner, 'Nature and Grace', 186.
16. H. de Lubac, *Le Mystère du surnaturel* (Lyon-Fourvière: Éditions Montaigne, 1965), 49.
17. Ibid., 236.
18. Ibid., 259.
19. Ibid., 336.
20. Ibid., 237.
21. Ibid., 421.
22. De Lubac, *Surnaturel* (Paris: Aubier-Montaigne, 1946), 486–7; 489, n.1.
23. Rahner, 'Concerning Nature and Grace', 303.
24. Ibid., 304.
25. Ibid., 309–10.
26. Theologically, this is a very technical argument which does not need to be rehearsed here again, but can be found in de Lubac, *Le Mystère*, 142, n.1, and Rahner, 'Concerning the Relationship between Nature and Grace'. The argument is precisely the onto-theological conflict between ontology and metaphysics. For Levinas, metaphysics is a metaphysics of desire, inspired by the other and intending the other, and desire has a particular structure and dynamic, which is otherwise than onto-theology. Similarly, de Lubac, argues the prevenience of the other as gift and grace which cannot be commanded or summoned, but which is experienced only as response and responsibility. The prevenience of grace places the subject in question.
27. Rahner, 'Concerning Nature and Grace', 317.
28. Ibid., 318.
29. Ibid., 317.
30. De Lubac, *Le Mystère*, 257.
31. Ibid., 271–2.
32. This transition from the *il y a* to *illeity* should not be seen as definitive or as 'once and for all'. The concupiscent subject lives in the midst of tendencies and attractions. Life in its entirety is intentional, and hangs between the threat and the horror of anonymous being and the challenge of excessive and ongoing response. What is clear in Levinas, however, is that the salvation of the self is only ever achieved by the self's responsive commitment to the prevenient advent of the other person.
33. The asymmetry of the relationship between the 'I' and the 'other person' is addressed by Levinas in his correspondence with Martin Buber. Levinas is critical of Buber for seeing the relationship between the 'I' and the 'Thou' as reversible, a community of equals. For Levinas, the other person is always the principal interlocutor.

34. What is in play here is the reversal of intentionality on the basis of a phe-
    nomenology of response and responsibility which contests the subject
    as origin. This has terribly practical implications. The confusion of the
    'who is speaking' and the 'what is being said', and the reduction of the
    'who' to a 'what' commodifies the unique individual within ontological
    structures, and thus there follows exclusion: the refugee, the stranger,
    the orphan, the person whose potential is pre-determined from within
    the womb, and whose challenge and appeal are silenced before ever a
    word is said. Exclusion is a function of ontology.

35. Levinas, 'Réflexions sur la "technique" phénoménologique', in *En
    découvrant l'existence avec Husserl et Heidegger* (Paris: J. Vrin, 1988), 115.

36. Marc Faessler, 'L'Intrigue du tout-autre, Dieu dans la pensée
    d'Emmanuel Levinas', in Jacques Rolland (ed.), *Les Cahiers de la nuit
    surveilée: E. Levinas* (Lagrasse: Editions Verdier, 1984), 141.

37. What is significant here is that God is not the counterpart of my respon-
    sibility for the other person, which might run the risk of privatising
    the relationship with God. What Levinas stresses is the arising of God
    as the counterpart of justice, and justice is the action of a community.
    An unbearable ethics of responsibility opens on to the need to enact
    justice as a community of responsible individuals, and the possibility of
    a relationship with God. Thus again is ethics first theology.

38. This is the reason why the demand of justice is difficult for it is the
    demand to make a comparison between incomparables, between the
    others who, signifying solely in terms of themselves, confound and
    confuse my confidence and ability, bestow significance, and compare.
    The effacement which is both the *illeity of the other person* and *the tra-
    cing of the divine* renders all others ethically equal on account of the
    universal parenthood of God, and the demand of a justice which is
    blind.

39. Levinas makes the point in *Existence and Existents* that form is that by
    which an object is given to us, and that even in their nudity, human beings
    'are clothed with a *form*' (40). But there is a more absolute nudity which
    form conceals and by which an object withdraws from the world. It is
    the relationship with this nudity, beyond form and so beyond exposition
    and comprehension, which is 'the true experience of the otherness of the
    other' (40). 'Since Aristotle we conceive of the world as a phenomenon of
    form cloaking a content completely . . . All the unfathomable mystery of
    a thing shows itself to us and is open to our grasp. By virtue of its forms
    the world is stable and made up of solids. Objects can be defined by
    their finitude: form is just this way of coming to an end [*finir*] where the
    finite [*le fini*] is the definite and is already exposed to being apprehended'
    (41–2). This absolute nakedness is the illeity of the other person.

40. Faessler, 'L'Intrigue du tout-autre', 141.

41. Levinas points out that 'a word is a nomination . . . a consecrating of the "this as this" or "this as that" by a saying which is also *understanding* and *listening*, absorbed in the said . . . Identification is ascription of meaning. But this already happens within a horizon. 'Entities . . . are not first given and thematized, and then receive a meaning; they are given by the meaning they have . . . in an *already said'* (*OB*, 37).

42. Levinas, 'Le Nom de Dieu d'après quelques textes talmudiques', in *L'Au-delà du verset* (Paris: Éditions de Minuit, 1982), 157.

43. Faessler, 'L'Intrigue du tout-autre', 140.

44. Ibid., 141.

6. THE LITURGICAL ORIENTATION OF THE SELF

1. J. Bloechl, *Liturgy of the Neighbour* (Pittsburgh: Duquesne University Press, 2000), 11.

2. For example, *Sacrosanctum Concilium* (*SC*), the Constitution on the Sacred Liturgy of the Second Vatican Council (4 December 1963), speaks of the two principal notes of the liturgy: the perfect glorification of God, and the sanctification of humanity. 'Christ, indeed, always associates the Church with himself in the great work in which God is perfectly glorified and men are sanctified. The Church is his beloved Bride who calls to her Lord, and through him offers worship to the Father' (Ibid., 7). Again, 'From the liturgy, therefore, especially the Eucharist, grace is poured forth upon us as from a fountain, and the sanctification of men in Christ and the glorification of God to which all other activities of the Church are directed, as towards their end, are achieved with maximum effectiveness' (*SC*, 10). The worship of God, however, is the liturgy's principal purpose. '[T]he sacred liturgy is principally the worship of the divine majesty . . .' (*SC*, 33). Commenting on the document, Louis Bouyer remarks that 'it is striking to notice that every mention of the sanctifying effect of the liturgy on those who take part in it is immediately complemented by a mention of the glorification of God thus achieved' (Louis Bouyer, *The Liturgy Revived: A Doctrinal Commentary on the Conciliar Constitution on the Liturgy* (London: Darton, Longman and Todd, 1965), 42). In fact, 'the sanctification of man consists of his being enabled to glorify God' (42–3). What is striking to note in Bouyer's comment is that 'the glorification of God' is *thus* achieved by the sanctification of humanity. Both aspects constitute a unity. The sanctification of humanity is the glorification of God. It should also be noted that it is in the doing of the liturgy that sanctification of humanity and the glorification of God takes place. Echoes here perhaps of 'we will do *in order* to understand' (Levinas, *Nine Talmudic Readings*, 42).

3. L Bouyer, *The Liturgy Revived*, 46, commenting upon *SC*, para. 8.

4. *Catechism of the Catholic Church* (London: Geoffrey Chapman, 1999), §1069. In French, '*Le mot "liturgie" signifie originellement "œuvre publique", "service de la part/en faveur du peuple". Dans la tradition chrétienne il veut signifier que le Peuple de Dieu prend part à "l'œuvre de Dieu" (Cf. Jn.17:4). Par la liturgie, le Christ, notre Rédempteur et Grand Prêtre, continue dans son Église, avec elle et par elle, l'œuvre de notre rédemption.*' The basis of the sense of liturgy as *œuvre* can be seen more clearly in the French version of the *Sacrosanctum Concilium* which one finds quoted in the more recent *Catéchisme de l'Église Catholique* (*Catéchisme de l'Église Catholique*, Texte typique latin (Citta de Vaticano: Libreria Editrice Vaticana, 1992; Paris: Mame/Plon, 1992), §1067), which, in French, formed the original text of the Catechism. Asking, '*pourquoi la liturgie?*' the Catechism responds, '*"Cette œuvre de la rédemption des hommes . . . le Christ Seigneur l'a accomplie principalement par le mystère Pascal (SC, 5)." C'est pourquoi, dans sa liturgie, l'Église célèbre principalement le mystère Pascal par lequel Christ a accompli l'œuvre de notre salut*' (§1067). See also Irené-Henri Dalmas, *Initiation à la liturgie*, Series La Pierre-qui-Vire (Paris: Desclée de Brouwer, 1960): '*Liturgie = œuvre du peuple* (λειτουργια = ἔργον τοῦ λαοῦ)' (15).

5. J. Jungmann, 'Liturgy', in *Encyclopaedia of Theology: A Concise Sacramentum Mundi* (London: Burns and Oates, 1975), 851.

6. See *Dictionnaire étymologique de la langue grecque* (Paris: Librairie C. Vlincksieck, 1938), where ἔργον is translated as '*action, œuvre, travail*'.

7. This notion is one which Chrétien exploits in his reflections on the immemorial, and the relation between remembrance and forgetting. See: *The Unforgettable and the Unhoped for* (Fordham: Fordham University Press, 2002); *L'Inoubliable et l'inespéré* (Paris: Desclée de Brower, 2000).

8. M. Blanchot, *The Space of Literature* (Lincoln and London: University of Nebraska Press, 1982), 13, 21.

9. This quote from *Totality* is, of course, an intentional adaptation of Rimbaud who, in *Une saison en enfer*, in *Délires I: Vierge folle – L'Epoux infernal*, writes '*La vraie vie est absente. Nous ne sommes pas au monde.*' It demonstrates Levinas' metaphysics as a commitment to the world.

10. Blanchot, *The Space of Literature*, 21–2.

11. Ibid., 23.

12. Chrétien, *The Unforgettable and Unhoped for*, 15–16.

13. J. Derrida, *Given Time* (Chicago: University of Chicago Press, 1994).

14. Ibid., 12.

15. Ibid., 11.

16. Ibid., 16.

17. Ibid., 12.

18. Ibid., 13.

19. Ibid., 13–14.
20. Ibid., 23.
21. Ibid., 13.
22. In *The Unforgettable and the Unhoped for*, Chrétien will explain this in terms of time, as does Derrida. The gift, precisely because it is immemorial and its meaning cannot be recuperated, is eschatological: 'its proper temporal dimension is the future – the opening and the gift of the future' (14). Again, 'the *forever* of love translates, at the other extremity of time, into the *always already* of the immemorial' (17). Time, then, is not so much a matter of chronological progression but is a being summoned into a future which is not our own but that of the other who, nonetheless, predates the subject. The eucharistic significance of this structure of giving and its temporality will be said later.
23. Derrida, *Given Time*, 57.
24. Ibid., 27.
25. Ibid., 28.
26. Ibid., 7.
27. Ibid.
28. See Derrida, 'At This Very Moment in This Work Here I Am', in R. Bernasconi and S. Critchley (eds.), *Re-Reading Levinas* (London: The Athlone Press, 1991), 11–48.
29. See J.-L. Marion, *God without Being* (Chicago: Chicago University Press, 1991), and *Idol and Distance* (New York: Fordham University Press, 2001). Also helpful is Robyn Harper's *Rethinking God as Gift: Marion, Derrida, and the Limits of Phenomenology* (New York: Fordham University Press, 2001).
30. Derrida, *Given Time*, 28.
31. Blanchot, *The Infinite Conversation* (Minneapolis: University of Minnesota Press, 1991), 73.
32. Ibid., 441.
33. Ibid., 76.
34. Derrida, *Given Time*, 31.
35. Ibid.
36. See Derrida, 'At This Very Moment in This Work Here I Am', 11–48.

7. EUCHARISTIC RESPONSIBILITY AND WORKING FOR JUSTICE

1. J.-L. Chrétien, *The Unforgettable and the Unhoped for* (New York: Fordham University Press, 2002), 29.
2. *O Sacrum convivium in quo Christus sumatur: recolitur memoria passionis eius, mens impletur gratia, et pignus futurae gloriae nobis datur.*
3. Levinas, 'A Man-God?' in *Entre nous*, 53–63.

4. K. Marx, *Contribution to the Critique of Hegel's Philosophy of Right*, in *On Religion* (Chico: Scholars Press, 1964), 50.
5. R. P. Blum, 'Emmanuel Levinas's Theory of Commitment,' *Philosophy and Phenomenological Research*, vol. 44, no. 2 (1983): 167.
6. M. Blanchot, *The Writing of the Disaster* (Lincoln: University of Nebraska Press, 1986), 25.
7. Levinas, *Of God who Comes to Mind*, 82.
8. Ibid.

Select bibliography

Bergo, Bettina, *Levinas between Ethics and Politics* (Pittsburgh: Duquesne University Press, 1999)
Re-Reading Levinas (London: Athlone Press, 1991)
Bernasconi, Robert, and Critchley, Simon, *The Provocation of Levinas: Rethinking the Other* (London: Routledge, 1988)
Blanchot, Maurice, *L'Entretien infini* (Paris: Gallimard, 1969)
L'Espace littéraire (Paris: Gallimard, 1955)
The Infinite Conversation, trans. Susan Hanson (Minneapolis: University of Minnesota Press, 1993)
The Space of Literature, trans. Ann Smock (Lincoln and London: University of Nebraska Press, 1982)
The Unavowable Community, trans. P. Joris (Barrytown: Station Hill, 1988)
Bloechl, J., *Liturgy of the Neighbor* (Pittsburgh: Duquesne University Press, 2000)
Boff, Clodovis, *Theology and Praxis, Epistemological Foundations* (Maryknoll: Orbis, 1987) (Originally, *Teologia e pratica: teologia do politico e suas mediaçôes* (Petropolis, 1978))
Burggraeve, R., *From Self-Development to Solidarity: An Ethical Reading of Human Desire in its Socio-Political Relevance according to Emmanuel Levinas* (Leuven: Centre for Metaphysics and the Philosophy of God/Peeters, 1985)
Mens en Medemens: Verantwoordlijkheid en God. De metafysische ethiek van E Levinas (Leuven: Acco, 1986)
The Wisdom of Love in the Service of Love (Marquette: Marquette University Press, 2002)
Caputo, John D., *Against Ethics* (Bloomington: Indiana University Press, 1993)
Caygill, Howard, *L'Appel et la réponse* (Paris: Éditions de Minuit, 1992)
De la fatigue, (Paris: Éditions de Minuit, 1996)
L'Effroi du beau (Paris: Éditions du Cerf, 1987)
L'Intelligence du feu (Paris: Bayard, 2003)

Levinas and the Political (London: Routledge, 2002)
Le Régard de l'amour (Paris: Desclée de Brower, 2000)
Chrétien, Jean-Louis, *The Unforgettable and the Unhoped for* (New York: Fordham University Press, 2002)
   La Voix nue: phénoménologie de la promesse (Paris: Éditions de Minuit, 1990)
Cohen, Richard (ed.), *Face to Face with Levinas* (Albany: State University of New York Press, 1986)
Dalgarno, Melvin, and Matthews, Eric, *The Philosophy of Thomas Reid* (Dordrecht: Kluwer Academic Publishers, 1989)
De Lubac, Henri, *Le Mystère du surnaturel* (Lyon-Fourvière: Éditions Montaigne, 1965)
   Surnaturel (Paris: Aubier-Montaigne, 1946)
Derrida, Jacques, *Adieu to Emmanuel Levinas*, trans. Pascale A. Brault (Stanford: Stanford University Press, 1999)
   Given Time: 1. Counterfeit Money, trans. P. Kamuf (Chicago: University of Chicago Press, 1994)
   Of Grammatology, trans. Gayatri Chakravorty Spivak (Baltimore: Johns Hopkins University Press, 1976) (Originally published as *De la grammatologie* (Paris: Éditions de Minuit, 1967))
Edie, J. M., *Edmund Husserl's Phenomenology: A Critical Commentary* (Bloomington: Indiana University Press, 1987)
Feron, Etienne, *De l'idée de transcendance à la question du langage: l'itinéraire philosophique d'Emmanuel Lévinas* (Grenoble: Éditions J. Millon, 1992)
Finkielkraut, Alain, *La Sagesse de l'amour* (Paris: Gallimard, 1984)
Forthomme, Bernard, *Une Philosophie de la transcendance: la métaphysique d'Emmanuel Levinas* (Paris: J. Vrin, 1979)
Gubal, F., *Et combien de dieux nouveaux: II. Emmanuel Levinas* (Paris: Aubier-Montaigne, 1980)
Hand, Sean, *Facing the Other: The Ethics of Emmanuel Levinas* (Richmond: Curzon Press, 1996)
Handelman, Susan, *Fragments of Redemption* (Bloomington: Indiana University Press, 1991)
Hart, Kevin, *The Trespass of the Sign: Deconstruction, Theology and Philosophy* (Cambridge: Cambridge University Press, 1989)
Heidegger, Martin, *An Introduction to Metaphysics*, trans. R Manheim (New Haven and London: Yale University Press, 1959)
   Being and Time, trans. J. McQuarrie and E. Robinson (London: Harper and Row, 1962)
Henry, Michel, *I am the Truth: Toward a Philosophy of Christianity* (Stanford: Stanford University Press, 2003)

Husserl, Edmund, *Cartesian Meditations: An Introduction to Phenomenology*, trans. D. Cairns (The Hague: M. Nijhoff, 1973)
Cartesianische Meditationen (The Hague: M. Nijhoff, 1950)
Méditations Cartésiennes, trans. G. Peiffer and E. Levinas (Paris: J. Vrin, 1986)
Johns, R. J., *Man in the World: The Political Theology of Johannes Baptist Metz* (Missoula: Scholars Press, 1976)
Kant, Immanuel, *Critique of Practical Reason*, trans. L. W. Beck (Indianapolis: Bobbs-Merrill, 1956)
Critique of Pure Reason, trans. N. Kemp Smith (London: Macmillan, 1982)
Prolegomena to Any Future Metaphysics, trans. Paul Carus, rev. James W. Ellington (Indianapolis: Hackett Publishing Company, 1977)
Janicaud, Dominique, *L'intentionalité en question* (Paris: J. Vrin, 1995)
The Theological Turn in French Phenomenology (New York: Fordham University Press, 2002)
Kelly, W. J. (ed.), *Theology and Discovery: Essays in Honor of Karl Rahner S. J.* (Milwaukee: Marquette University Press, 1980)
Laruelle, François, *Les Philosophies de la différance* (Paris: Presses Universitaires, 1986)
Textes pour Emmanuel Levinas (Paris: Jean-Michel Place, 1980)
Levinas, Emmanuel, *Autrement que savoir* (Paris: Osiris, 1988)
Autrement qu'être ou au-delà de l'essence (The Hague: M. Nijhoff, 1974)
Basic Philosophical Writings (Bloomington: Indiana University Press, 1996)
Collected Philosophical Papers, ed. A Lingis (The Hague: M. Nijhoff, 1987)
De Dieu qui vient à l'idée (Paris: J. Vrin, 1986)
De l'évasion (Montpellier: Fata Morgana, 1982)
De l'existence à l'existant (Paris: Fontaine, 1947)
Dieu, la mort et le temps (Paris: Bernard Grasset, 1993)
Difficile liberté: essais sur le judaïsme (Paris: Éditions Albin Michel, 1963, 1976)
Difficult Freedom: Essays on Judaism trans. S. Hand (London: Athlone Press, 1990)
Du sacré au saint (Paris: Éditions de Minuit, 1977)
En découvrant l'existence avec Husserl et Heidegger (Paris: J. Vrin, 1988)
Entre nous: essais sur le penser-à-l'autre (Paris: Grasset, 1991)
Ethics and Infinity: Conversations with Philippe Nemo, trans. R. A. Cohen (Pittsburgh: Duquesne University Press, 1985)
Éthique et infini (Paris: Fayard, 1982)
Exercises de la patience, No.1: Levinas (Paris: Obsidiane, 1980)
Existence and Existents (The Hague: M. Nijhoff, 1978)
Four Talmudic Readings, trans. N. Poller (Bloomington: Indiana University Press, 1990)

God, Death, and Time, trans. B. Bergo (Stanford: Stanford University Press, 2000)

Hors sujet (Montpellier: Fata Morgana, 1987)

Humanisme de l'autre homme (Montpellier: Fata Morgana, 1972)

Humanism of the Other (Urbana and Chicago: University of Illinois Press, 2003)

Is it Righteous to be? Interviews with Emmanuel Levinas, ed. Jill Robbins (Stanford: Stanford University Press, 2001)

L'Au-delà du verset (Paris: Éditions de Minuit, 1982)

New Talmudic Reading (Pittsburgh: Duquesne University Press, 1999)

Nine Talmudic Readings, trans. A. Aronowitcz (Bloomington: Indiana University Press, 1994)

Nommes propres (Montpellier: Fata Morgana, 1976)

Of God who Comes to Mind, 2nd edn. (Stanford: Stanford University Press, 1998)

On Escape, trans. B. Bergo (Stanford: Stanford University Press, 2003)

Otherwise than Being or Beyond Essence, trans. Alphonso Lingis (The Hague: M. Nijhoff, 1981)

Proper Names, trans. M. B. Smith (Stanford: Stanford University Press, 1996)

Quatre lectures talmudiques (Paris: Éditions de Minuit, 1968)

Quelques réflexions sur la philosophie de l'hitlérisme (Paris: Éditions Payot et Rivages, 1997)

Sur Maurice Blanchot, (Montpellier: Fata Morgana, 1975)

Le Temps et l'autre (Montpellier: Fata Morgana, 1979)

La Théorie de l'intuition dans la phénomenologie de Husserl (Paris: Librairie F. Lacan, 1930)

The Theory of Intuition in Husserl's Phenomenology, trans. A. Orianne (Evanston: Northwestern University Press, 1973)

Time and the Other, trans. R. A. Cohen (Pittsburgh: Duquesne University Press, 1987)

Totalité et infini: essai sur l'extériorité (The Hague: M. Nijhoff, 1961)

Totality and Infinity, An Essay on Exteriority, trans. Alphonso Lingis (The Hague: M. Nijhoff, 1979)

Transcendance et intelligibilité (Geneva: Labor et Fides, 1984)

'Useless Suffering', in R. Bernasconi and D. Wood (eds.), *The Provocation of Levinas: Rethinking the Other* (London: Routledge, 1988)

Libertson, James, *Proximity: Levinas, Blanchot, Battaille and Communication* (The Hague: M. Nijhoff, 1982)

Lonergan, Bernard, *Insight: A Study of Human Understanding* (London: Darton, Longman and Todd, 1958)

Malka, Salmon, *Lire Levinas* (Paris: Éditions du Cerf, 1989)

Idol and Distance (New York: Fordham University Press, 2001)

Manning, Robert J. S., *Idol and Distance* (New York: Fordham University Press, 2001)
Interpreting Otherwise than Heidegger: Emmanuel Levinas's Ethics as First Philosophy (Pittsburgh: Duquesne University Press, 1993)
Maréchal, Joseph, *Le Point de départ de la métaphysique: leçons sur le développement historique et théorique du problème de la connaissance, V: Le Thomisme devant la philosophie critique* (Brussels: Editions Universelles, 1949)
Marion, Jean-Luc, *In Excess: Studies of Saturated Phenomena* (New York: Fordham University Press, 2000)
Reduction and Givenness (Evanston: Northwestern University Press, 1998)
Moran, Dermot, *Introduction to Phenomenology* (London: Routledge, 2000)
Peperzak, Adriaan T., *Ethics as First Philosophy: The Significance of Emmanuel Levinas for Philosophy, Literature and Religion* (New York and London: Routledge, 1995)
Piclin, Michel, *La Notion de transcendance* (Paris: Armand Colin, 1969)
Rahner, Karl, *Foundations of Christian Faith: An Introduction to the Idea of Christianity* (London: Darton, Longman and Todd, 1978)
Geist in Welt: Zur Metaphysik der endlichen Erkenntnis bei Tomas Von Aquin (Munich: Kosel-Verlag, 1964)
Grundkurs des Glaubens: Einführung in den Begriff des Christentums (Freiburg, Herder, 1976)
Hörer des Wortes (Munich: Kosel-Verlag, 1963)
Nature and Grace, trans. D. Wharton (London: Sheed and Ward, 1963)
A Rahner Reader, trans. G. McCool (London: Darton, Longman and Todd, 1975)
Reed, Charles, *The Problem of Method in the Philosophy of Emmanuel Levinas*, Ph.D. Dissertation, Yale University, 1983 (Ann Arbor: University Microfilms International)
Reeder, H. P., *The Theory and Practice of Husserl's Phenomenology* (Lanham: University Press of America, 1986)
Reid, Thomas, *Essays on the Intellectual Powers of Man* (London: Charles Griffin and Company, 1865)
An Inquiry into the Human Mind (Edinburgh: Bell and Bradfute, 1810)
Thomas Reid's Inquiry and Essays, ed. R. Beanblossom and K. Lehrer (Indianapolis: Hackett Publishing Company, 1983)
Richardson, W. J., *Heidegger: Through Phenomenology to Thought* (The Hague: M. Nijhoff, 1963)
Sheehan, Thomas, *Karl Rahner: The Philosophical Foundations* (Athens: Ohio University Press, 1987)
Spiegelberg, Herbert, *The Phenomenological Method: A Historical Introduction*, 3rd edn. (The Hague: M. Nijhoff, 1984)
Tracy, David, *The Analogical Imagination* (London: SCM Press, 1981)

Valevicius, Andreas, *From the Other to the Totally Other* (New York: Peter Lang, 1988)

Ward, Graham, *Barth, Derrida and The Language of Theology* (Cambridge: Cambridge University Press, 1995)

Wright, Tamra, *The Twilight of Jewish Philosophy* (Amsterdam: Harwood Academic Publishers, 1999)

Wyschogrod, Edith, *Emmanuel Levinas: The Problem of Ethical Metaphysics* (The Hague: M. Nijhoff, 1974)